1960s Counterculture

DOCUMENTS DECODED

The ABC-CLIO series **Documents Decoded** guides readers on a hunt for new secrets through an expertly curated selection of primary sources. Each book pairs key documents with in-depth analysis, all in an original and visually engaging side-by-side format. But *Documents Decoded* authors do more than just explain each source's context and significance—they give readers a front-row seat to their own investigation and interpretation of each essential document line by line.

1960s Counterculture
DOCUMENTS DECODED

Jim Willis

Documents Decoded

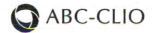 ABC-CLIO

Library of Congress Cataloging-in-Publication Data

Willis, Jim, 1946 March 19–
    1960s counterculture : documents decoded / Jim Willis.
        pages cm. — (Documents decoded series)
    Includes index.
    ISBN 978-1-61069-522-0 (alk. paper) — ISBN 978-1-61069-523-7 (ebook) 1. United States—Social conditions—1960–1980. 2. United States—Civilization—1945– 3. United States—History—1961–1969. 4. Protest movements—United States—History—20th century—Sources. 5. Social movements—United States—History—20th century—Sources. 6. Counterculture—United States—History—20th century—Sources. I. Title.
    HN59.W525 2015
    303.48'40973—dc23   2014034984

ISBN: 978-1-61069-522-0
EISBN: 978-1-61069-523-7

19 18 17 16 15   1 2 3 4 5

This book is also available on the World Wide Web as an eBook.
Visit www.abc-clio.com for details.

ABC-CLIO, LLC
130 Cremona Drive, P.O. Box 1911
Santa Barbara, California 93116-1911

This book is printed on acid-free paper ∞
Manufactured in the United States of America

This book is dedicated to my fellow alumni of the remarkable class of 1964 at Midwest City High School.

What a decade the 1960s proved to be, and what a special class of Oklahomans this was.

Contents

Introduction: Seeds of the 1960s Protest Movement

America is a nation born out of protest.

It is a nation that grew, and continues to grow, out of protest.

Protest is built into the DNA of Americans. I think it is part of every nation to some extent, but it only had a chance to express itself and flourish in a nation that is pluralistic: one that welcomes (and is often exasperated by) the open display of disagreement.

As a journalist who now teaches and writes about a profession that focuses on needed change and upsetting a status quo that sometimes isn't working, I understand that America's values are embedded in the stories that writers tell. It has always been so, in all cultures. The power of the narrative is that the best stories resonate with readers or viewers because they tap into the values that those people have. The story may be about someone who upholds those values or someone who threatens them, but either way the values themselves are embedded in the tale. Sometimes those stories are not published for mass consumption but are simple lessons passed on by parent to child. They encase a value or maybe even an entire morality. So, along with the story comes a moral.

Take, for example, Norman Maclean's moving life story that was made into a Robert Redford film, *A River Runs through It.* In the opening scenes we see Norman and his younger brother Paul as children who are learning about life under the tutelage of their father, a Presbyterian minister, in Missoula, Montana. Some of what they learn comes through homeschooling, but some of it comes another way: their father schools them in the art of fly fishing. In that art, the boys learn larger lessons about patience, following a plan, and following through on what you start.

Years ago, Columbia sociologist Herbert Gans set out to find what American values might be embedded in the stories that journalists write.[1] For his project, he selected many stories published in some of the top newspapers and magazines and aired on network television newscasts. After assembling them, he began the process of content analysis, looking specifically for evidence of consistent human values that the stories were built upon. Gans reasoned that if the top news media were reporting these stories and if people were reading or watching them, there must be value in the stories that people were connecting with. He found eight such values and called them "enduring values" because they seemed embedded in the fabric of Americans. The values were, in no particular order, ethnocentrism, altruistic democracy, responsible capitalism, leadership, order, small-town pastoralism, moderatism, and rugged individualism.

From my own journalistic experience, I believe that it is this last value—rugged individualism—that is probably the strongest of the list. At least, rugged individualism is the value that often resonates strongest with readers. Americans love to read about someone who fights the good fight, who challenges greater odds especially in the pursuit of something valuable to that individual. Isn't this the story of America itself? Why else would the earliest of adventurers and settlers in the New World have braved hardship and death when others were telling them that they could not succeed? Why else would the descendants of those settlers have pushed west into the frontier, all the way to the Pacific Ocean, when so many harsh conditions were opposing them along the way? It was as if this massive protest was expressing itself in the conquering of the wilderness that was America.

And through it all, the history of this protest was being conveyed to others who would follow, and this conveyance came through stories and written documents. For those who would follow in the footsteps of the pioneers, these stories and documents formed a kind of guidebook that was rich in insight and instruction. The documents went past the "what" of the pioneering movement to the "why," the "how," and the "so what" of it. Most of these documents were never meant to be published, nor did the writers know they would become the inspiration they did to later generations. Some of these papers were personal journals that were later published, some were official reports of expeditions, some were letters, and some were transcripts of official proceedings. They were mostly meant for purposes of the moment or the era, but this massive accumulation of documents has gone far beyond serving the needs of those times; they have become a lasting footprint of different eras through which America has passed: times in which the country struggled mightily; times in which it failed to meet its ideals, as expressed in documents such as the Declaration of Independence and even the U.S. Constitution; times in which it did succeed; and times in which it needed to reach down deep to its values to pull through against formidable opponents. These moments are all there in these documents.

The premise of this book is that the history of America can be found in its artifacts and—in this case—in the documents left behind by previous generations. Specifically, this book looks at the documents from the 1960s. This was the decade that spilled over into the 1970s, which will forever be known as the "era of protest," in which America reexamined itself and its values related to a wide range of issues. These issues included the status of free speech in America, the reasons for—and value of involvement in—the Vietnam War, the equal treatment of African Americans, the equal treatment of women, the relationship of the country to its Native American population and the debts owed to that population, the way America felt about homosexuality, and the plight of Mexican Americans working as migrant farm laborers.

All of these issues became points of protest during the 1960s, and they were not all separate or exclusive. Indeed, like different labor unions that show support for striking workers in another union, members of each of these protest movements voiced support for other movements. African Americans seeking equality were quick to show support for women seeking equal rights, and vice versa; leaders such as Cesar Chavez of the United Farm Workers were invoking the name of Dr. Martin Luther King Jr. in his struggle for civil rights. The interconnectedness of the protest movements sometimes resembled a spider web, all tied together by a common spirit of struggle for equal rights under the law.

The protest era of the 1960s didn't just happen; it did not arise from a vacuum. There was a progression of events that made it reasonable to assume that such an era would lie ahead. Certainly the precursors of some of the protests that erupted in the 1960s were there in earlier decades. The struggle for women's rights dates back to the turn of the twentieth century in America and, in the case of rights for black Americans, the abolition movement, Lincoln's Emancipation Proclamation, and the end of the Civil War in the 19th century all started the ball rolling on that issue. The struggle for free speech in America is as old as America itself. But progress on these and other issues was stalled in the first four decades of the 20th century by two world wars and the Great Depression. When World War II ended, the country moved into a decade of domestic recovery, the return to peacetime conditions (except for the Korean War), and the start of the baby boomer generation as families reunited after being separated by the war. Political concerns in the early 1950s were focused mostly on the perceived threat of communism and not on U.S. governmental policies that might be seen as oppressive or unequal in their application.

That began to change as early as 1954, however, with the Supreme Court ruling in *Brown v. Board of Education of Topeka, Kansas* that public school segregation was unconstitutional. Three years later in high drama on the front steps of Central High School in Little Rock, Arkansas, America saw its public schools begin to be integrated, over the objections of southern governors such as Orval Faubus of Arkansas and George Wallace of Alabama. The civil rights movement was starting, ready or not, and would reach a crescendo in the 1960s, moving Congress to pass the landmark Civil Rights Act under President Lyndon Johnson.

The impetus of the protest era of the 1960s came largely from those baby boomers who had grown up in the relatively stable and sanguine 1950s. In the 1960s they entered college and turned their university campuses into public forums on the controversial issues of the day. American involvement in Vietnam, coupled with the existence of the military draft, gave many college students a vested interest in what their government was doing, especially regarding foreign policy in Southeast Asia. The forms that these protests took usually involved questions of the right to speak and protest openly on state campuses, and that led into the free speech movement, which opened other doors of protest as well.

The 1960s evokes strong—and often polarized—emotions in the minds of many who lived through that era. To some, it was an exciting decade when experimentation and protest were the order of the day. It was a golden era when the old traditions of morality, authority, and discipline were questioned. It was a time of revolution. But to others, it was a decade that represented the undermining of the enduring values of America, a time of self-denunciation of a nation that was still considered to be the best democracy on Earth. It was a time when extremist groups were moving the country away from a prized moderatism and a time when the fear of communism—as a driver of that extremism—was still present. America had never really questioned the reasons for wars it had been involved in (a false idea, since isolationists had questioned America's entry into both World War I and the Korea War), but now there was a national debate over the validity of sending troops to Vietnam. America was not presenting the united front that it had in World War II, and this troubled many traditionalists. It was a decade when young college men were joining the Reserve Officers' Training Corps (ROTC) because they knew they would probably be drafted after graduation anyway, but they sometimes had to step over the prone bodies of student protestors who lined sidewalks between the campus armory and drill field.

Into this mix would come those young people who were so frustrated with the "establishment" that they adopted the slogan of "turn on [to drugs] and drop out." Drugs, it was sometimes said, were for those who couldn't handle reality.

For other young people—many of whom came from upper-middle-class families—it was a time to beat the boredom of their suburban lives by entering into a different kind of world of hippies, liberal sexual morality, psychedelic colors and dreams, free-spiritedness, and a chance to maybe stand up for something more meaningful than the hypocrisy they were trying to escape back home. Growing up the 1950s, many young people developed a growing resentment in their teenage years to such things as a rigid social hierarchy, unequal treatment of minorities and women, and an overrespect for authority in the family, in business, and in government. In the world of the arts, conformity and a sense of blandness in music and films would give rise to a new age of rock music and edgy films that dealt with real-life issues that were confronting everyone but were being discussed by only a few brave souls.

In his book *The Sixties,* Arthur Marwick asked if it is legitimate to compare and draw contrasts between the decades of the 1950s, 1960s, and 1970s or whether what happened in one of those decades was just a link in the evolutionary change of events of the larger era. He writes:

> In historical study we do need a concept of periods, or eras, or ages, though such periods do not automatically coincide with decades or with centuries, nor do they have any immanent or natural existence, independent of the analytical needs of historians. Periodization, the chopping up of the past into chunks or periods, is essential because the past in its entirety is so extensive and complex; but different historians will identify different chunks, depending upon their interests and the countries they are dealing with—a periodization which suits the study of Western Europe will not suit the study of Africa or Japan. The implication of periodization is that particular chunks of time contain a certain unity, in that events, attitudes, values, social hierarchies within the chosen "period" seem to be closely integrated with each other, to share common features, and in that there are identifiable points of change when a "period" defined in this way gives way to a "new period."[2]

That said, however, Marwick goes on to explain that there is "prima facie evidence" that a self-contained and cohesive era did exist that we call the 1960s and that this period did produce a uniqueness, in nature and effect, on American history.[3] Those effects would leave a legacy for the rest of the 20th century and into the 21st century as well. Furthermore, that effect was felt not just in America but in Europe and other parts of the world as well. The fashion, music, openness to new ideas, and tolerance for those with differing lifestyles and the sense of injustice for those minority groups being treated unequally all became American exports to other developed countries in the 1960s and beyond. Marwick concludes by saying that "I believe that the sixties were a mini-renaissance in which the right of individual expression was encouraged, applauded and nurtured by a generation whose naive belief was that all we needed was love."[4]

Historians such as Marwick believe that the following developments emerged from and characterized the decade of the 1960s. This is not a complete listing of all such developments but includes some of the key ones that were brought on by the young people of the era:

- The 1960s brought about new movements and subcultures that were usually—but not always—protesting established traditions and expressions of values in American society.
- The decade also energized young people into launching many creative enterprises; in a way it was a new era of capitalism created by the very generation that was protesting established capitalism in America as being hypocritical. But these young entrepreneurs were not greedy, sold at prices that would generally only cover their costs, and provided some services for free in return for support and donations. These ventures included the founding of clubs, boutiques, theaters, book shops, cafés, art galleries, magazines, and art studios.
- The 1960s brought many young people into role model positions of influence, not just in the performing arts or in the world of fashion but also in the political realm. Keep in mind that many of these young political firebrands were featured on television news and so became celebrities to other young people as well.
- The era certainly turned concepts of class, race, and family relationships upside down. The unifying theme here was one of protesting established ideas of authority and hierarchy. Indeed, one of the most popular bumper stickers of the day read simply "Question Authority."
- The experimentations that were going on among young people in the 1960s occurred in an atmosphere of general permissiveness. In the area of sexual relationships, the traditional ideal of no sex before marriage was spun around 180 degrees, as free love (love without marital commitment) became a popular mantra. After all, marriage itself was seen as part of the hypocrisy of the establishment, so why embrace it or imbue it with more importance than it deserved?
- Along with the newfound sexual experimentation (or at least the public acknowledgment that it existed) came new forms of self-presentation. A key aspect of this was fashion itself. No one could confuse the tie-dyed and psychedelic clothing of the 1960s with the button-downed shirts, slacks, and dresses of the 1950s. Some of this fashion statement drew attention to natural attributes of the body as something to admire rather than be ashamed of.

- The culture of young people in the 1960s was more participatory, and the thread that provided unity for the culture was its music, which evolved from folk to folk-rock to hard rock.
- Last and probably most important on this abbreviated list is that the 1960s brought new understanding of the need for civil rights among all oppressed groups in America. It also brought a generation of young people willing to risk some of their own personal freedom (jail time was a possibility for protestors) in pursuit of larger goals of equality and freedom for others.

The chapters that follow each focus on documents, nearly all of which come out of the decade of the 1960s, that are artifacts of this protest era. In order, they deal with (1) the campus free speech movement, (2) the hippie culture, (3) the Vietnam War, (4) the civil rights struggle, (5) the struggle for women's rights, (6) the gay rights movement, (7) the American Indian movement, and (8) the protests of Mexican American migrant farmworkers. The concluding chapter assesses where young people of the millennial generation stand, in comparison to the baby boomers, on the spirit of protest and seeking changes in society. The entire project is meant to show how the decade of the 1960s defined itself and how it made the footprint it did in the long trail of American history.

Notes

1. Herbert J. Gans, *Deciding What's News* (Evanston, IL: Northwestern University Press, 2005).

2. Arthur Marwick, *The Sixties: Cultural Revolution in Britain, France, Italy, and the United States* (London: Oxford University Press, 1998), excerpt accessed at http://www.nytimes.com/books/first/m/marwick-sixties.html.

3. Ibid.

4. Ibid.

Chapter 1

Raised Voices: The Berkeley Free Speech Movement

Introduction

While the group Students for a Democratic Society was busy gathering the support of college students around the country, a separate movement exploded onto the public scene in 1964 on the campus of the University of California at Berkeley. This was the Free Speech Movement (FSM) that was inspired by the American struggle for civil rights and grew quickly into a protest of U.S. involvement in Vietnam.[1] The opening salvo of the FSM came when Cal-Berkeley students protested the university's ban on political activity on campus in the fall of 1964, a ban that simultaneously extended the campus boundaries. Students were demanding the right to organize politically—pass out literature, collect money, recruit members, and advocate political action—while standing on what was now deemed to be campus property.

This protest grew into a large movement that inspired an unprecedented and prolonged period of student involvement and activism at Cal-Berkeley. That movement quickly spread to campuses nationwide over the ensuing months. The epicenter on the Berkeley campus for this protest was Sproul Plaza, where students would rise to offer protests similar to those found in the Port Huron Statements of the Students for a Democratic Society. The Berkeley FSM made headlines around the world and resulted in polarized feelings about whether these student protesters were helping or hurting America. The 1964 Berkeley protests lasted more than two months and concluded when 773 protestors (students and other supporters) were arrested for a massive sit-in at the administration building. After the sit-in, the faculty voted on December 8, 1964, by a huge margin, to uphold the students' position—that the university should not restrict the content of speech but should only determine rules for time, place, and manner of political activity so as to not interfere with the normal educational functions of the university. During the months to follow the administration, while agreeing to observe the First and Fourteenth Amendments of the U.S. Constitution, tried to reassert additional limitations on political activity, but the students successfully opposed them. Although the regents never formally accepted the faculty's "December 8th Resolution," continuing to maintain their right to punish advocacy leading to illegal actions (such as sit-ins), the administration did not attempt to do so during the years of massive antiwar protests that were about to occur.

Freedom of Speech

The First Amendment to the U.S. Constitution

Ratified December 15, 1791

INTRODUCTION

Over the centuries, this one amendment has stood as the bulwark to freedom of speech and freedom of the press in America. Ironically, it is one of the shortest guarantees of free speech in any nation's constitution in the world.

While other countries have felt the need to operationally define what "freedom" in relation to "speech" and "press" means, the U.S. Constitution does not. Over the years, the Supreme Court has generally upheld the amendment to mean that there is to be no prior restraint on speech or on the press in America. This was the key constitutional guarantee that the students at Cal-Berkeley were demanding be applied to their political speech and debate on campus.

Congress shall make no law respecting an establishment of religion, or prohibiting the free exercise thereof; or abridging the freedom of speech, or of the press; or the right of the people peaceably to assemble, and to petition the Government for a redress of grievances.

Source: National Archives.

"A Spectre Is Haunting the University"

Leaflet from the FSM Steering Committee

December 1964

INTRODUCTION

This was a leaflet written to draw the attention of students at the University of California at Berkeley to the perceived need to join in protesting the university's sanctioning of student leaders and organizations protesting what they felt were oppressive measures directed at the Cal students. The letter, and other rhetoric like it, was part of the prologue to the student march on Sproul Hall a couple of months later.

A spectre is haunting the University of California: the spectre of student resistance to arbitrary administrative power. The board of regents has used Chancellor Strong to attack leaders of the Free Speech Movement.

Chancellor Strong has summoned Arthur Goldberg, Mario Savio and Jackie Goldberg before his Faculty Committee on Student Conduct. These three students have been singled out—from among thousands—for their participation in the demonstrations of October 1st and 2nd.

The demonstration referred to was actually the beginning of the Free Speech Movement at the University of California at Berkeley, which gave rise to a larger nationwide university campus-based movement. The incident sparking the demonstration occurred when a former UC grad student, Jack Weinberg, was manning a table for the Congress of Racial Equality (CORE) and refused to show his student ID to a campus police officer. Weinberg was arrested, and a massive student demonstration ensued and lasted into the next day. Charges against Weinberg were ultimately dropped.

The administration has also initiated disciplinary action against these student organizations: Campus CORE, Young Socialist Alliance, Slate, Women for Peace, W.E.B. DuBois Club, University Friends of SNCC.

We demand the following action be taken by Wednesday noon:

That disciplinary procedures against Arthur Goldberg, Mario Savio, Jackie Goldberg and the student political organizations be halted.

That the Administration guarantee there will be no further disciplining of students or organizations for political activity that occurs before a final settlement is reached.

That Freedom of Political Activity be protected by revision of present University policy so that:

- Only the courts regulate the content of political expression.
- Faculty, students, and Administration jointly determine and enforce all regulations governing the form of political expression.
- All regulations which unnecessarily restrict political activity be repealed.

Independents for Free Speech [will meet] Thursday, 7:30 p.m., Hillel. Elections will be held. Graduate Coordinating Committee [will meet] today at 4 p.m., 100 Cal. All students (including undergraduates) and all faculty members are urged to attend. *Final Strike Preparations will be made.*

The Sproul Hall steps were the favorite gathering place for student and faculty speeches and protests at the University of California during the counterculture era of the 1960s and especially during the days of the Free Speech Movement in 1964–1965.

A mass meeting [will be held] today at noon, Sproul Hall steps.

Source: Courtesy of the Free Speech Movement Archives, http://www.fsm-a .org/FSM%20Documents/FSM%20Dec%20Documents/Webpages/detail.np/ detail-01.html.

"The Bodies upon the Gears"

Mario Savio's Speech on the Sproul Hall Steps, UC-Berkeley
December 2, 1964

INTRODUCTION

Mario Savio was a student at the University of California at Berkeley who held a deep social conscience and earlier in life had planned to become a Catholic priest. As head of Campus Friends of SNCC—the Student Nonviolent Coordinating Committee—Savio had already emerged as a spokesperson for the political organizations protesting the ban. When ex–grad student Jack Weinberg, manning a table on campus sponsored by the Congress of Racial Equality (CORE), was arrested just before the planned noon rally and put into a police car in the middle of Sproul Plaza, several students in the crowd shouted "sit down," and hundreds immediately did. With the car immobilized, Savio, who had been sitting on its hood, removed his shoes and climbed on top of the car to speak. During the ensuing 32 hours of the car blockade, dozens of students spoke about freedom, democracy, higher education, and civil disobedience, but Savio's eloquence and clarity of reasoning, as well as his ability to express the moral issues involved in the conflict, made him the leading spokesperson for the movement. His most famous speech came on the steps of Sproul Hall on December 2, 1964, before a crowd of 4,000, when he urged students to occupy the administration building of Sproul Hall. He was following another student speaker who was asking his classmates to follow campus rules.

You know, I just want to say one brief thing about something the previous speaker said. I didn't want to spend too much time on that because I don't think it's important enough. But one thing is worth considering.

He's the . . . nominal head of an organization supposedly representative of the undergraduates, whereas in fact under the Kerr directives it derives its authority, its delegated power, from the Administration. It's totally unrepresentative of the graduate students and TAs [teaching assistants].

But he made the following statement, I quote: "I would ask all those who are not definitely committed to the FSM cause to stay away from demonstration." All right, now, listen to this: "For all upper division students who are interested in alleviating the TA shortage problem, I would encourage you to offer your services to department chairmen and advisors." That has two things: a strikebreaker and a fink.

I'd like to say . . . one other thing about a union problem. Upstairs, you may have noticed already on the second floor of Sproul Hall, Locals 40 and 127 of the Painters' Union are painting the inside of the second floor of Sproul Hall. Now, apparently that action had been planned sometime in the past. I've tried to contact those unions. Unfortunately, and it tears my heart out—they're as bureaucratized as the administration—it's difficult to get through to anyone in authority there. Very sad. We're still . . . making an attempt. Those people up there have no desire to interfere with what we're doing. I would ask that they be considered and that they not be heckled in any way. And I think that . . . while there's unfortunately no sense of solidarity at this point between unions and students, there at least need be no . . . excessively hard feelings between the two groups.

Now, there are at least two ways in which sit-ins, and civil disobedience, and whatever, at least two major ways in which it can occur. One, when a law exists, is promulgated, which is totally unacceptable to people and they violate it again and again and again until it's rescinded, repealed.

All right, but there's another way.

Sometimes the form of the law is such as to render impossible its effective violation as a method to have it repealed. Sometimes the grievances of people are more, extend . . . to more than just the law, extend to a whole mode of arbitrary power, a whole mode of arbitrary exercise of arbitrary power. And that's what we have here.

Although protestors such as Savio saw the university campus as the best hope for change in America, it is obvious that they did not include everyone on campus as equally committed to the fight against establishment values. As Savio notes here, the university administration at Cal-Berkeley and those students who followed the administration's rules were perceived as corporate management and lackeys: the very types of individuals whom the student protestors were railing against. The call went out for change to begin occurring on the college campus itself, demanding that college administrators grant the students their rights as American citizens in freely engaging in public speech and political debate.

We have an autocracy which runs this university. It's managed! We were told the following: If President Kerr actually tried to get something more liberal out of the regents in his telephone conversation, why didn't he make some public statement to that effect? And the answer we received, from a well-meaning liberal, was the following. He said: "Would you ever imagine the manager of a firm making a statement publicly in opposition to his Board of Directors?" That's the answer! Now I ask you to consider: if this is a firm, and if the Board of Regents are the board of directors, and if President Kerr in fact is the manager, then I'll tell you something, the faculty are a bunch of employees, and we're the raw materials! But we're a bunch of raw materials that don't

mean to . . . have any process upon us, don't mean to be made into any product, don't mean . . . to end up being bought by some clients of the University, be they the government, be they industry, be they organized labor, be they anyone! We're human beings!

And that . . . brings me to the second mode of civil disobedience. There's a time when the operation of the machine becomes so odious, makes you so sick at heart that you can't take part; you can't even passively take part! And you've got to put your bodies upon the gears and upon the wheels, upon the levers, upon all the apparatus, and you've got to make it stop! And you've got to indicate to the people who run it, to the people who own it, that unless you're free, the machine will be prevented from working at all!!

That doesn't mean—and it will be interpreted to mean, unfortunately, by the bigots who run the [*San Francisco*] *Examiner,* for example—. . . that you have to break anything. One thousand people sitting down someplace, not letting anybody by, not letting anything happen, can stop any machine, including this machine! And it will stop!!

The allusions that Savio makes to the "operation of the machine" and "put[ting] your bodies upon the gears" resulted in this speech often being called later "The Bodies upon the Gears" speech. He is saying that the machine of the establishment has run amok and is hurting people and that brave individuals must sacrifice themselves to shut the machine down for the good of all. If this sacrifice is done in the proper (i.e., nonviolent) way, it will not cause physical damage but will stop the machine so that corrections can be made. It was an effective articulation that resonated with idealists of the day. Also, his framing of the *San Francisco Examiner* management as "bigots" disparages one of the city's two largest newspapers that was perceived as editorially conservative and thus a tool of the establishment.

We're going to do the following, and the greater the number of people, the safer they'll be and the more effective it will be. We're going, once again, to march up to the second floor of Sproul Hall. And we're going to conduct our lives for a while in the second floor of Sproul Hall.

We'll show movies, for example. We tried to get *Un Chant d'Amour.* Unfortunately, that's tied up in the courts because of a lot of squeamish moral mothers for a moral America and other people on the outside, the same people who get all their ideas out of the *San Francisco Examiner.* Sad, sad. But, Mr. Landau . . . has gotten us some other films.

Un Chant d'Amour (A Song of Love) was a 1976 film by French writer Jean Genet that he directed in 1950. It is a short 26-minute film with explicit homosexual content about two prisoners held in isolation, separated by a brick wall, who find an unusual way of communicating their feelings for each other. The film was banned as pornographic in most of the world, although many critics sing its praises. Savio wanted to show the film as an example of how society stifles free speech, especially about provocative subjects. The reference to "Mr. Landau" is to Saul Landau, a liberal journalist and filmmaker who was sympathetic to the Berkeley FSM.

Student protestors were championing their rights not only under the First Amendment but also under the Fourteenth Amendment. This is an amendment five times the length of the First Amendment and guarantees several constitutional rights. The key right for these protesters was the right for individual Americans to have due process under the law if they feel their constitutional liberties have been violated. The students were stating that their right to free speech and assembly (under the First Amendment) had been violated by the campus administration and that they were offered no due process to challenge that violation.

Joan Baez, who was only 23 years old in 1964, had already made a name for herself as one of America's leading folk singers and was also an emerging voice for the counterculture movement of the 1960s. In her career she wrote a number of protest songs, and she was a staunch critic of America's involvement in Vietnam and a staunch supporter of civil rights in America. Baez had been catapulted to worldwide protest fame by being asked to sing "Oh Freedom!" by Dr. Martin Luther King Jr. just before he delivered his famous "I Have a Dream" speech in Washington, D.C., in August 1963. She was arrested in 1967 as part of an antiwar rally but was soon released. Baez remains committed to human rights causes today and has released 30 albums, many of them containing songs of protest.

Likewise, we'll do something . . . that hasn't occurred at this University in a good long time. We're going to have real classes up there. There are going to be Freedom Schools conducted up there. We're going to have classes on [the] First and Fourteenth amendments! We're going to spend our time learning about the things this University is afraid that we know! We're going to learn about freedom up there, and we're going to learn by doing!!

Now, we've had some good long rallies. We've had some good long rallies, and I think I'm sicker of rallies than anyone else here. It's not going to be long. I'd like to introduce one last person . . . before we enter Sproul Hall. And the person is Joan Baez.

Source: Mario Savio, "Bodies upon the Gears." Used by permission of Lynne Hollander Savio.

The Function of the University in Time of Crisis

Noam Chomsky's Speech on the Role of the University
1969

INTRODUCTION

Noam Chomsky, professor emeritus of linguistics at MIT, is a leading liberal voice in America and the author of more than 100 books. He has often described himself as a libertarian socialist. He is a staunch defender of freedom of speech, even for opinions that he himself disagrees with. Chomsky believes that either one defends free speech vigorously for differing views or rejects it and chooses repressive standards instead, whether an individual is from movements on the Left or the Right. He has spent most of his life on or around university campuses, and he published this essay on the role of the university during the turbulent 1960s. Chomsky was 41 years old at the time.

Writing 150 years ago, the great liberal reformer and humanist Wilhelm von Humboldt defined the university as "nothing other than the spiritual life of those human beings who are moved by external leisure or internal pressures toward learning and research." At every stage of his life, a free man will be driven, to a greater or lesser extent, by these "internal pressures."

Chomsky begins by offering a broad definition of a university as a state of mind rather than a physical setting. He also links learning directly to freedom, which is a telling connection: only the individual who lives in a free society has the chance to openly and actively question things and pursue the discovery of truth. The impetus for that journey is embedded within a free individual and forms the internal pressure of which he or she speaks.

The society in which he lives may or may not provide him with the "external leisure" and the institutional forms in which to realize this human need to discover and create, to explore and evaluate and come to understand, to refine and exercise his talents, to contemplate, to make his own individual contribution to contemporary culture, to analyze and criticize and transform this culture and the social structure in which it is rooted.

Even if the university did not exist formally, Humboldt observes, "one person would privately reflect and collect, another join with men of his own age, a third find a circle of disciples.

Such is the picture to which the state must remain faithful if it wishes to give an institutional form to such indefinite and rather accidental human operations."

[One measure of the level of civilization]

10

Here Chomsky lays out his thesis of what a physical university should be: an institution that provides an atmosphere for individuals to respond positively and openly to that internal pressure to learn and research, which allows the individual to become self-fulfilled in this regard. He concludes the passage by praising the student counterculture movement of the 1960s as the catalyst to wake up the university administration to providing this kind of open, learning atmosphere.

The extent to which existing institutional forms permit these human needs to be satisfied provides one measure of the level of civilization that a society has achieved. One element in the unending struggle to achieve a more just and humane social order will be the effort to remove the barriers—whether they be economic, ideological, or political—that stand in the way of the particular forms of individual self-fulfillment and collective action that the university should make possible. It is the great merit of the student movement of the 1960s to have helped shatter the complacency that had settled over much of American intellectual life, both with regard to American society and to the role of the universities within it. The renewed concern with university reform is in large measure a consequence of student activism.

A great deal of energy has been directed to problems of "restructuring the university": democratizing it, redistributing "power" in it, reducing constraints on student freedom as well as the dependence of the university on outside institutions. I suspect that little can be achieved of real substance along these lines. Formal changes in the university structure will have little effect on what a student does with his life, or on the relation of the university to the society. To the extent that reform does not reach the heart of the university—the content of the curriculum, the interaction between student and teacher, the nature of research, and, in some fields, the practice that relates to theory—it will remain superficial.

"[S]ociety must undergo drastic changes if civilization is to advance—perhaps even to survive."

But it is doubtful that these matters will be significantly affected by the kinds of structural reforms that are now being actively debated on many campuses. It is pointless to discuss the "function of the university" in abstraction from concrete historical circumstances, as it would be a waste of effort to study any other social institution in this way. In a different society entirely different questions might arise as to the function of the university and the problems that are pressing. To one who believes, as I do, that our society must undergo drastic changes if civilization is to advance—perhaps even to survive—university reform will appear an insignificant matter except insofar as it contributes to social change.

Apart from this question, improvements in the university can no doubt take place within the framework of the presently existing institutional forms, and drastic revision of these forms will contribute little to it. It is never an easy matter to determine to what extent deficiencies of a particular institution can actually be overcome through internal reform and to what extent they reflect characteristics of society at large or matters of individual psychology that are relatively independent of social forms.

[Sharing of discovery and mutual assistance]

Consider, for example, the competitiveness fostered in the university, in fact, in the school system as a whole. It is difficult to convince oneself that this serves an educational purpose. Certainly it does not prepare the student for the life of a scholar or scientist. It would be absurd to demand of the working scientist that he keep his work secret so that his colleagues will not know of his achievements and not be helped by his discoveries in pursuing their own studies and research. Yet this demand is often made of the student in the classroom.

In later life, collective effort with sharing of discovery and mutual assistance is the idea; if it is not the norm, we rightly interpret this as an inadequacy of those who cannot rise above personal aggrandizement and to this extent are incompetent as scholars and teachers. Yet even at the most advanced level of graduate education, the student is discouraged by university regulation from working as any reasonable man would certainly choose to do: individually, where his interests lead him; collectively, where he can learn from and give aid to his fellows. Course projects and examinations are individual and competitive. The doctoral dissertation not only is required to be a purely individual contribution; beyond this questionable requirement, there is a built-in bias toward insignificance in the requirement that a finished piece of work be completed in a fixed time span. The student is obliged to set himself a limited goal and to avoid adventuresome, speculative investigation that may challenge the conventional framework of scholarship and, correspondingly, runs a

Leading up to this highlighted passage, Chomsky discusses the different levels of university structure that he feels can and cannot be changed and those that will benefit the student most. In this highlighted example, he urges change in the university philosophy that promotes individual, competitive scholarship among students and faculty and discourages (or penalizes) students and faculty for working collaboratively on research. Instead of promoting the goal of shared learning and more valid discoveries through such open learning and collaboration, Chomsky chides the university structure (which he says is reflective of competitive American society) for valuing individual accomplishment and public aggrandizement for both the individual researcher as well as the prestige and reputation the university derives from having its individual students and faculty achieve. One such mark of pride for universities, for example, is the way they tout the number of individual Fulbright scholarships their students and faculty accumulate or the number of National Merit Scholarship finalists they have among their freshman student body.

high risk of failure. In this respect, the institutional forms of the university encourage mediocrity.

Perhaps this limitation is one reason why it is so common for a scholar to devote his career to trivial modifications of what he has already done. The patterns of thinking imposed in his early work, the poverty of conception that is fostered by too-rigid institutional forms, may limit his imagination and distort his vision. That many escape these limitations is a tribute to the human ability to resist pressures that tend to restrict the variety and creativity of life and thought. What is true even at the most advanced levels of graduate education is far more significant at earlier stages, as many critics have eloquently demonstrated. Still, it is not evident, even in this case, to what extent the fault is one of the universities and to what extent it is inherent to the role assigned them in a competitive society, where pursuit of self-interest is elevated to the highest goal. Some of the pressures that impoverish the educational experience and distort the natural relation of student and teacher clearly have their origin in demands that are imposed on the school. Consider, for example, the sociological problem defined by Daniel Bell: "Higher education has been burdened with the task of becoming a gatekeeper—perhaps the only gatekeeper—to significant place and privilege in society . . . it means that the education system is no longer geared to teaching but to judging."[2]

Jencks and Riesman make a similar point: "College is a kind of protracted aptitude test for measuring certain aspects of intelligence and character." The result: "Reliance on colleges to preselect the upper-middle class obviously eliminates most youngsters born into lower-strata families, since they have 'the wrong attitudes' for academic success."[3]

The effect is that the university serves as an instrument for ensuring the perpetuation of social privilege.

[Open to any person, at any stage of life]

The same, incidentally, holds for later life. To achieve the Humboldtian ideal, a university should be open to any man, at any stage of life, who wishes to avail himself to this institutional form for enhancing his "spiritual life."

To some extent true across America, Chomsky's observations have been even truer in certain regions of the country. In New England, for example, the stress levels of high school students can reach a fever pitch in fighting for a space in the "right" elite college or university, with that "rightness" being defined by the benchmarks of the day, such as the *U.S. News & World Report* college guide, or even simple word of mouth from students' peers. Another aspect of Chomsky's theory that a key function of colleges is to perpetuate the divide among social classes is this: During the Vietnam War era, a young man would receive an automatic four-year deferment from military service (hence fighting in Vietnam) simply by going to college and maintaining a 2.0 grade point average. And upon graduation—especially if he had taken the Reserve Officers' Training Course (ROTC)—he could be ensured of entering the military as an officer, with higher pay and status, than one who decided not to attend college. Here is how one U.S. Census Bureau official, Rosaline R. Bruno, put it: "College attendance to maintain a draft deferment most likely caused an increase in college enrollment rates among young men in the 1960's, and the elimination of the draft in the early 1970's probably had some negative impact on enrollment rates in succeeding years."[4]

So, to many young men facing the prospect of fighting in a distant war they didn't understand, the function of college was not only education but also served as a refuge from that war and as hope that it would be over by the time of graduation. If not, at least a man's chance of becoming an officer in the military was heavily increased. A final note in this comment on students in the ROTC comes

In fact, there are programs for bringing corporate executives or engineers from industry to the university for specialized training or simply for broadening their cultural background, but none, to my knowledge, for shoemakers or industrial workers, who could, in principle, profit no less from these opportunities. Evidently, it would be misleading to describe these inequities merely as defects of the university. In general, there is little if any educational function to the requirement that the university be concerned with certification as well as with education and research. On the contrary, this requirement interferes with its proper function. It is a demand imposed by a society that ensures, in many ways, the preservation of certain forms of privilege and elitism.

as a personal observation when this editor was in the naval ROTC at the University of Oklahoma during 1964–1968. It is an indelible memory of the contrast that existed on college campuses during this time: Each Tuesday afternoon the various ROTC units would spend two hours on the drill field, in full uniform. That drill field was several blocks from the campus armory, and we would march in company formation to that field. Sometimes along the way, student protestors would lay down on the street in front of us. We were instructed to keep marching and to step over them as we continued on our way to the drill field. That is just what we did. Many felt badly about doing that, and still do. We were not physically hurting them, but each of us was making our own statement, and it must have been demeaning for those protestors.

Or consider the often-voiced demand that the universities serve the needs of the outside society—that its activities be "relevant" to general social concerns. Put in a very general way, this demand is justifiable. Translated into practice, however, it generally means that the universities provide a service to those existing social institutions that are in a position to articulate their needs and to subsidize the effort to meet these needs. It is not difficult for members of the university community to delude themselves into believing that they are maintaining a "neutral, value-free" position when they simply respond to demands set elsewhere. In fact, to do so is to make a political decision, namely, to ratify the existing distribution of power, authority, and privilege in the society at large, and to take on a commitment to reinforce it. The Pentagon and the great corporations can formulate their needs and subsidize the kind of work that will answer to them. The peasants of Guatemala or the unemployed in Harlem are in no position to do so, obviously. A free society should encourage the development of a university that escapes the not-too-subtle compulsion to be "relevant" in this sense. The university will be able to make its contribution to a free society only to the extent that it overcomes the temptation to conform unthinkingly to the prevailing ideology and to the existing patterns of power and privilege.

Chomsky here articulates part of the ongoing debate about whether universities should be engaged more in "pure" or "applied" education. Sometimes this debate is framed as whether a school should pursue an academic mission or a vocational mission. Chomsky's belief is that a true university should be one that is free of controls or influence by the needs and demands of industry or the government. He argues that a university should offer equally resourced opportunities for its students to pursue careers in both profit and nonprofit sectors and encourage them as much to help the underprivileged as to help the privileged institutions to maintain the status quo and thus their control of society. This mission is made infinitely more difficult because the needed private funding for universities usually comes from the private industries that are looking for graduates who can meet their needs. And the research funding often comes from the same industries that are looking for research and development help from universities that can supply the brains and manpower via their students. This kind of self-interested alliance between the university, which needs the money, and the industry, which needs the help, runs counter to what Chomsky sees as the mission of a "free" university, a term that does not refer to how much it costs to attend the school but to how free the school is to pursue a mission of pure education. This debate between free and applied education was especially intense during the 1960s, an era when much of young America was protesting the influence of the establishment (business and government) in America.

"[A] free university should be expected to be, in a sense, 'subversive.'"

Chomsky continues his theme here and expands it to include the role of the university as protector—if not champion—of the social rebel. He sees this individual as one who is lonely in a society that is influenced so heavily by the institutions that work to suppress free thinking and instead encourage applied thought that meets their own demands.

[A center of intellectual stimulation: ("subversive" challenges of orthodoxy)]

In its relation to society, a free university should be expected to be, in a sense, "subversive." We take for granted that creative work in any field will challenge prevailing orthodoxy. A physicist who refines yesterday's experiment, an engineer who merely seeks to improve existing devices, or an artist who limits himself to styles and techniques that have been thoroughly explored is rightly regarded as deficient in creative imagination. Exciting work in science, technology, scholarship, or the arts will probe the frontiers of understanding and try to create alternatives to the conventional assumptions. If, in some field of inquiry, this is no longer true, then the field will be abandoned by those who seek intellectual adventure. These observations are cliché's that few will question—except in the study of man and society. The social critic who seeks to formulate a vision of a more just and human social order, and is concerned with the discrepancy—more often, the chasm—that separates this vision from the reality that confronts him, is a frightening creature who must "overcome his alienation" and become "responsible," "realistic," and "pragmatic." To decode these expressions: he must stop questioning our values and threatening our privilege. He may be concerned with technical modifications of existing society that improve its efficiency and blur its inequities, but he must not try to design a radically different alternative and involve himself in an attempt to bring about social change. He must, therefore, abandon the path of creative inquiry as it is conceived in other domains. It is hardly necessary to stress that this prejudice is even more rigidly institutionalized in the state socialist societies. Obviously, a free mind may fall into error; the social critic is no less immune to this possibility than the inventive scientist or artist. It may be that at a given stage of technology, the most important activity is to improve the internal combustion engine, and that at a given stage of social evolution, primary attention should be given to the study of fiscal measures that will improve the operation of the system of state capitalism of the Western democracies. This is possible, but hardly obvious, in either case.

The universities offer freedom and encouragement to those who question the first of these assumptions, but more rarely to those who question the second. The reasons are fairly clear. Since the dominant voice in any

society is that of the beneficiaries of the status quo, the "alienated intellectual" who tries to pursue the normal path of honest inquiry—perhaps falling into error on the way—and thus often finds himself challenging the conventional wisdom, tends to be a lonely figure. The degree of protection and support afforded him by the university is, again, a measure of its success in fulfilling its proper function in society. It is, furthermore, a measure of the willingness of the society to submit its ideology and structure to critical analysis and evaluation, and of its willingness to overcome inequities and defects that will be revealed by such a critique. . . .

Such problems as these, which will never cease to exist, so long as human society continues—have become somewhat more critical in the last few years for a number of reasons. In an advanced industrial society, the linkage between the university and external social institutions tend to become more tight and intricate because of the utility of the "knowledge that is produced" (to use a vulgar idiom) and the training that is provided. This is a familiar insight.

Half a century ago, Randolph Bourne noted that the world war had brought to leadership a liberal, technical intelligentsia "immensely ready for the executive ordering of events, pitifully unprepared for the intellectual interpretation or the idealistic focusing of ends," pragmatic intellectuals who "have absorbed the secret of scientific method as applied to political administration" and who readily "lined up in the service of the war technique." Turning to the university, and taking Columbia University as the prototype, he described it as "a financial corporation, strictly analogous, in its motives and responses, to the corporation which is concerned in the production of industrial commodities. . . . The university produces learning instead of steel or rubber, but the nature of the academic commodity has become less and less potent in insuring for the academic workman a status materially different from that of any other kind of employee." The trustees, he claimed, define their obligation in this way: "to see that the quality of the commodity which the university produces is such as to seem reputable

Randolph Silliman Bourne was a left-wing intellectual and progressive writer in the early 20th century who died in 1918 at the young age of 32. He was a graduate of Columbia University and was a staunch protestor of America's involvement in World War I, advocating against the use of war as a tool to bring peace. Bourne was often cited by intellectual protestors of the Vietnam War in the 1960s and early 1970s because his thinking on war was consistent with the rhetoric of the anti-war movement during the Vietnam War era.

to the class which they represent." "Under trustee control," Bourne went on, "the American university has been degraded from its old, noble ideal of a community of scholarship to a private commercial corporation."[5]

Bourne's characterization of the university can be questioned in many respects, but it nevertheless has an unpleasant ring of authenticity, today even more than at the time when he wrote. . . .

Lionel Trilling was a 20th-century social critic who wrote for publications supporting liberal and even communistic ideologies. He denounced right-wing reactionary ideas and encouraged more free thinking and intellectualism in American society.

Lionel Trilling, in a recent interview, pointed out that he cannot draw on his own experience as a student to help him comprehend the motivation of the "militant students" at Columbia:

Like all my friends at college, I hadn't the slightest interest in the university as an institution: I thought of it, when I thought of it at all, as the inevitable philistine condition of one's being given leisure, a few interesting teachers, and a library. I find it hard to believe that this isn't the natural attitude.[6]

Chomsky's view, stated in 1969, was that football and fraternities were not the magnetic force for colleges that they had been 20 years earlier. That is a difficult assertion to support, however, and even historians look at a place such as New York University—not generally thought of as a football or party school—and find that fraternity life was thriving during the Vietnam War years. The same was true for many other colleges and universities around the country, both public and private. At schools such as the University of Oklahoma and Southern Methodist University, Greek life and football were huge draws for students. Some saw them as an escape, albeit a temporary one, from the worries about the horrible and seemingly unsolvable problem of the Vietnam War. To be sure, intellectualism existed alongside these distractions, but much of that seemed centered in the graduate schools. At the undergraduate level, this intellectualism largely asserted itself through the various student protest demonstrations on campus. Often led by a relatively small number of dissidents, these protests nevertheless were often loud and drew media attention.

We skip to the concluding paragraphs of Chomsky's essay, wherein he discusses how to address the conflict involving the proper function of the university

This is an apt comment. In the past, it was for the most part the football and fraternity crowd who had an interest in the university as such. But in this respect there have been substantial changes. Now it is generally the most serious and thoughtful students who are concerned with the nature of the universities and who feel hurt and deprived by its failings. Twenty years ago [in 1949], these students—in an urban university at least—would have looked elsewhere for the intellectual and social life that they now expect the university to provide. Personally, I feel that the sharp challenges that have been raised by the student movement are among the few hopeful developments of these troubled years.

. . . "Restructuring the university" is unlikely to be effective in eliminating the features of the institution that have sparked student criticism. In fact, many of the concrete proposals that I have seen are, I suspect, likely to have the opposite effect; namely, they may lead toward a system of enforceable regulations that may appear democratic on paper but will limit the individual freedom that exists in an institution that is highly decentralized and rather loose in its structure of decision making and administration, hence fairly responsive to the wishes of its members. It is possible to imagine useful reforms; I suspect, however, that they will have at best a small effect on the way the university functions. The real problem is a much deeper one: to change the choices and personal commitment of the individuals who make up the university. This is much harder than modification of formal structures and is not likely to be effected by such restructuring in any very serious way.

More to the point, I believe, is the view expressed in the Port Huron Statement of 1962, more or less the founding document of SDS [Students for a Democratic Society]: The university is located in a permanent position of social influence. Its educational function makes it indispensable and automatically makes it a crucial institution in the formation of social attitudes. In an unbelievably complicated world, it is the central institution for organizing, evaluating, and transmitting knowledge. . . . Social relevance, the accessibility to knowledge, and internal openness—these together make the university a potential base and agency in the movement of social change.

The primary barrier to such development will not be the unwillingness of administrators or the stubbornness of trustees. It will be the unwillingness of students to do the difficult and serious work required and the fear of the faculty that its security and authority, its guild structure, will be threatened.

In concluding, Chomsky does not call for what he feels would be a superficial restructuring of the university but instead issues a clarion call to liberal-minded students and faculty to resist what he perceives as administrators and trustees who are oriented toward the status quo and are held in the grip of the extrauniversity institutions that stifle free thinking and real innovation in America. He aligns his worldview with that of the Port Huron Statement of the Students for a Democratic Society, detailed in Chapter 3 of this book.

Source: C. P. Otero, ed., *Chomsky on Democracy and Education* (New York: RoutledgeFalmer, 2003), 178–194. Used by permission.

Notes

1. Jo Freeman, "The Berkeley Free Speech Movement," University of Illinois at Chicago, http://www.uic.edu/orgs/cwluherstory/jofreeman/sixtiesprotest/berkeley.htm.

2. Daniel Bell, "The Scholar Concerned," *American Scholar,* 37(3) (1968): 401–406.

3. Christopher Jencks and David Riesman, *The Academic Revolution* (New York: Doubleday, 1968), 104, 100.

4. "College Enrollment Linked to Vietnam War," *New York Times,* September 2, 1984, http://www.nytimes.com/1984/09/02/us/college-enrollment-linked-to-vietnam-war.html.

5. Lillian Schlissel, ed., *The World of Randolph Bourne* (New York: E. P. Dutton, 1965), 198, 85, 87.

6. Ibid.

Chapter 2

Flowers in Their Hair: Voices of the Hippie Movement

Introduction

This chapter looks at documents focusing on the uniquely 1960s culture in America known as hippies. What is a hippie? Many observers of the decade focus on the outward appearances of those in the 1960s who were demonstrating for various causes. There was the psychedelic clothing, the beards on men, the flowers in the hair, the flowers on clothing and cars—ubiquitous flowers. There were the peace signs on chains around the neck, the wide-brimmed floppy hats, the painted VW buses, and more. There was also the revolutionary rock and folk-rock music, and there were the drugs: marijuana, LSD, ecstasy, and more. But the hippie movement was much more than the sum of its outward protest-screaming appearance. One of its champions of the time, Dr. Timothy Leary, said the following about it *The Politics of Ecstasy* (1968): "Hippy is an establishment label for a profound, invisible, underground, evolutionary process. For every visible hippy, barefoot, beflowered, beaded, there are a thousand invisible members of the turned-on underground. Persons whose lives are tuned in to their inner vision, who are dropping out of the TV comedy of American life."[1]

"The Class Structure of Hippie Society"

Dr. Sherry Cavan's Article on the Economics of Hippie Society
October 1972

INTRODUCTION

The following is an excerpt from Dr. Sherry Cavan's article "The Class Structure of Hippie Society," published in the October 1972 issue of *Urban Life and Culture,* a multivolume set of reference books looking at life in America. In this essay, Cavan depicts hippies as a group focusing on "counter-development." By this she means that hippies attempted to simplify the structure of their society. This goes against the grain of most cultures, she writes, that develop by adding to the complexity of society. Cavan's essay focuses on the "underground economy" and splits the hippie movement into different segments of workers and earners, including "craftsmen, peddlers, [and] merchants." Each of these segments, she explains, occupies a different level of prestige within the hippie society.

It is interesting that Dr. Cavan focuses on the economic aspect of the hippie movement, because most other analyses focus on the idealism of the hippies. Any movement—no matter how political or idealistic—has pragmatic concerns, and the hippie movement was no different. Was idealism at the heart of the movement? There is no doubt about that. But practical concerns were there too, issues such as where the money, food, and housing would come from to fund the daily existence of its members and how to distribute those resources to members.

Hippie society is ideally conceived of as a place where personal interest is served; where the individual is free to "do his own thing" and to "find where he's at." In its utopian version, it is a world where each, in accordance with personal disposition, acts in terms of his individual interests; and all, in sharing similar interests, act in concert. Thus how any individual chooses to orient himself toward the means of production and distribution ultimately rests on matters of personal disposition. Some hippies live as idlers, as persons who drift aimlessly, without ambition. Others homestead and focus their attention on "getting by." Yet others desire to secure various advantages for themselves and their kin—and in so desiring they may direct their attention and interest towards the marketplace.

Resources—whether they be skill or cash, stamina or guile—are what the individual brings to the marketplace.

Dr. Cavan raises a point that is often overlooked as people discuss revolutionary movements: that while the concept of an ideal society may serve as the reason for bringing individuals into the movement—and provide an underlying justification for staying there—it isn't long before individual ambitions and expectations surface. Concerns such as "What is my place in this society going to be?" and "How am I going to eat and pay the rent?" begin raising their heads and demanding answers. When these individual practical issues confront idealism, group dynamics and interpersonal conflict are affected.

Many never think about the concept of a "rich hippie," but many who joined the movement came from upper-middle-class families, and some came from wealthy families. In both cases, their access to personal resources was much greater than those who came from different backgrounds. It is important not to overstate the notion, often exaggerated by more conservative politicians, that most hippies came from privileged backgrounds and used protest as a means of eradicating boredom from their lives. For example, in her book *Hardhats, Hippies, and Hawks: The Vietnam Anti-War Movement as Myth and Memory,* sociologist Penny Lewis says that most of the hippies came from working-class backgrounds. Lewis asserts that many in the country's working class embraced the antiwar sentiment and became active in the counterculture movement. She adds, however, that these working classes did not always articulate their views in the rhetoric of class politics.[2]

Regardless of how he came by them, resources provide bargaining power. Where resources are scant, the individual's position in the market situation is low, and what assets he has are likely to be expropriated by others. Those whose resources are more substantial are correspondingly more free to pursue life in accordance with personal disposition. And they sometimes do so at a profit.

Resources are also necessary to build a new society. The hippies constitute a subordinate culture that must engage in daily transactions with the dominant group. The alternatives they have available for the reconstruction of societal forms are those that are compatible with, if not identical to, the dominant culture. So, even though they make frequent use of barter among themselves, their transactions with the conventional culture necessitate a source of revenue. The three main sources of revenue in hippie society are public assistance, family allotments and members' own labor. Within the context of members' own labor would include dealing dope, rip-offs, and business.

In the present paper, I have focused only on business. Business holds an important place in the new society. It is used to supplement revenue from other sources, even where it does not supplant them. It accounts for the largest cash flow in the counter-culture. Finally, though economic exchange, business brings together large numbers of individuals in routinized patterns of conduct. In turn, these routine patterns of economic exchange create a particular societal form: the underground marketplace.

As Belshaw (1965) notes with respect to peasant economies, the market does not come into existence to enable persons to dispose of surplus. It comes into existence as a function of the division of labor. The mode this division takes among the hippies is five class-like social groups: vagabonds (explained in the article as individuals who drift between settlements in a nomadic fashion), peddlers, craftsmen, merchants, and entrepreneurs.

"Craftsmanship forms the backbone of the underground economy . . ."

Craftsmanship forms the backbone of the underground economy and the skilled craftsman holds the most esteemed place in hippie society. Ideally, his creativity is an expressive rather than instrumental act. But nonetheless, it is understood that he has the right to market his wares. It is also understood that some craftsmen do not desire to market their own wares directly, and hence arrangements for distribution exist. Both peddlers and merchants act as traders within the economy, although these two groups are distinguished from one another in a variety of ways: by the complexity and permanence of their enterprise, by the dominant nature of their repute in both the counter-culture and the dominant culture, and by their relations with the class of craftsmen.

This complex of three roles forms the core of the economy. Between them, goods are produced and distributed and money begins to circulate. However, the underground market extends beyond this core, to incorporate vagabonds, whose personal assets consist of interest, if not skill, and entrepreneurs, whose personal interest goes beyond trade to promotion.

Movement across these class lines is fluid. Craftsmen may peddle their own wares; vagabonds may learn a skill; merchants and entrepreneurs are sometimes interchangeable. However, the classes exist as observable features of the underground marketplace. They constitute concrete forms of exchange that have become routinized in the counter-culture, and, in their routinization, they have provided that culture with some measure of economic stability.

Yet that measure of economic stability comes at a cost to cultural consistency. In the context of "ordinary business," values stressed by the ideology are subverted by everyday practice. Principles of altruism begin to give way to those of chicanery; bluffing replaces up-front transactions; planning and organization supplant spontaneity and psychic whim.

Source: Sherri Cavan, "The Class Structure of Hippie Society," *Urban Life and Culture,* October 1972, 235–237. © 2009 Sage Publications. Used by permission of Sage Publications.

While Dr. Cavan looks at the role of the economy within hippie society and the effect that economic engine had on members of that group, it is worth noting that economic issues have often driven revolutionary movements in the world and still do today. Indeed, it is economic depravity and the chasm between the haves and have-nots that often has driven everyday people to the point of risking their lives to redress their grievances. Such was the case in America's own Revolutionary War. Here, much of the impetus for going to war with England came from everyday colonial businesspeople who were frustrated over having to compete in a marketplace stacked by Mother England and designed to benefit British-produced goods over American products. This was the whole point of the most visible of the American prewar protests against England: the Boston Tea Party, when tons of English tea were dumped into Boston Harbor straight from the decks of the ships importing it to the colonies.

"The Gathering of the Tribes"

Promotional Article in the *San Francisco Oracle*
January 1967

INTRODUCTION

In her book *The Dissident Press,* journalistic historian Lauren Kessler talks about the role of the counterculture media during the 1960s and 1970s. About the disparate groups giving birth to these publications, she writes that "Unlike short-lived special-interest groups . . . these groups struggled for years. During their struggle they produced an impressive variety and number of publications."[3] These publications, such as the *Berkeley Barb, Ramparts,* the *Village Voice,* and the *San Francisco Oracle,* had many functions, but one of them was certainly informing hippies of upcoming protest events or happenings.

While the four publications noted were leaders in this underground press movement, most were little more than newsletters printed on home mimeograph machines on shoestring budgets. Whether resource rich or resource poor, however, they provided a vital service to the counterculture movement in announcing events, reporting on them, and advocating for the protest movement.

This brief article, "The Gathering of the Tribes," was published in the January 1967 issue of the *San Francisco Oracle.* In journalistic parlance it is known as an advance, which is a story done to announce an upcoming event. The article is promoting the Human Be-In, which turned out to be one of the earliest of the large-scale gatherings of hippies and like-minded Vietnam War protestors in the city that became the epicenter of the hippie movement in America. These promotional articles often used the tone and vocabulary of the counterculture society they were trying to reach.

Any traditional journalist would find it hard not to cringe when reading the text of this article because it violates so many norms of objective reporting, which is the standard—at least the ideal—of the mainstream media. Even a casual reading of the article makes that apparent, and it happens from the very first phrase: "A union of love and activism previously separated by categorical dogma and label mongering will finally occur ecstatically." The blend of the hippie worldview and hyperbole over the event's anticipation make mincemeat of journalistic training when it comes to detachment and objectivity.

A union of love and activism previously separated by categorical dogma and label mongering will finally occur ecstatically when Berkeley political activists and hip community and San Francisco's spiritual generation and contingents from the emerging revolutionary generation all over California meet for a Gathering of the Tribes for a Human Be-In at the Polo Field in Golden Gate Park on Saturday, January 14, 1967, from 1 to 5 p.m.

Twenty to fifty thousand people are expected to gather for a joyful Pow-Wow and Peace Dance to be celebrated with leaders, guides, and heroes of our generation: Timothy Leary will make his first Bay Area public appearance; Allen Ginsberg will chant and read with Gary Snyder, Michael McClure, and Lenore Kandel; Dick Alpert, Jerry Rubin, Dick Gregory, and Jack Weinberg will speak. Music will be played by all the Bay Area rock bands, including the Grateful Dead, Big Brother and the Holding Co., Quicksilver Messenger Service, and many others. Everyone is invited to bring costumes, blankets, bells, flags, symbols, cymbals, drums, beads, feathers, flowers.

Now in the evolving generation of America's young, the humanization of the American man and woman can begin in joy and embrace without fear, dogma, suspicion, or dialectical righteousness. A new concert of human relations being developed within the youthful underground must emerge, become conscious, and be shared so that a revolution of form can be filled with a Renaissance of compassion, awareness, and love in the Revelation of the unity of all mankind. The Human Be-In is the joyful, face-to-face beginning of the new epoch.

The twin concepts of revolution and renaissance are stressed here, and again the rhetoric is rife with value statements of the hippie movement. It is important to remember, however, that objective reporting was not what the underground press was all about. The journalism of the underground press was *advocacy* journalism, and the press felt that the mainstream media's idea of objectivity had underrepresented the hippie goals and ideals and instead focused on establishment values. These, of course, were the very values that the hippie movement was against. That view is similar to the views of many right-wing ideologues today who feel that there is nothing wrong with having a television network such as Fox deliver a conservative slant to the news, inasmuch as the mainstream media—in the minds of conservatives—bases its stories on liberal values and denigrates conservatism.

"Trip without a Ticket"

The Digger Papers
August 1968

INTRODUCTION

Coming on the heels of the last article looking at some economic realities within the hippie society, this next article, "Trip without a Ticket," is very representative of the idealistic economic view of young counterculture revolutionaries of the 1960s. Published in 1967, it warns readers of being caught up in what the hippies called "the establishment" and promotes instead a kind of free-store mentality whereby none of the rules of capitalism (seen as a manipulated evil) apply. Just as love was meant to be free of costs in the 1960s, so were goods and services. They were to be distributed to anyone who needed them. The article would go on to become part of "The Digger Papers" the following year. The Diggers were those hippies who believed in free stores, argued against ownership and private property (holding beliefs similar to Native Americans in the early days of America), and described their lifestyle as "street theater." The diggers were in fact largely made up of street artisans who performed spontaneously their improvisations on the street (free of charge but accepting donations), displayed their art, and pushed for a free exchange of goods and services.

Nembutal is a barbiturate used as a sedative, hypnotic, and/or antispasmodic drug. This writer uses "Nembutals" as a metaphor for the state of those living in the world of the establishment, meaning those who embrace capitalism and refuse to question whether they are being manipulated by the power elite who manufacture goods and exploit the populace by selling at a high profit. This is a common mantra of the hippie movement of the 1960s.

Our authorized sanities are so many Nembutals. "Normal" citizens with store-dummy smiles stand apart from each other like cotton-packed capsules in a bottle. Perpetual mental out-patients. Maddeningly sterile jobs for strait-jackets, love scrubbed into an insipid "functional personal relationship" and Art as a fantasy pacifier.

Everyone is kept inside while the outside is shown through windows: advertising and manicured news. And we all know this.

In the hippie worldview, advertising, public relations, and the news media itself are held in the grip of the power elite, who use all of it to manipulate thoughts and emotions of everyday people, all with the purpose of getting them to buy products, ideas, or even wars they are pushing for their own self-interest.

How many TV specials would it take to establish one Guatemalan revolution? How many weeks would an ad agency require to face-lift the image of the Viet Cong? Slowly, very slowly we are led nowhere. Consumer circuses are held in the ward daily. Critics are tolerated like exploding novelties. We will be told which burning Asians to take seriously. Slowly. Later.

But there is a real danger in suddenly waking a somnambulistic patient. And we all know this.

What if he is startled right out the window?

No one can control the single circuit-breaking moment that charges games with critical reality. If the glass is cut, if the cushioned distance of media is removed, the patients may never respond as normals again. They will become life-actors. Theater is territory. A space for existing outside padded walls. Setting down a stage declares a universal pardon for imagination.

But what happens next must mean more than sanctuary or preserve. How would real wardens react to life-actors on liberated ground? How can the intrinsic freedom of theater illuminate walls and show the weak-spots where a breakout could occur?

Guerrilla theater intends to bring audiences to liberated territory to create life-actors. It remains light and exploitative of forms for the same reasons that it intends to remain free. It seeks audiences that are created by issues. It creates a cast of freed beings. It will become an issue itself.

"Guerrilla theater intends to bring audiences to liberated territory to create life-actors."

This is theater of an underground that wants out. Its aim is to liberate ground held by consumer wardens and establish territory without walls. Its plays are glass cutters for empire windows.

The Concept of a Free Store

The Diggers are hip to property. Everything is free, do your own thing. Human beings are the means of exchange. Food, machines, clothing, materials, shelter and props are simply there. Stuff. A perfect dispenser would be an open Automat on the street. Locks are time-consuming. Combinations are clocks.

So a store of goods or clinic or restaurant that is free becomes a social art form. Ticketless theater. Out of money and control.

Changing the economic base of society is seen as resulting in changing human nature and the kind of society that citizens make up as they go along, relying on their own resourcefulness.

Diggers assume free stores to liberate human nature. First free the space, goods and services. Let theories of economics follow social facts. Once a free store is assumed, human wanting and giving, needing and taking, become wide open to improvisation.

"Someone asked how much a book cost. How much did he think it was worth?"

Someone asked how much a book cost. How much did he think it was worth? 75 cents. The money was taken and held out for anyone. "Who wants 75 cents?" A girl who had just walked in came over and took it.

A basket labeled Free Money.

No owner, no manager, no employees and no cash-register. A salesman in a free store is a life-actor. Anyone who will assume an answer to a question or accept a problem as a turn-on.

Question (whispered): "Who pays the rent?"

Answer (loudly): "May I help you?"

Who's ready for the implications of a free store? Welfare mothers pile bags full of clothes for a few days and come back to hang up dresses. Kids case the joint wondering how to boost.

Fire helmets, riding pants, shower curtains, surgical gowns and World War I Army boots are parts for costumes. Nightsticks, sample cases, water pipes, toy guns and weather balloons are taken for props. When materials are free, imagination becomes currency for spirit.

So, here the question of where these goods will come from if no one is paying for them is answered. They are simply donated by people who no longer want them or who want to trade them for other goods. Think of the concept of a Goodwill Store, although one where you don't even have to pay a few dollars for a shirt or pair of pants. Actually, Goodwill International was set up on a premise similar to this in 1902 by a Methodist minister in Boston. Collect unwanted goods, hire unemployed workers to repair and clean them, then distribute them at basement-level prices to the needy. Left unanswered is whether store employees are paid (it is assumed not) and who in fact pays the rent for the store.

Where does the stuff come from? People, persons, beings. Isn't it obvious that objects are only transitory subjects of human value? An object released from one person's value may be destroyed, abandoned or made available to other people. The choice is anyone's.

The question of a free store is simply: What would you have?

Street Events

Pop Art mirrored the social skin. Happenings X-rayed the bones. Street events are social acid heightening consciousness of what is real on the street. To expand eye-ball implications until facts are established through action.

The Mexican Day of the Dead is celebrated in cemeteries. Yellow flowers falling petal by petal on graves. In moonlight. Favorite songs of the deceased and everybody gets loaded. Children suck deaths-head candy engraved with their names in icing.

Dia de Muertos is a holiday celebrated primarily in Mexico from October 31 to November 2 when family and friends gather in cemeteries to pray for, remember, and celebrate friends and family members who have died. It is often a festive event with more of a focus on celebration than mourning.

A Digger event. Flowers, mirrors, penny-whistles, girls in costumes of themselves, Hell's Angels, street people, Mime Troupe.

Angels ride up Haight with girls holding Now! signs. Flowers and penny-whistles passed out to everyone.

A chorus on both sides of the street chanting Uhh!—Ahh!—Shh be cool! Mirrors held up to reflect faces of passersby.

The burial procession. Three black-shrouded messengers holding staffs topped with reflective dollar signs. A runner swinging a red lantern. Four pall bearers wearing animal heads carry a black casket filled with blowups of silver dollars. A chorus singing Get Out Of My Life Why Don't You Babe to Chopin's Death March. Members of the procession give out silver dollars and candles.

Now more reality. Someone jumps on a car with the news that two Angels were busted. Crowd, funeral cortege and friends of the Angels fill the street to march on Park Police Station. Cops confront 400 free beings: a growling poet with a lute, animal spirits in black, candle-lit girls singing Silent Night. A collection for bail fills an Angel's helmet. March back to Haight and street dancing.

Street events are rituals of release. Reclaiming of territory (sundown, traffic, public joy) through spirit. Possession. Public NewSense.

Not street-theater, the street is theater. Parades, bank robberies, fires and sonic explosions focus street attention. A crowd is an audience for an event. Release of crowd spirit can accomplish social facts.

Riots are a reaction to police theater. Thrown bottles and over-turned cars are responses to a dull, heavy-fisted,

Here the writer makes reference to police, who were often disparaged by hippies, as being the muscle for the power elite intent on silencing the voices of the "liberated." During the 1960s, protestors denigrated police by calling them "pigs," a term of uncertain origin or meaning. Some believe that it refers to what a police officer looks like in a gas mask as he is dispersing a crowd with tear gas. Others feel that it is a reference to the pigs who were in charge of the animal farm in George Orwell's book of that name.

mechanical and deathly show. People fill the street to express special public feelings and hold human communion. To ask "What's Happening?"

The alternative to death is a joyous funeral in company with the living.

Who paid for your trip?

Concern over abuse of the environment became a growing part of the protest movement of the 1960s, and the creation of synthetic materials that were not biodegradable infuriated many hippies. A classic line from the movie that defined the 1960s generation of young people, *The Graduate*, showed a businessman trying to interest an innocent young college graduate, Ben, in a career in plastics.

Industrialization was a battle with 19th-century ecology to win breakfast at the cost of smog and insanity. Wars against ecology are suicidal. The U.S. standard of living is a bourgeois baby blanket for executives who scream in their sleep. No Pleistocene swamp could match the pestilential horror of modern urban sewage. No children of White Western Progress will escape the dues of peoples forced to haul their raw materials.

But the tools (that's all factories are) remain innocent and the ethics of greed aren't necessary. Computers render the principles of wage-labor obsolete by incorporating them. We are being freed from mechanistic consciousness. We could evacuate the factories, turn them over to androids, clean up our pollution. North Americans could give up self-righteousness to expand their being.

Our conflict is with job-wardens and consumer-keepers of a permissive loony-bin. Property, credit, interest, insurance, installments, profit are stupid concepts. Millions of have-nots and drop-outs in the U.S. are living on an overflow of technologically produced fat. They aren't fighting ecology, they're responding to it. Middle-class living rooms are funeral parlors and only undertakers will stay in them. Our fight is with those who would kill us through dumb work, insane wars, dull money morality.

Give up jobs, so computers can do them! Any important human occupation can be done free. Can it be given away?

Revolutions in Asia, Africa, South America are for humanistic industrialization. The technological resources of North America can be used throughout the world. Gratis. Not a patronizing gift, shared.

Our conflict begins with salaries and prices. The trip has been paid for at an incredible price in death, slavery, psychosis.

An event for the main business district of any U.S. city. Infiltrate the largest corporation office building with life-actors as nymphomaniacal secretaries, clumsy repairmen, berserk executives, sloppy security guards, clerks with animals in their clothes. Low key until the first coffee-break and then pour it on.

Secretaries unbutton their blouses and press shy clerks against the wall. Repairmen drop typewriters and knock over water coolers. Executives charge into private offices claiming their seniority. Guards produce booze bottles and playfully jam elevator doors. Clerks pull out goldfish, rabbits, pigeons, cats on leashes, loose dogs.

The hypocrisy of the establishment was often a focus of protest and derision among members of the hippie culture. The solution was to not buy into the establishment, in effect dropping out of that society. This theme has been revised numerous times since the 1960s, most recently in the nonfiction story and movie *Into the Wild* about a young Chris McCandless who sought freedom apart from the civilized world in 1992, only to find death instead.

At noon 1,000 freed beings singing and dancing appear outside to persuade employees to take off for the day. Banners roll down from office windows announcing liberation. Shills in business suits run out of the building, strip and dive in the fountain. Elevators are loaded with incense and a pie fight breaks out in the cafeteria. Theater is fact/action.

Give up jobs. Be with people. Defend against property.

"Give up jobs. Be with people."

Source: Originally published by the Diggers, ca. Winter 1966–1967. Reprinted by the Communication Company SF 2nd Edition 6/28/67. Included in The Digger Papers, August 1968. Available online at http://www.diggers.org/digpaps68/twatdp.html.

"The Community of the Tribe"

Tom Law's Article on Hippie Culture

1967

INTRODUCTION

It is ironic that although the hippie movement began and thrived in the cities, especially on the West Coast, it wasn't long before many hippies began seeing urban life as incompatible with the simplicity and communitarian nature of their newfound values. Dropping out of the establishment, living in an environment of a "free store," and pursuing pleasure for its own sake seemed like it would be easier to do in rural America than in the crowded and expensive cities.

San Francisco was especially expensive and, since this city was the epicenter of the hippie movement, voices arose for hippies to move out of the cities and into the more uninhabited areas to set up hippie communes and live off the land. This became one of the themes of the movement and was expressed in counterculture publications such as the *San Francisco Oracle*. Part of the function of the news media—whether mainstream or advocate—is to orient people to their own culture, even as that culture is developing. Such was the case with the underground press of the 1960s. It existed not only to announce and promote upcoming events and then report on them afterward but also to promulgate tenets of the hippie philosophy to others in the movement and to new and would-be converts. This article by Tom Law serves just that purpose.

The concept of centering is an interesting one with regard to the hippie movement. The word "center" was a dominant theme, for example, in one of the signature works of writer Joan Didion in 1967: "Slouching towards Bethlehem." Her essay describes in various ways the vulnerability of both the individuals' and society's centers to forces trying to pull it one direction or another.

In this phase of our organic growth we must all center, letting the forces and energies that are happening within us draw us together. By doing so we render impotent the cop without as well as the cop within.

We must then consciously enforce that centering to avoid the ugly games of power and prejudice which erode the community spirit, feeling, and effort. In times of decision this centering is the process of dipping, beyond images of the intellect, into the wellspring of the divine within every man and there finding the next natural step in the process of creating our new world.

The comparison of hippie culture to the tribe—especially that of Native American tribes—is a common theme in hippie rhetoric. Indeed, many of the concepts embraced by hippies are those developed and practiced by tribes of American Indians in the days of the American frontier.

We thereby respect each other and the environment which we find ourselves creating for the Tribe. The Tribe then is. Without pushing or pointing it grows organically.

The organic growth of love and cooperation in us is the balancing factor of nature. To every facet of hate we must reflect love and to know this we must practice it unceasingly in all directions.

Guard carefully against feeling that we are a special, new or unique tribe. We are the ancient tribal consciousness of man in harmonious relationship with nature. The distended machine is the mutant.

We are all—squares and the psychedelically enlightened alike—involved in our world of now. To take up the call, to respond to the cosmic forces, we must *be* the hard-working, harmonious, respectful, honest, diligent, co-operative family of man. Our words are inspired. Our devotion is strong. The precious revelations which have come through us with increasing magnitude must be fathomed until we are one with each other and can extend our awareness beyond the tribe to our entire planet.

This is an interesting passage, given the earlier warning about not feeling special. There was, in fact, a feeling among hippies that they were especially imbued with a kind of spiritual light that set them apart from those in the established society.

What is the natural karmic duty of a generation whose brother, neighbors, and childhood friends now promote hate by killing innocent human beings around the world? It is to balance their jive and immature actions with the light of intelligent goodness; fearlessly to deal with the money-mad machine in order to release its hold on our bowels—the bowels of mankind.

Practically, this means that all excess profit is turned back into the community. That means all money, material things, food, etc., which are beyond the basic necessities of a happy, healthy, human existence: loyal to the turn-on. While profit is only to be made on those people led and fed by the machine. By more and more of us approaching this new level of awareness within, and by giving to each other, we quite naturally are open to receive. We all become our creative selves, creating our society within this massive mess of victims of greed, indulgence, possessiveness, and hate. If our souls are mirrors, does not hate reflect hate?

"[A]ll excess profit is turned back into the community."

So we must change the entire environment, dealing within and for the community which we create. *Do* that love with those who'll do love with you: the promoter, artist, editor, concessionaire, musician, shopkeeper, carpenter, plumber, dishwasher cook, monk, and all the other masters of smoke, color, and the all-knowing center.

In a real sense, this phrase sums up the goals ....
of the hippie culture: stressing love, avoiding
the "plastic" society, embracing nature, and
being one with the "awakening" within.

Without offending the Plastic-Zip population, we can create our own communities and ashrams and love environments where we can turn on and tune into the real cosmic dream of awakening, once again, to nature; where we can live in health within our needs both practical and spiritual.

"Let's make Haight Love together, and then move to the country . . ."

Let's make Haight Love together, and then move to the country where love is hanging out waiting. Love-Ashbury will then exist as our trade capital, our funnel to the world, and we can occasionally share a natural sunset together, steadying our lives with both the active and the passive changes.

Source: Tom Law, "The Community of the Tribe," *San Francisco Oracle* 6: 15. © 2009 Regent Press. Used by permission of the estate of Allen Cohen and Regent Press, as originally printed in *The San Francisco Oracle*, and collected in the book/CD/DVD *The San Francisco Oracle Facsimile Edition: The Psychedelic Newspaper of the Haight Ashbury* (Berkeley, CA: Regent Press, 2005).

"Marxism and Nonviolence"

A Conversation with Isaac Deutscher

May 1966

INTRODUCTION

The question sometimes arises about where hippies stood in their views in relation to Marxist doctrine. Most of the hippie protest was directed at the establishment, or the power elite and its traditional value structure that hippies saw as hypocritical and often oppressive. Was this not the same view that Marxists had? Although there were similarities between some of the tenets of Marxism and hippie-ism, there were also differences. Similarities included the hippie hope to eliminate class systems and strive for equality and an equitable distribution of wealth and resources in society. Hippies favored socialism over capitalism as a general rule. However, most hippies did not believe in overthrowing the bourgeoisie or in forcing their ideologies onto other countries, as Marxists believed. But there was another difference: Marxism did not seem to promote nonviolent protest, while most hippies believed in nonviolence. Indeed, the universal symbol of hippies was the peace symbol, and love was seen as the means to achieving peace, as in the ubiquitous saying "Make love, not war." So, the question arose that if hippies were Marxists, why were so many of them pushing nonviolent means of reaching their utopian goals? After all, nonviolence did not seem to be a hallmark of Marxist teachings. The following essay, which was a transcript of an audio tape of Isaac Deustcher made in May 1966, looks at the question of nonviolence and how it related to Marxism. Deutscher was a Polish-born writer and academic whose books and studies made him an authority on Marxism, Joseph Stalin, Leon Trotsky, and the Russian Revolution. Deutscher lectured frequently at top American universities. These remarks were made in a conversation with Dave Dellinger, an influential political activist and proponent of nonviolence, and A. J. Muste, a Dutch-born clergyman and activist.

I must admit that talk about the challenge of nonviolence tends at the beginning to stare at all my deep-seated Marxist bias against this kind of argument. I am at once aroused to suspect some wishy-washy idealistic generalizations that lead us politically, analytically and morally nowhere.

But as I listen to your [David Dellenger's] argument [in favor of nonviolent protest] I become increasingly aware that my bias is directed against an opponent who doesn't stand in front of me at all; my bias is directed against the escapism of absolute pacifism.

Even against the high principles of absolute pacifism it is difficult to argue without feeling a certain moral

As a historian and pragmatist, Deutscher seems to find some value in the principles of nonviolence but sees the overall idea of pacifism as an unrealizable and unworkable ideal, one that will not achieve the goals that hippies are seeking.

embarrassment, because one would like the absolute pacifist— who denies absolutely any positive role of violence in history—to be right. And yet one knows that he isn't right and that this is a very dangerous escapism.

Therefore, one tends to react, if one is a Marxist, with a certain venom. But you are not romantic creatures of nonviolence.

Deutscher asks the question of how hippies can protest the violence of U.S. involvement in Vietnam while defending the violence that the North Vietnamese and Viet Cong exhibit themselves, whether in defense of their beliefs or not.

To my mind, and I hesitate to use strong words, you have taken a heroic stand over the war in Vietnam. When you started your protest you could not have foreseen that you would be backed by such wide popular response: you have taken great risks in order to express not only your opposition to the violence used by American power, by American imperialism, but also to defend to some extent, morally, the violence to which the Vietnamese have to resort in order to save their own dignity, their own interests, their own present and their own future.

"One might say that there is an inconsistency in your attitude . . ."

One might say that there is an inconsistency in your attitude, a contradiction in your preaching nonviolence and yet accepting morally to some extent the violence applied by the Vietcong in Vietnam and probably by the FLN in Algeria. But I think that this is a creative inconsistency, a creative contradiction in your attitude.

Although you start from an idealistic and, to my mind, a somewhat metaphysical principle, nevertheless your inconsistency opens for you an important horizon into the realities of our age. I think that you are carrying out something like truthful self-criticism. It is the self-criticism of a variety of pacifism which is not afraid of bringing its own apparent formal inconsistency into the open in order to achieve a greater moral and political consistency in action.

And may I say that arguing philosophically from places partly opposed, I admit a similar, but a much larger, perhaps a more tragic inconsistency in the history of revolution, in the history of Communism and Marxism.

The fact is that there is a whole dialectic of violence and nonviolence implied in the Marxist doctrine from its beginnings and throughout all its historic metamorphosis from 1848–1966. As Marxists we have always preached proletarian dictatorship, and the need to overthrow capitalism by force. We have always tried to impress on the working classes of all countries that they would have to be prepared to struggle, even in civil wars, against their oppressing and ruling classes. We were quite devastating in our rejoinders to all those who doubted the right or questioned the need for all those preachings.

But here is the dialectical contradiction: after all what has been the idea of Marxism? That of the classless society in which man is no longer exploited and dominated by man, a stateless society. So many people of the left consider this the Utopian element in Marxism, the aspiration to transform societies in such a way that violence should cease forever as the necessary and permanent element in the regulation of the relationship between society and individuals, between individuals and individuals.

Here Deutscher lays out a parallel inconsistency—if not outright contradiction—in Marxism regarding violence and nonviolence as means to achieve utopian goals. So, he is criticizing not only the hippies' inconsistent thinking regarding nonviolence but also the contradictions found in Marxist history regarding necessary means to achieve an end. Every follower of any doctrine or political ideology, while preferring that doctrine over others, generally finds inconsistencies and problems within her or his preferred belief system. Indeed, democracy itself has often been described as "the worst kind of government in the world . . . except for all the others."[4]

In embracing the vision of a nonviolent society, Marxism, I maintain, has gone further and deeper than any pacifist preachers of nonviolence have ever done. Why? Because Marxism laid bare the roots of violence in our society, which the others have not done.

Marxism has set out to attack those roots; to uproot violence not just from human thoughts, not just from human emotions, but to uproot them from the very bases of the material existence of society. Marxism has seen violence fed by class antagonism in society—and here Marxism should be assessed against the two-thousand-year record of futile Christian preaching of nonviolence. I say futile in the sense that it has led to no real consequences, to no real diminution of violence. After two millennia of "love thy brother" we are in this situation; that those who go to church throw the napalm bombs and the others who were also brought up in a Christian tradition, the Nazis, have sent the six million descendents of Christ's countrymen to the gas chambers. After two millennia the preaching of nonviolence has led to this!

"After two millennia of 'Love thy brother,' we are still in this situation."

Acknowledging that Marxism is inconsistent in its application of nonviolence, Deutscher still prefers it over what Christianity has done in its attempts at producing a nonviolent society. He believes that Marxism has done a better job of getting to the reasons for violence in the first place, and the main one of these is a society of classes where competition and violence are built into the system. Deutscher believes that producing a nonviolent society must be predicated on eradicating those classes and evolving into a classless society. He notes that if Marxism has had problems reaching its goal of nonviolence, then look at how far the Christian-based thinking has fallen short: two world wars and a holocaust.

One of the reasons for this is that the roots of violence have never been attacked, never been dug up. Class society has persisted and therefore these preachings, even when most sincere, even when the Christian teacher put both his heart and soul in them, were bound to be futile, because they attacked only the surface of the nonviolence. But then the dialectic of Marxism has also been at fault; Marxism itself, throughout its history of deep and tragic contradictions.

How strong the dream of nonviolence lay at the root of the Russian Revolution one can find out if one studies Lenin's statement on Revolution which is written in outwardly a very dogmatic form, almost like an ecclesiastical text interpreting Biblical verses. Behind these somewhat ecclesiastical formulas there is the deep well of the dream of the stateless society constantly welling up.

The October insurrection was carried out in such a way that, according to all the hostile eyewitnesses such as the Western ambassadors who were then in Petrograd, the total number of victims on all sides was ten. That is the total number of victims of that great revolutionary October insurrection. The men who directed this insurrection: Lenin, Trotsky, the members of the military revolutionary committee, gave some thought to the question of violence and nonviolence and organized this tremendous upheaval, with a very profound although unspoken concern for human lives, for the lives of their enemies as well as for their own people.

Here Deutscher reveals something that is startling to most people who think of the Russian Revolution as being a bloody and violent chapter in Russian history. And he distinguishes between the concepts of violent rhetoric and violent action. The October Revolution brought much of the former but very little of the latter. In the next paragraph, he contrasts this revolution with the cost in lives during World War I.

The Russian Revolution, in the name of which so much violence has been committed, was the most nonviolent act of this scale in the whole history of the human race! The revolution was won not with guns, but with words, with argument, persuasion. The words were very violent, the words were terribly forceful, but this is the violence of emotion in the revolt against the actuality of violence, of a world war which cost millions of human beings.

All those people nowadays who take it upon themselves to preach morality to the makers of the Russian Revolution assume, of course, that there was a kind of good and angelic status quo, an angelic nonviolence which was upset by those Dostoyevskian possessed fiends, the revolutionaries who appropriated to themselves the right to dispose of human lives. Nearly ten million people had perished in the trenches of the First World War when the Bolsheviks carried out that great revolution which cost ten victims.

The deep universal humanism inherent in what you call the challenge of nonviolence has been there in Marxism as its most essential element. We were a little more shy about talking about humanism—we are more shy about this because what scoundrel in world history hasn't spoken about humanism—hasn't Stalin, hasn't Hitler, hasn't Goebbels? I always get more than a little shocked when I hear left-wingers and ex-Marxists suggest that Marxism needs to be supplemented by Humanism. Marxism only needs to be true to itself.

But what happened really after this very promising beginning of the Russian Revolution, after Lenin had written The State and Revolution, which is the great revolutionary dream about nonviolence expressed in Marxist terms, what happened? The others who preached nonviolence, for instance Kerensky, preached nonviolence to the oppressed by reintroducing the death penalty for soldiers who were refusing to fight on the front. Perhaps in the nature of people who really detest violence there is a greater shyness about speaking about nonviolence. I distrust those who have so many noble words on their lips. I very often trust more those who speak frankly and even brutally about the necessities of the political struggle as long as they don't get carried away by their own righteousness.

These are interesting thoughts, especially about those who detest violence the most being the ones who are often the shyest when it comes to speaking out for nonviolence. He seems to be suggesting, with this and the statement following this, that those who make such a point of pontificating about the problem of violence are to be less trusted than those who just speak candidly about it in a balanced way.

Then came the intervention, the Civil war. Violence had to be used on an increasing scale, just as the Vietcong today has to use violence on an increasing scale. They can't help it; they're either to go under or they use the violence. But even in the civil war what did the Bolsheviks do? Again they tried to keep a balance between argument, persuasion and violence; a balance in [which] they still attached far greater importance to persuasion and argument than to the gun. In sheer arms they were infinitely inferior to the British, the French, and the Americans (who sent both troops and munitions for the White armies in Russia). The Red army led by Trotsky at that time was far inferior. What happened?

They agitated, they appealed to the consciousness of the soldiers, of the workers in uniform in those interventionist armies. The French Navy, sent to suppress the revolution, rose in mutiny in Odessa and refused to fight against the Bolsheviks; another triumph of nonviolence in the civil war. This revolt of the sailors was the result of what was called Bolshevik propaganda, but this "subversion" prevented violence. (In Britain in 1920 during the intervention, during the Russo-Polish war [when Poland was White Poland] the dockers of London struck and refused to send arms against Russia and the docks of London were immobilized—this was nonviolence.)

Then comes the great tragedy of the isolation of the Russian Revolution; of its succumbing to incredible, unimaginable destruction, poverty, hunger, and disease as a result of the wars of intervention, the civil wars, and of course the long and exhausting world war which was not of Bolshevik making. As a result of all this, terror was let loose on Russia. Men lost their balance. They lost, even the leaders, the clarity of their thinking and of their minds. They acted under overwhelming and inhuman pressures. I don't undertake to judge them, to blame them or to justify them. I can only see the deep tragedy of this historic process the result of which was the glorification of violence.

But what was to have been but a glassful of violence became buckets and buckets full, and then rivers of violence. That is the tragedy of the Russian Revolution.

The dialectics of violence and nonviolence in Marxism were so upset that in the end the nonviolent meaning of Marxism was suppressed under the massive, crushing weight of Stalinism. It wasn't a matter of chance that Stalin implicitly denounced the Leninist and Marxist idea of the withering away of the state. It was on that idea that the whole Marxist nonviolence was epitomized. The Stalinist regime couldn't tolerate, couldn't bear the

These examples provide formidable evidence of the power of persuasion and argument over the power of military force. In every war, starting in America with the Revolutionary War, leaders have realized that guns alone are not going to win the war. Morale among the troops is needed, and so is public support to continue fighting, even when the odds look bad. It was writers such as Thomas Paine, author of the pamphlets *Common Sense* and *The Crisis,* that kept the fighting spirit of the Colonial Army going and eventually spurred it on to victory over the British.

To Deutscher, most of the violence that people attribute to Marxism should be more rightly attributed to Stalin and his willingness to use all means—violence included—to reach the goals of communism.

survival of that dream. It had to crush it out of human minds in order to justify its own violence. I'm not saying this to blame the whole thing on single individuals. It was more than that. It was the tragedy of an isolated and poverty-ridden revolution incapable of fulfilling its promise in isolation and poverty: a revolution caught in this tragic situation—of the irreconcilable contradiction between promise and fulfillment, between dream and reality, sunk into irrationality.

To what extent is Marxism, as such, responsible for this? It would be wrong to identify Stalinism with Marxism, and to blame Marxism for the things that have been done under Stalinism. On the other hand, it would show a lack of moral courage in Marxism to draw the formal line of dissociation and say that we are not responsible for Stalinism, that that wasn't what we aimed at.

You see, in a way Marxism is as responsible for Stalin as Christianity was responsible for the Borgias. The Borgias are not Christianity, but Christianity cannot bleach the Borgias from its records. We cannot delete Stalinism from our records although we are not responsible for Stalinist crimes.

The Borgia family was from Valencia and became influential during the Italian Renaissance in church and state affairs in the 15th and 16th centuries. They abused their power and are blamed for a variety of crimes, including adultery, theft, bribery, and murder. They carried out their actions under the banner of Christianity.

To some extent we (and when I say we I mean that generation of Marxists with which I as an individual identify morally, I mean Lenin, Trotsky, Bukharin, Zinoviev, the early Communist leaders in Europe) participated in this glorification of violence as a self-defense mechanism. Rosa Luxemburg understood this when she criticized the first faint signs of this attitude.

But the issue is larger and deeper than just human intentions. The violence isn't rooted in human intentions. The human intentions are, shall we say, the mechanism, the psychological, the ideal mechanism through which material factors and material necessities transmit their pressures. Marxism had not made any allowance for the possibility of such tremendous outgrowth of violence, of such tremendous abuse of violence that would be done in the name of Marxism, for a simple reason. Marxism

"Marxism had not made any allowance for the . . . tremendous outgrowth of violence . . ."

assumed that revolution would always be an act of change in society carried out violently, but with the support of immense popular majorities.

The thinking here is that violence is not simply a matter of human intention but instead comes in response to oppression by the elite and powerful. If Marxism doesn't produce a changed, classless society—both in the East and the West—then the reaction of the populace could become violent in the face of oppression and exploitation. To Deutscher, the ideals of Marxism—including nonviolence—only work in such classless societies.

It assumed revolution in an industrialized West carried out by working classes committed to socialism, supporting the revolution with all their heart and confronting as their enemies a really small minority consisting of the exploiters. In such a confrontation of revolutionary majorities with counter-revolutionary minorities, the need to use violence would indeed have been very limited and the dream of nonviolence would have had all this hope for fulfillment.

It is said that Marxism suits the underdeveloped countries but not the advanced and industrial west. I still maintain that the original dream of Marxism and the real original inspiration and hope of Marxism still suits the industrial west much better than it can suit the underdeveloped countries, even if revolution in certain phases is the job of great majorities as it was in Russia in 1917, as it was in China in 1949, as it is in Vietnam today.

"In underdeveloped countries there comes a moment after the revolution when again there is this breach between promise and fulfillment . . ."

In underdeveloped countries there comes a moment after the revolution when again there is this breach between promise and fulfillment, of making the people accomplish what they had set out to accomplish or they can accomplish it only partly, very inadequately. Therefore there come frustrations, explosive dissonances and the desire of the post-revolutionary rulers to secure the revolution as they understand it and are able to secure it. The more underdeveloped the country, the more bound to come, after the revolution, a moment of bitter truth and violence.

However, I think that the violence in China already is much smaller than it was in Russia. The irrationality of the Chinese Revolution, though goodness knows there is a lot of irrationality, so far is much less, I think, than what came to the top in the Russian Revolution. But then the Chinese Revolution wasn't the first pioneer, wasn't the isolated revolution: it was already assisted by Stalinist Russia, and this reduced the amount of irrationality. I think that with the spread of revolution, with the advance of the industrial and technological aspects of revolutionary societies, with the growth of their wealth, with the rising in their standards of living, with a relative contentment in the popular masses, the irrational element will decrease.

The final vindication of the dream of nonviolence in Marxism will come with socialism gaining the advanced countries. That is my belief, and it is not a belief of wishful thinking; it is the whole theoretical structure of Marxism that leads me to this conclusion. I think that the de-Stalinization carried out in Russia, partial, self-contradictory, inadequate, hypocritical as it has been, has already somewhat reestablished the balance between the contradictory elements in the Russian Revolution by reducing the violence and giving more scope to the nonviolent element in Marxism.

Marxists such as Deutscher pinned their hopes largely on the West's embracing socialism, and he credited de-Stalinization in Russia with the decrease of violence that country was experiencing as he uttered these remarks.

You have asked me what I meant when I spoke about the negative effect on the Communist World of the war in Vietnam. The war in Vietnam may or may not be a prelude to new confrontations of violence surging back from the Western world and flooding the world again. The fear of the ultimate violence promotes a recrudescence of the authoritarian and violent trend within Russia and in China. I made an analogy between the effects of the Vietnamese War in the Communist part of the world and the repercussions of the Korean War in the last years of Stalin's era.

"The war in Vietnam may or may not be a prelude to new confrontations of violence . . . flooding the world again."

The fears and panic let loose by the Korean War expressed themselves in Russia in the insanity of Stalin's rule in the last years, in the repetition of the witches' sabbath of the thirties. I don't foresee and I'm not afraid of something as terrible as that in Russia in response to the American aggression in Vietnam, but we have already seen some recrudescence of the authoritarian trend. The Twenty-third congress of the Communist Party testifies to this. The trials of Daniel and Sinyevsky were symptomatic of the partial return of the authoritarian trend.

On the other hand I don't think that one can say that the Korean War had only one effect, i.e. the encouragement of domestic violence in the Soviet Union and China. It also had a positive effect parallel to the effect that it had in our part of the world. It gave one a sense of human solidarity with a small nation so ruthlessly attacked, so ruthlessly crushed by the most powerful, the greatest, the richest nation in the world. The Korean War disposed of certain illusions which Khruschevism spread, namely the illusion about the possibility of the peaceful transition from capitalism to socialism in such countries as France or Italy. Try to go now to French and Italian workers and tell them that they can accomplish this miracle when in such small nations as Korea and Vietnam it is so resisted by the great capitalist powers.

Source: "Archives: Marxism and Nonviolence (1966)," Hippyland, http://www .hippy.com/modules.php?name=News&file=article&sid=365.

Notes

1. Quoted in Skip Stone, "Hippies from A to Z: The Way of the Hippy," Hip Planet, http://www.hipplanet.com/books/atoz/ way.htm.

2. See Penny Lewis, "Hardhats and Hippies: An Interview with Penny Lewis," *Jacobin: A Magazine of Culture and Polemic*, http://jacobinmag.com/2013/06/hardhats-hippies-and-hawks-an -interview-with-penny-lewis/.

3. Lauren Kessler, *The Dissident Press: Alternative Journalism in American History* (Beverly Hills: Sage, 1984), 16.

4. Winston Churchill, *Churchill by Himself* (New York: Rosetta Books, 2013), 574.

Chapter 3

Hell No, We Won't Go: Protesting the Vietnam War

Introduction

Although there were numerous threads to the fabric of the counterculture movement of the 1960s, the dominant one was provided by America's first televised war and the most controversial of wars that the United States has been involved in: the Vietnam War. This war polarized America like no other had for at least three reasons:

1. It was, in fact, beamed into every living room on a nightly basis at a time when television had hit its stride and found its critical mass in America.
2. Thanks to the existence of the military draft, every young man 18 years and older was vulnerable to being pressed into action in this war, with the very real possibility of coming back injured or dead.
3. The war took place in a country that few had ever heard of that was not seen as a direct threat to the security of the United States, and so our reasons for being there were confusing to many and unethical to others.

The Vietnam War, or more accurately the Vietnam conflict since war was never officially declared, plunged America into a protracted and expensive military action that squared the country off against the communist regime of North Vietnam and its allies in South Vietnam who called themselves the Viet Cong. The United States joined forces with the government of South Vietnam to repel the communist influence from South Vietnam. Although the regional conflicts began as early as the mid-1940s, the rise to power of Ho Chi Minh in North Vietnam in the early 1950s took the conflict to a higher level. France became heavily involved in repelling the advances of North Vietnam and then suffered a major defeat and exited, whereupon the United States entered the conflict. The war was played out against the larger context of the Cold War between America and the Soviet Union as the latter supplied arms to North Vietnam. The United States originally supplied military advisers to help South Vietnam and then began committing frontline fighting troops in large numbers under Presidents John F. Kennedy, Lyndon B. Johnson, and Richard M. Nixon. By 1969, more than 500,000 American troops were in Vietnam. Some 58,000 Americans would lose their lives in the fighting. Most of those killed were young men in their late teens or their 20s, and the threat of going to Vietnam was very real for any American male who passed his 18th birthday. Mounting opposition to the conflict reached a crescendo, dividing the country in the 1960s and early 1970s until Nixon ordered the removal of all U.S. troops in 1973. In the end, many wonder what the benefit of U.S. involvement really was, given the high casualty count and the fact that in 1975 communist forces seized control of the South Vietnamese capital of Saigon when the last of the U.S. troops finally exited the country. Vietnam was unified as the Socialist Republic of Vietnam in 1976.

America's young people had an immediate and strong vested interest in the Vietnam War that was not only ideologically grounded but also grounded in their desire not to fight a war they didn't want and in which they would have to devote a year of their life, with the possibility of being killed. Altogether, there was great motivation for many young Americans to become hippies. And since young men could be deferred for four years from military service by simply going to college, it is no surprise that the hippie movement was largely populated by college students. College provided an intersection of intellectual thought that spurred critical analysis of reasons for America's involvement in the war and provided an opportunity for those facing the draft to hopefully force the government's hand in ending that involvement before they graduated.

The documents in this section reflect the tenor of the 1960s with regard to this overarching debate about America's involvement in the Vietnam War. Much heat was generated on both sides, and much violence erupted on college campuses and in cities across the country, alongside the more peaceful sit-ins and love-ins staged by the more moderate elements of the hippie movement.

The Port Huron Statement

Students for a Democratic Society's Manifesto

June 1962

INTRODUCTION

The so-called Port Huron Statement of the Students for a Democratic Society (SDS) was one of the original written protests of America's growing involvement in the Vietnam War. In 1961 when American troop strength was tripled under President John Kennedy (and then tripled again the next year), the decibel level of war protests arose loudly in America. Leading the charge on the college campuses was the SDS. The group had formed in 1960 on the University of Michigan campus, and the Port Huron Statement was its official political manifesto, adopted at the first SDS Convention in 1962. The entire document runs more than 20,000 words; key parts are excerpted here.

INTRODUCTION: AGENDA FOR A GENERATION

We are people of this generation, bred in at least modest comfort, housed now in universities, looking uncomfortably to the world we inherit.

This opening statement lays out the brief history of the generation we know today as the baby boomers who grew up in the placid 1950s in an America that was the envy of the world, having waged a successful war against the Nazi threat and the threat of the Japanese Army. That placidity, however, would give way to other national and international threats (referred to often here as paradoxes), and the SDS states its position regarding these threats in the remainder of the document. One of these threats is internal—a growing sense of hypocrisy that SDS leaders saw in the U.S. government and American business.

When we were kids the United States was the wealthiest and strongest country in the world: the only one with the atom bomb, the least scarred by modern war, an initiator of the United Nations that we thought would distribute Western influence throughout the world. Freedom and equality for each individual, government of, by, and for the people—these American values we found good, principles by which we could live as men. Many of us began maturing in complacency.

As we grew, however, our comfort was penetrated by events too troubling to dismiss. First, the permeating and victimizing fact of human degradation, symbolized by the Southern struggle against racial bigotry, compelled most of us from silence to activism. Second, the enclosing fact of the Cold War, symbolized by the presence of the Bomb, brought awareness that we ourselves, and our friends, and millions of abstract "others" we knew more directly because of our common peril, might die at any time. We might deliberately ignore, or avoid, or fail to feel all other human problems, but not these two, for these were too immediate and crushing in their impact, too challenging in the demand that we as individuals take the responsibility for encounter and resolution.

While these and other problems either directly oppressed us or rankled our consciences and became our own subjective concerns, we began to see complicated and disturbing paradoxes in our surrounding America. The declaration "all men are created equal . . ." rang hollow before the facts of Negro life in the South and the big cities of the North. The proclaimed peaceful intentions of the United States contradicted its economic and military investments in the Cold War status quo.

"The declaration 'all men are created equal . . .' rang hollow . . ."

We witnessed, and continue to witness, other paradoxes. With nuclear energy, whole cities can easily be powered, yet the dominant nation-states seem more likely to unleash destruction greater than that incurred in all wars of human history. Although our own technology is destroying old and creating new forms of social organization, men still tolerate meaningless work and idleness.

While two-thirds of mankind suffers undernourishment, our own upper classes revel amidst superfluous abundance. Although world population is expected to double in forty years, the nations still tolerate anarchy as a major principle of international conduct and uncontrolled exploitation governs the sapping of the earth's physical resources. Although mankind desperately needs revolutionary leadership, America rests in national stalemate, its goals ambiguous and tradition-bound instead of informed and clear, its democratic system apathetic and manipulated rather than "of, by, and for the people."

Here, the SDS calls for "revolutionary leadership" in the face of national apathy that gives the federal government free rein in manipulating the citizenry. The SDS calls for a return to basic democratic principles of the Constitution and a rebellion against government manipulation. These are common themes not only with the SDS in this era but also with other protestors and groups of the time.

Not only did tarnish appear on our image of American virtue, not only did disillusion occur when the hypocrisy of American ideals was discovered, but we began to sense that what we had originally seen as the American Golden Age was actually the decline of an era. The worldwide outbreak of revolution against colonialism and imperialism, the entrenchment of totalitarian states, the menace of war, overpopulation, international disorder, supertechnology—these trends were testing the tenacity of our own commitment to democracy and freedom and our abilities to visualize their application to a world in upheaval.

In this phrasing, the SDS sees itself and the generation it represents as being "imbued" with light and a sense of urgency. While the rest of America—most notably older generations and those who have bought into traditional ways—may be asleep, the SDS is issuing a wake-up call to the young generations to change the course of history. This would become a magnetic message that would galvanize young baby boomers into protests and action across the country. The epicenter of that activity would be the college campus.

Our work is guided by the sense that we may be the last generation in the experiment with living. But we are a minority—the vast majority of our people regard the temporary equilibriums of our society and world as eternally-functional parts. In this is perhaps the outstanding paradox: we ourselves are imbued with urgency, yet the message of our society is that there is no viable alternative to the present. Beneath the reassuring tones of the politicians, beneath the common opinion that America will "muddle through", beneath the stagnation of those who have closed their minds to the future, is the pervading feeling that there simply are no alternatives, that our times have witnessed the exhaustion not only of Utopias, but of any new departures as well. Feeling the press of complexity upon the emptiness of life, people are fearful of the thought that at any moment things might thrust out of control. They fear change itself, since change might smash whatever invisible framework seems to hold back chaos for them now. For most Americans, all crusades are suspect, threatening.

The fact that each individual sees apathy in his fellows perpetuates the common reluctance to organize for change. The dominant institutions are complex enough to blunt the minds of their potential critics, and entrenched enough to swiftly dissipate or entirely repel the energies of protest and reform, thus limiting human expectancies. Then, too, we are a materially improved society, and by our own improvements we seem to have weakened the case for further change. . . .

Values

"Making values explicit . . . has been devalued and corrupted."

Making values explicit—an initial task in establishing alternatives—is an activity that has been devalued and corrupted. The conventional moral terms of the age, the politician moralities—"free world", "people's democracies"—reflect realities poorly, if at all, and seem to function more as ruling myths than as descriptive principles. But neither has our experience in the universities brought us moral enlightenment. Our professors and administrators sacrifice controversy to public relations; their curriculums change more slowly than the living events of the world; their skills and silence are purchased by investors in the arms race; passion is called unscholastic. The questions we might want raised—what is really important? can we live in a different and better way? if we wanted to change society, how would we do it?—are not thought to be questions of a "fruitful, empirical nature", and thus are brushed aside.

Unlike youth in other countries we are used to moral leadership being exercised and moral dimensions being clarified by our elders. But today, for us, not even the liberal and socialist preachments of the past seem adequate to the forms of the present. Consider the old slogans; Capitalism Cannot Reform Itself, United Front Against Fascism, General Strike, All Out on May Day. Or, more recently, No Cooperation with Commies and Fellow Travellers, Ideologies Are Exhausted, Bipartisanship, No Utopias. These are incomplete, and there are few new prophets. It has been said that our liberal and socialist predecessors were plagued by vision without program, while our own generation is plagued by program without vision. All around us there is astute grasp of method, technique—the committee, the ad hoc group, the lobbyist, that hard and soft sell, the make, the projected image—but, if pressed critically, such expertise is incompetent to explain its implicit ideals. It is highly fashionable to identify oneself by old categories, or by naming a respected political figure, or by explaining "how we would vote" on various issues.

"[T]here are few new prophets."

Theoretic chaos has replaced the idealistic thinking of old—and, unable to reconstitute theoretic order, men have condemned idealism itself. Doubt has replaced hopefulness—and men act out a defeatism that is labeled realistic. The decline of utopia and hope is in fact one of the defining features of social life today. The reasons are various: the dreams of the older left were perverted by Stalinism and never recreated; the congressional stalemate makes men narrow their view of the possible; the specialization of human activity leaves little room for sweeping thought; the horrors of the twentieth century, symbolized in the gas-ovens and concentration camps and atom bombs, have blasted hopefulness. To be idealistic is to be considered apocalyptic, deluded. To have no serious aspirations, on the contrary, is to be "toughminded".

In suggesting social goals and values, therefore, we are aware of entering a sphere of some disrepute. Perhaps

As this statement progresses, the separation by the SDS of its movement from past liberal movements becomes more obvious. Not only are its leaders separating themselves from contemporary conservatism, but they are also separating themselves from progressives of the past who had passion and vision but no program. So, the SDS defines itself as having both, starting with the need to build on a set of values that, as the next passage will show, focuses on the central importance of the human being as an end in itself, not a means to an end. To philosophers, this suggests part of the thinking of Immanuel Kant, the 18th-century ethicist who defined the need to treat humans as ends in and of themselves. The fact that the SDS leadership came together in Port Huron and drafted a 26,000-word statement of values, principles, and action shows that they were serious about defining both their vision and their program.

matured by the past, we have no sure formulas, no closed theories—but that does not mean values are beyond discussion and tentative determination. A first task of any social movement is to inconvenience people that the search for orienting theories and the creation of human values is complex but worthwhile. We are aware that to avoid platitudes we must analyze the concrete conditions of social order. But to direct such an analysis we must use the guideposts of basic principles. Our own social values involve conceptions of human beings, human relationships, and social systems.

We regard men as infinitely precious and possessed of unfulfilled capacities for reason, freedom, and love. In affirming these principles we are aware of countering perhaps the dominant conceptions of man in the twentieth century: that he is a thing to be manipulated, and that he is inherently incapable of directing his own affairs. We oppose the depersonalization that reduces human beings to the status of things—if anything, the brutalities of the twentieth century teach that means and ends are intimately related, that vague appeals to "posterity" cannot justify the mutilations of the present. We oppose, too, the doctrine of human incompetence because it rests essentially on the modern fact that men have been "competently" manipulated into incompetence—we see little reason why men cannot meet with increasing skill the complexities and responsibilities of their situation, if society is organized not for minority, but for majority, participation in decision-making.

There is a lot in this passage that provides philosophic underpinning to the thinking of the antiwar protests that were a constant part of American life during the Vietnam War. Again, the emphasis on the individual human being is front and center and includes emphasis on individuals' abilities to think for themselves and realize their own potential. None of that is possible if individuals blindly subordinate themselves to "authority" or to the status and values of contemporary society. One must think for oneself in order to be "authentic." In philosophy, when one thinks of the importance of authenticity to the concept of virtue, ethicists such as Aristotle and the 20th-century philosopher Charles Taylor come to mind. To Aristotle, authenticity is linked to the "supreme good," and he defines that good as the essential inner being of an individual that cannot be taken from her or him without that person's permission.

Men have unrealized potential for self-cultivation, self-direction, self-understanding, and creativity. It is this potential that we regard as crucial and to which we appeal, not to the human potentiality for violence, unreason, and submission to authority. The goal of man and society should be human independence: a concern not with image of popularity but with finding a meaning in life that is personally authentic: a quality of mind not compulsively driven by a sense of powerlessness, nor one which unthinkingly adopts status values, nor one which represses all threats to its habits, but one which has full, spontaneous access to present and past experiences, one which easily unites the fragmented parts of personal

history, one which openly faces problems which are troubling and unresolved: one with an intuitive awareness of possibilities, an active sense of curiosity, an ability and willingness to learn.

This kind of independence does not mean egoistic individualism—the object is not to have one's way so much as it is to have a way that is one's own. Nor do we deify man—we merely have faith in his potential.

Human Relationships

Human relationships should involve fraternity and honesty. Human interdependence is contemporary fact; human brotherhood must be willed, however, as a condition of future survival and as the most appropriate form of social relations. Personal links between man and man are needed, especially to go beyond the partial and fragmentary bonds of function that bind men only as worker to worker, employer to employee, teacher to student, American to Russian.

Loneliness, estrangement, isolation describe the vast distance between man and man today. These dominant tendencies cannot be overcome by better personnel management, nor by improved gadgets, but only when a love of man overcomes the idolatrous worship of things by man.

As the individualism we affirm is not egoism, the selflessness we affirm is not self-elimination. On the contrary, we believe in generosity of a kind that imprints one's unique individual qualities in the relation to other men, and to all human activity. Further, to dislike isolation is not to favor the abolition of privacy; the latter differs from isolation in that it occurs or is abolished according to individual will. Finally, we would replace power and personal uniqueness rooted in possession, privilege, or circumstance by power and uniqueness rooted in love, reflectiveness, reason, and creativity.

Participatory Democracy

As a social system we seek the establishment of a democracy of individual participation, governed by two central aims: that the individual share in those social decisions determining the quality and direction of his life; that society be organized to encourage independence in men and provide the media for their common participation.

"[T]he object is not to have one's way . . . as it is to have a way that is one's own."

A key part of SDS thinking was that a democracy should be truly participatory, wherein the individual has an identifiable and effective role in making government policy. Furthermore, the SDS believed that these government policies should be directed at helping individuals achieve their maximum potential and at bringing individuals out of isolation and into harmony with other individuals. Violence and the making of war have no place in this kind of democracy, according to SDS thinking. The entirety of the social protest movements of the 1960s was based on the premise that everyone should have a voice in the formation of public policy and foreign policy, especially if those policies lead to or involve questions about continuing war.

In a participatory democracy, the political life would be based in several root principles:

- **that decision-making of basic social consequence be carried on by public groupings;**

- **that politics be seen positively, as the art of collectively creating an acceptable pattern of social relations;**

- **that politics has the function of bringing people out of isolation and into community, thus being a necessary, though not sufficient, means of finding meaning in personal life;**

- **that the political order should serve to clarify problems in a way instrumental to their solution; it should provide outlets for the expression of personal grievance and aspiration; opposing views should be organized so as to illuminate choices and facilities the attainment of goals; channels should be commonly available to related men to knowledge and to power so that private problems—from bad recreation facilities to personal alienation—are formulated as general issues.**

The Economic System

The economic sphere would have as its basis the principles:

- that work should involve incentives worthier than money or survival. It should be educative, not stultifying; creative, not mechanical; self-direct, not manipulated, encouraging independence; a respect for others, a sense of dignity and a willingness to accept social responsibility, since it is this experience that has crucial influence on habits, perceptions and individual ethics;

- that the economic experience is so personally decisive that the individual must share in its full determination;

- that the economy itself is of such social importance that its major resources and means of production should be open to democratic participation and subject to democratic social regulation.

"[I]nstitutions . . . should be generally organized with the well being and dignity of man as the essential measure of success."

Like the political and economic ones, major social institutions—cultural, education, rehabilitative, and others—should be generally organized with the well-being and dignity of man as the essential measure of success.

In social change or interchange, we find violence to be abhorrent because it requires generally the transformation of the target, be it a human being or a community of people, into a depersonalized object of hate. It is imperative that the means of violence be abolished and the institutions—local, national, international—that encourage nonviolence as a condition of conflict be developed.

These are our central values, in skeletal form. It remains vital to understand their denial or attainment in the context of the modern world.

The University and Social Change

There is perhaps little reason to be optimistic about the above analysis. True, the Dixiecrat-GOP coalition is the weakest point in the dominating complex of corporate, military and political power. But the civil rights and peace and student movements are too poor and socially slighted, and the labor movement too quiescent, to be counted with enthusiasm.

From where else can power and vision be summoned? We believe that the universities are an overlooked seat of influence.

First, the university is located in a permanent position of social influence. Its educational function makes it indispensable and automatically makes it a crucial institution in the formation of social attitudes. Second, in an unbelievably complicated world, it is the central institution for organizing, evaluating, and transmitting knowledge. Third, the extent to which academic resources presently is used to buttress immoral social practice is revealed first, by the extent to which defense contracts make the universities engineers of the arms race. Too, the use of modern social science as a manipulative tool reveals itself in the "human relations" consultants to the modern corporation, who introduce trivial sops to give laborers feelings of "participation" or "belonging", while actually deluding them in order to further exploit their labor. And, of course, the use of motivational research is

Nonviolence was a major philosophy among many of the protest groups of the 1960s. Leaders such as Dr. Martin Luther King Jr. and Cesar Chavez drew inspiration from international leaders such as Mahatma Gandhi who insisted on nonviolent behavior in reaction to perceived oppression. Not all protest groups—or all factions within these groups—advocated nonviolence as a means to achieve the end of equality and greater participation in the democratic process. In this passage, however, the SDS lays down its principle that violence is abhorrent for any institution, including the federal government. The SDS makes an interesting point about reducing sectors of humanity to targets or objects of hate. This depersonalization surfaced a lot in the 1960s.

There follows a very long section of the Port Huron Statement that goes into detail about what is wrong with American society, capitalism, and warmongering but also separates the SDS vision and program from communism, which it derides as oppressive and unhelpful in realizing democratic goals. The statement concludes by bringing the spotlight to those who are in the best position to bring the SDS vision to reality. These are the university students of the 1960s.

This passage shows how much value the SDS places on the university campus as the catalyst for change and revolution. As is noted earlier in the statement, however, that change will come not from the professors (whom the SDS perceives as selling out to the establishment and traditional thinking) but instead from the students themselves. The fact that these young people exist in a critical mass on university campuses, plus the fact that they have the most to gain—or lose—from social and governmental change, makes them an ideal catalyst for that change.

already infamous as a manipulative aspect of American politics. But these social uses of the universities' resources also demonstrate the unchangeable reliance by men of power on the men and storehouses of knowledge: this makes the university functionally tied to society in new ways, revealing new potentialities, new levers for change. Fourth, the university is the only mainstream institution that is open to participation by individuals of nearly any viewpoint.

These, at least, are facts, no matter how dull the teaching, how paternalistic the rules, how irrelevant the research that goes on. Social relevance, the accessibility to knowledge, and internal openness together make the university a potential base and agency in a movement of social change.

[The SDS then discusses its ideas of what is needed to bring change through college campuses.]

1. Any new left in America must be, in large measure, a left with real intellectual skills, committed to deliberativeness, honesty, reflection as working tools. The university permits the political life to be an adjunct to the academic one, and action to be informed by reason.

"A new left must be distributed . . . throughout the country."

2. A new left must be distributed in significant social roles throughout the country. The universities are distributed in such a manner.

3. A new left must consist of younger people who matured in the postwar world, and partially be directed to the recruitment of younger people. The university is an obvious beginning point.

4. A new left must include liberals and socialists, the former for their relevance, the latter for their sense of thoroughgoing reforms in the system. The university is a more sensible place than a political party for these two traditions to begin to discuss their differences and look for political synthesis.

5. A new left must start controversy across the land, if national policies and national apathy are to be reversed. The ideal university is a community of controversy, within itself and in its effects on communities beyond.

6. A new left must transform modern complexity into issues that can be understood and felt close-up by every human

being. It must give form to the feelings of helplessness and indifference, so that people may see the political, social and economic sources of their private troubles and organize to change society. In a time of supposed prosperity, moral complacency and political manipulation, a new left cannot rely on only aching stomachs to be the engine force of social reform. The case for change, for alternatives that will involve uncomfortable personal efforts, must be argued as never before. The university is a relevant place for all of these activities.

But we need not indulge in illusions: the university system cannot complete a movement of ordinary people making demands for a better life. From its schools and colleges across the nation, a militant left might awaken its allies, and by beginning the process towards peace, civil rights, and labor struggles, reinsert theory and idealism where too often reign confusion and political barter. The power of students and faculty united is not only potential; it has shown its actuality in the South, and in the reform movements of the North.

The bridge to political power, though, will be built through genuine cooperation, locally, nationally, and internationally, between a new left of young people, and an awakening community of allies. In each community we must look within the university and act with confidence that we can be powerful, but we must look outwards to the less exotic but more lasting struggles for justice.

Here, the SDS explains that students can be effective catalysts for change, but they themselves will not be able to sustain it without like-minded allies from the faculty and those beyond the university campus. So, the SDS calls for a grounded cooperation between allies to produce lasting change in America. To some extent, this is what happened in America in the 1960s: the clarion call for revolution began on college campuses across the country, and the message was heard by a growing number of other adults from all walks of life who lent their voices to the steady drumbeat of protest.

The Students

In the last few years, thousands of American students demonstrated that they at least felt the urgency of the times. They moved actively and directly against racial injustices, the threat of war, violations of individual rights of conscience and, less frequently, against economic manipulation. They succeeded in restoring a small measure of controversy to the campuses after the stillness of the McCarthy period. They succeeded, too, in gaining some concessions from the people and institutions they opposed, especially in the fight against racial bigotry.

The significance of these scattered movements lies not in their success or failure in gaining objectives—at least not yet. Nor does the significance lie in the intellectual "competence" or "maturity" of the students involved—as some pedantic elders allege. The significance is in the fact the students are breaking the crust of apathy and overcoming the inner alienation that remain the defining characteristics of American college life.

Here the SDS makes an interesting point in setting aside the results or goals of the student protest movement as the most important aspect of these movements. His point, and this editor experienced it himself on a large state university campus in the 1960s, is that the protest movement's real value was in bringing self-satisfied students out of themselves and into a larger public debate on issues of extreme significance to all people living in America. What happened on college campuses in the 1960s was a culture clash between the traditional students who were oriented toward Greek life, parties, and athletics and the new breed of activist students who felt that the point of life was larger than this and that education should spill out of the classroom and onto the campus ovals in public debate and action focused on controversial issues of the day.

If student movements for change are rarities still on the campus scene, what is commonplace there? The real campus, the familiar campus, is a place of private people, engaged in their notorious "inner emigration." It is a place of commitment to business-as-usual, getting ahead, playing it cool. It is a place of mass affirmation of the Twist, but mass reluctance toward the controversial public stance. Rules are accepted as "inevitable", bureaucracy as "just circumstances", irrelevance as "scholarship", selflessness as "martyrdom", politics as "just another way to make people, and an unprofitable one, too."

Almost no students value activity as a citizen. Passive in public, they are hardly more idealistic in arranging their private lives: Gallup concludes they will settle for "low success, and won't risk high failure." There is not much willingness to take risks (not even in business), no setting of dangerous goals, no real conception of personal identity except one manufactured in the image of others, no real urge for personal fulfillment except to be almost as successful as the very successful people. Attention is being paid to social status (the quality of shirt collars, meeting people, getting wives or husbands, making solid contacts for later on); much too, is paid to academic status (grades, honors, the med school rat-race). But neglected generally is real intellectual status, the personal cultivation of the mind.

"Students don't even give a damn about the apathy," one has said. Apathy toward apathy begets a privately-constructed universe, a place of systematic study schedules, two nights each week for beer, a girl or two, and early marriage; a framework infused with personality, warmth, and under control, no matter how unsatisfying otherwise.

Under these conditions university life loses all relevance to some. Four hundred thousand of our classmates leave college every year. But apathy is not simply an attitude; it is a product of social institutions, and of the structure and organization of higher education itself. The extracurricular life is ordered according to in loco parentis theory, which ratifies the Administration as the moral guardian of the young. The accompanying "let's pretend" theory of student extracurricular affairs validates student government as a training center for those who want to spend their lives in political pretense, and discourages initiative from more articulate, honest, and sensitive students. The bounds and style of controversy are delimited before controversy begins. The university "prepares" the student for "citizenship" through perpetual rehearsals and, usually, through emasculation of what creative spirit there is in the individual.

The academic life contains reinforcing counterparts to the way in which extracurricular life is organized. The academic world is founded in a teacher-student relation analogous to the parent-child relation which characterizes in loco parentis. Further, academia includes a radical separation of student from the material of study. That which is studied, the social reality, is "objectified" to sterility, dividing the student from life—just as he is restrained in active involvement by the deans controlling student government. The specialization of function and knowledge, admittedly necessary to our complex technological and social structure, has produced and exaggerated compartmentalization of study and understanding. This has contributed to: an overly parochial view, by faculty, of the role of its research and scholarship; a discontinuous and truncated understanding, by students, of the surrounding social order; a loss of personal attachment, by nearly all, to the worth of study as a humanistic enterprise.

There is, finally, the cumbersome academic bureaucracy extending throughout the academic as well as extracurricular structures, contributing to the sense of outer complexity and inner powerlessness that transforms so many students from honest searching to ratification of convention and, worse, to a numbness of present and future catastrophes. The size and financing systems of the university enhance the permanent trusteeship of the administrative bureaucracy,

As this passage and the following one explain, the "in loco parentis theory" (Latin for "in place of parents") was prevalent among university administrators until the mid-1960s. The theory essentially posited that when parents send their students away to college, they do so with the understanding that the university leaders will watch over their children when they are there, acting as a sort of parental guardian. This philosophy also gave the university the power to sanction students for not following curfew regulations, for not keeping their rooms clean, for being too noisy in the dorms, and even for public displays of affection. The beginning of the end for in loco parentis came with a 1961 landmark court case, *Dixon v. Alabama,* when the U.S. Court of Appeals for the Fifth Circuit found that Alabama State College could not expel a student without due process. The ruling struck a blow for students' individual civil liberties at colleges and universities. In the years following that case, state universities began doing away with their policies that bespoke guardianship rights over their students. In my own case as a student at the University of Oklahoma, my college career began with these restrictive policies in place on campus and ended four years later with no curfew, the beginnings of co-ed dorms, and dorm counselors transitioning to the position of resident advisers. However, at public secondary schools, in loco parentis still holds as the guiding philosophy that school administrators follow. The court ruling affected only higher education.

their power leading to a shift to the value standards of business and administrative mentality within the university. Huge foundations and other private financial interests shape under-financed colleges and universities, not only making them more commercial, but less disposed to diagnose society critically, less open to dissent. Many social and physical scientists, neglecting the liberating heritage of higher learning, develop "human relations" or "morale-producing" techniques for the corporate economy, while others exercise their intellectual skills to accelerate the arms race.

A growing criticism of the university role in society—certainly one expressed by MIT's Noam Chomsky (see Chapter 1)—is that it has ceased becoming an institution pushing the boundaries of knowledge and instead perpetuated old "truths," especially ones that were politically safe and correct and would not irritate benefactors of the university. As a result, the university had failed at its most basic mission of education.

Tragically, the university could serve as a significant source of social criticism and an initiator of new modes and molders of attitudes. But the actual intellectual effect of the college experience is hardly distinguishable from that of any other communications channel—say, a television set—passing on the stock truths of the day. Students leave college somewhat more "tolerant" than when they arrived, but basically unchallenged in their values and political orientations. With administrators ordering the institutions, and faculty the curriculum, the student learns by his isolation to accept elite rule within the university, which prepares him to accept later forms of minority control. The real function of the educational system—as opposed to its more rhetorical function of "searching for truth"—is to impart the key information and styles that will help the student get by, modestly but comfortably, in the big society beyond.

To turn these possibilities into realities will involve national efforts at university reform by an alliance of students and faculty. They must wrest control of the educational process from the administrative bureaucracy. They must make fraternal and functional contact with allies in labor, civil rights, and other liberal forces outside the campus. They must import major public issues into the curriculum—research and teaching on problems of war and peace is an outstanding example. They must make debate and controversy, not dull pedantic cant, the common style for educational life. They must consciously build a base for their assault upon the loci of power.

As students, for a democratic society, we are committed to stimulating this kind of social movement, this kind of vision and program in campus and community across the country. If we appear to seek the unattainable, it has been said, then let it be known that we do so to avoid the unimaginable.

Source: Tom Hayden, "The Port Huron Statement of the Students for a Democratic Society," Matrix, the Center for Digital Humanities and Social Sciences, http://coursesa.matrix.msu.edu/~hst306/documents/huron.html.

"If we appear to seek the unattainable . . . we do so to avoid the unimaginable."

"The Incredible War"

Paul Potter's Essay on the Vietnam War
April 7, 1965

INTRODUCTION

Paul Potter was the president of Students for a Democratic Society (SDS) in 1964, following in the leadership role of Tom Hayden, the original president of the SDS. In April 1965 when it was clear that the White House was making a major commitment of American troops to Vietnam, Potter wrote his essay, "The Incredible War." It picks up on several of the themes from the Port Huron Statement but focuses much more specifically on the Vietnam War and why America's involvement in it was such a mistake.

Potter invokes the name of U.S. senator Wayne Morse, a Republican turned Independent turned Democrat from Oregon who staunchly opposed America's entry into the Vietnam War and believed strongly that President Johnson's decision to wage an undeclared war on North Vietnam was unconstitutional. That decision was the outcome of the Gulf of Tonkin Resolution, which authorized America's entry into Vietnam without a formal declaration of war because of an alleged attack on a U.S. warship that was patrolling the waters in the Gulf of Tonkin. Morse, himself an ardent anticommunist, was one of only two senators opposing that resolution. Alaska senator Ernest Gruening was the other. Morse perceived the Vietnam War as a conflict of doubtful merit and as an outcome of an overly aggressive military policy by the United States. He believed that waging war in Vietnam brought America closer to an ultimate, cataclysmic nuclear showdown with China or Russia, or both. Morse was reelected to a second term in the Senate but eventually paid the political price for his opposition to the war, losing in the 1968 election to Bob Packwood. Morse remained an outspoken critic of the Vietnam War, however, and openly joined demonstrations and protests involving other antiwar critics such as Dr. Benjamin Spock and Coretta Scott King.

Most of us grew up thinking that the United States was a strong but humble nation, that involved itself in world affairs only reluctantly, that respected the integrity of other nations and other systems, and that engaged in wars only as a last resort. This was a nation with no large standing army, with no design for external conquest, that sought primarily the opportunity to develop its own resources and its own mode of living. If at some point we began to hear vague and disturbing things about what this country had done in Latin America, China, Spain and other places, we somehow remained confident about the basic integrity of this nation's foreign policy. The Cold War with all of its neat categories and black and white descriptions did much to assure us that what we had been taught to believe was true.

But in recent years, the withdrawal from the hysteria of the Cold War era and the development of a more aggressive, activist foreign policy have done much to force many of us to rethink attitudes that were deep and basic sentiments about our country. The incredible war in Vietnam has provided the razor, the terrifying sharp cutting edge that has finally severed the last vestige of illusion that morality and democracy are the guiding principles of American foreign policy.

The saccharine self-righteous moralism that promises the Vietnamese a billion dollars of economic aid at the very moment we are delivering billions for economic and social destruction and political repression is rapidly

61

losing what power it might ever have had to reassure us about the decency of our foreign policy. The further we explore the reality of what this country is doing and planning in Vietnam the more we are driven toward the conclusion of Senator Morse that the United States may well be the greatest threat to peace in the world today. That is a terrible and bitter insight for people who grew up as we did—and our revulsion at that insight, our refusal to accept it as inevitable or necessary, is one of the reasons that so many people have come here today.

The President says that we are defending freedom in Vietnam. Whose freedom? Not the freedom of the Vietnamese. The first act of the first dictator, Diem, the United States installed in Vietnam, was to systematically begin the persecution of all political opposition, non-Communist as well as Communist. The first American military supplies were not used to fight Communist insurgents; they were used to control, imprison or kill any who sought something better for Vietnam than the personal aggrandizement, political corruption and the profiteering of the Diem regime. The elite of the forces that we have trained and equipped are still used to control political unrest in Saigon and defend the latest dictator from the people.

And yet in a world where dictatorships are so commonplace and popular control of government so rare, people become callous to the misery that is implied by dictatorial power. The rationalizations that are used to defend political despotism have been drummed into us so long that we have somehow become numb to the possibility that something else might exist. And it is only the kind of terror we see now in Vietnam that awakens conscience and reminds us that there is something deep in us that cries out against dictatorial suppression.

The pattern of repression and destruction that we have developed and justified in the war is so thorough that it can only be called cultural genocide. I am not simply talking about

The Diem regime, to which Potter refers, was the highly controversial dictatorship of General Ngo Dinh Diem. A native of Vietnam whose family had converted to Christianity in the 17th century under the influence of French missionaries, Diem attended French Catholic schools and became an administrator for the French in their colony of Vietnam. He rose to the position of provincial governor at age 25 and associated internationally with high-profile Catholics such as President John F. Kennedy. Diem told Kennedy that he was an ardent anticommunist who would make an effective leader of Vietnam if the French would choose to withdraw.

That withdrawal came in 1954 after the Vietnamese nationalists defeated French forces at the Battle of Dien Bien Phu, ending 100 years of French colonial rule and temporarily divided Vietnam into south and north at the 17th Parallel, with reunification to take place in 1956. Using its position as part of the Southeast Asia Treaty Organization (SEATO), the United States envisioned creating a new and democratic South Vietnam in 1954. The first thing it did was to back Diem's candidacy as ruler of South Vietnam, encountering opposition from the French, who felt that Diem was maniacal and incapable of such leadership.[1]

Once in office Diem proved the French correct, and he began amassing power and rejecting advice from the United States, much to the detriment of his own South Vietnamese people. The White House felt that it needed him as a stopper to communism in South Vietnam, however, so it let him stay. When he was reminded by North Vietnam that a general election for president of a unified Vietnam, north and south, was to be held in 1956, he rejected that warning and began arresting, imprisoning (reports indicate some 100,000), and even killing his political opponents, angering many South Vietnamese, who would join with the North Vietnamese Army (becoming the so-called Viet Cong) when war broke out and escalated to the point of involving American troops.[2]

Eventually, Kennedy saw that Diem was doing more harm than good, was not the man to unite South Vietnam, and ordered the Central Intelligence Agency to provide $40,000 to South Vietnamese generals to carry out a coup against Diem. That coup was accomplished in 1963, and Diem was executed.[3] He was replaced by Nguyen Van Thieu, who was the chief of staff of the Armed Forces of South Vietnam. In 1965, regular forces of the U.S. Army engaged the regular North Vietnamese Army for the first time in the Battle of Ia Drang Valley, starting a bloody decade of war between the two countries.

napalm or gas or crop destruction or torture, hurled indiscriminately on women and children, insurgent and neutral, upon the first suspicion of rebel activity. That in itself is horrendous and incredible beyond belief. But it is only part of a larger pattern of destruction to the very fabric of the country. We have uprooted the people from the land and imprisoned them in concentration camps called "sunrise villages." Through conscription and direct political intervention and control, we have destroyed local customs and traditions, trampled upon those things of value which give dignity and purpose to life.

What is left to the people of Vietnam after 20 years of war? What part of themselves and their own lives will those who survive be able to salvage from the wreckage of their country or build on the "peace" and "security" our Great Society offers them in reward for their allegiance? How can anyone be surprised that people who have had total war waged on themselves and their culture rebel in increasing numbers against that tyranny? What other course is available? And still our only response to rebellion is more vigorous repression, more merciless opposition to the social and cultural institutions which sustain dignity and the will to resist.

Not even the President can say that this is a war to defend the freedom of the Vietnamese people. Perhaps what the President means when he speaks of freedom is the freedom of the American people.

The "White Paper" that Potter refers to was written in 1961 under the instruction of President Kennedy, who sent a fact-finding team to Vietnam. The report said that an increase in U.S. aid was needed to help South Vietnam and proposed the introduction of many American military "advisers" to help support the Diem regime and crush the National Liberation Front (NLF), a new movement consisting of anyone in Vietnam who wanted the country reunified and Diem out. Further white papers showed that the White House perceived the NLF as a puppet of North Vietnamese communists and a danger to noncommunist South Vietnam.[4] Antiwar dissidents disagreed the NLF was a puppet movement of the communists. It was this depiction by the White House of the NLF (which became known by America as the Viet Cong) that war critics labeled subterfuge and White House propaganda designed to manipulate the American public into supporting the war.[5] As a result of the 1961 White Paper, Kennedy was presented with a choice to increase U.S. involvement or do as some of his advisers urged: withdraw completely. He chose a compromise, ordering more military supplies and advisers but not sending large forces of American troops. The strategy would not succeed, as the opposition forces in Vietnam proved too strong for limited U.S. support.

WHAT IN FACT has the war done for freedom in America? It has led to even more vigorous governmental efforts to control information, manipulate the press and pressure and persuade the public through distorted or downright dishonest documents such as the White Paper on Vietnam. It has led to the confiscation of films and other anti-war material and the vigorous harassment by the FBI of some of the people who have been most outspokenly active in their criticism of the war. As the war escalates and the administration seeks more actively to gain support for any initiative it may choose to take, there has been the beginnings of a war psychology unlike anything that has burdened this country since the 1950s. How much more of Mr. Johnson's freedom can we stand? How much freedom will be left in this country if there is a major war in Asia? By what weird logic can it be said that the freedom of one people can only be maintained by crushing another?

In many ways this is an unusual march because the large majority of people here are not involved in a peace movement as their primary basis of concern. What is exciting about the participants in this march is that so many of us view ourselves consciously as participants as well in a movement to build a more decent society.

There are students here who have been involved in protests over the quality and kind of education they are receiving in growingly bureaucratized, depersonalized institutions called universities; there are Negroes from Mississippi and Alabama who are struggling against the tyranny and repression of those states; there are poor people here—Negro and white—from Northern urban areas who are attempting to build movements that abolish poverty and secure democracy; there are faculty who are beginning to question the relevance of their institutions to the critical problems facing the society. Where will these people and the movements they are a part of be if the President is allowed to expand the war in Asia?

It is important to remember, as this passage shows, that the counterculture movement of the 1960s was not just a protest of the Vietnam War, although that was always the centerpiece. And it was not just a movement of white Americans. It became a protest against all conditions perceived as unjust and inequitable in America, and key among those was the treatment of minorities and of women.

What happens to the hopeful beginnings of expressed discontent that are trying to shift American attention to long-neglected internal priorities of shared abundance, democracy and decency at home when those priorities have to compete with the all-consuming priorities and psychology of a war against an enemy thousands of miles away?

The President mocks freedom if he insists that the war in Vietnam is a defense of American freedom. Perhaps the only freedom that this war protects is the freedom of the warhawks in the Pentagon and the State Department to experiment with counter-insurgency and guerilla warfare in Vietnam.

Vietnam, we may say, is a laboratory run by a new breed of gamesmen who approach war as a kind of rational exercise in international power politics. It is the testing ground and staging area for a new American response to the social revolution that is sweeping through the impoverished downtrodden areas of the world. It is the beginning of the American counter-revolution, and so far no one—none of us—not the N.Y. Times, nor 17 Neutral Nations, nor dozens of worried allies, nor the United States Congress have been able to interfere with the freedom of the President and the Pentagon to carry out that experiment.

"Vietnam . . . is a laboratory run by a new breed of gamesmen . . ."

. . . I believe that the administration is serious about expanding the war in Asia. The question is whether the people here are as serious about ending it. I wonder what it means for each of us to say we want to end the war in Vietnam—whether, if we accept the full meaning of that statement and the gravity of the situation, we can simply leave the march and go back to the routines of a society that acts as if it were not in the midst of a grave crisis. Maybe we, like the President, are insulated from the consequences of our own decision to end the war. Maybe we have yet really to listen to the screams of a burning child and decide that we cannot go back to whatever it is we did before today until that war has ended.

"There is no simple way to attack something that is deeply rooted in the society."

There is no simple plan, no scheme or gimmick that can be proposed here. There is no simple way to attack something that is deeply rooted in the society. If the people of this country are to end the war in Vietnam, and to change the institutions which create it, then the people of this country must create a massive social movement—and if that can be built around the issue of Vietnam then that is what we must do.

Source: Used by permission of Leni Wildflower.

"The Great Silent Majority"

President Richard Nixon's Address to the American People
November 3, 1969

INTRODUCTION

Richard Nixon won a landslide election to become president in 1968, partly because he promised the American people that he had a "secret plan" to end the war in Vietnam, which had ensnared full-scale American military involvement since 1965. To many Americans, this meant that Nixon planned to withdraw American troops soon. That was not his plan, however, as he feared a loss of American leadership if—in his words—"it betrays its allies, and lets down its friends." In October 1969 almost a year after Nixon's election, protestors staged a large demonstration in the nation's capital and demanded withdrawal of American troops from Vietnam. Shortly afterward on November 3, President Nixon went on the air to deliver what was billed as a major address on his Vietnam policy. It would not be the policy that protestors wanted to hear. Instead, Nixon revealed his policy of "Vietnamization," which purported to call for reduced troop strength but also called for continued fighting and "peace with honor." He issued a call for America's "great silent majority" to support him and this policy.

Good evening, my fellow Americans:

Tonight I want to talk to you on a subject of deep concern to all Americans and to many people in all parts of the world—the war in Vietnam.

I believe that one of the reasons for the deep division about Vietnam is that many Americans have lost confidence in what their Government has told them about our policy. The American people cannot and should not be asked to support a policy which involves the overriding issues of war and peace unless they know the truth about that policy.

Tonight, therefore, I would like to answer some of the questions that I know are on the minds of many of you listening to me.

- How and why did America get involved in Vietnam in the first place?
- How has this administration changed the policy of the previous administration? What has really happened in the negotiations in Paris and on the battlefront in Vietnam?
- What choices do we have if we are to end the war?
- What are the prospects for peace?

Now, let me begin by describing the situation I found when I was inaugurated on January 20.

- The war had been going on for 4 years.
- 31,000 Americans had been killed in action.
- The training program for the South Vietnamese was behind schedule.
- 540,000 Americans were in Vietnam with no plans to reduce the number.
- No progress had been made at the negotiations in Paris and the United States had not put forth a comprehensive peace proposal.
- The war was causing deep division at home and criticism from many of our friends as well as our enemies abroad.

In view of these circumstances there were some who urged that I end the war at once by ordering the immediate withdrawal of all American forces. From a political standpoint this would have been a popular and easy course to follow. After all, we became involved in the war while my predecessor was in office. I could blame the defeat which would be the result of my action on him and come out as the peacemaker. Some put it to me quite bluntly: This was the only way to avoid allowing Johnson's war to become Nixon's war.

But I had a greater obligation than to think only of the years of my administration and of the next election. I had to think of the effect of my decision on the next generation and on the future of peace and freedom in America and in the world.

President Nixon uses some effective rhetorical devices here. First, he raises the argument for withdrawal as an option to end the war. He frames that option as "politically safe" and then, in rejecting that argument, frames himself as a heroic risk taker, determined to achieve a higher goal of lasting peace worthy of those troops who are fighting there. Second, he points out that his administration didn't start the war; he only inherited it. Still, he tells America, he's going to shoulder the responsibility and again reject the "safe" strategy of withdrawing and blaming defeat on Lyndon Johnson, even though people might incorrectly refer to Vietnam as "Nixon's war."

Let us all understand that the question before us is not whether some Americans are for peace and some Americans are against peace. The question at issue is not whether Johnson's war becomes Nixon's war.

The great question is: How can we win America's peace?

Well, let us turn now to the fundamental issue. Why and how did the United States become involved in Vietnam in the first place?

Fifteen years ago North Vietnam, with the logistical support of Communist China and the Soviet Union, launched a campaign to impose a Communist government on South Vietnam by instigating and supporting a revolution.

In response to the request of the Government of South Vietnam, President Eisenhower sent economic aid and military equipment to assist the people of South Vietnam in their efforts to prevent a Communist takeover. Seven years ago, President Kennedy sent 16,000 military personnel to Vietnam as combat advisers. Four years ago, President Johnson sent American combat forces to South Vietnam.

It is interesting that President Nixon begins his interpretation of Vietnam with the statement that the rebellion against Diem in South Vietnam was led by communist forces. That was one of the key points under debate by many who perceived the rebellion as a popular uprising of South Vietnamese against the dictatorial rule of Diem and the brutal campaign he waged against those opposed to his repressive policies. In framing the start of the war in this way, Nixon sets it up as a fight against communist takeover and thus a just war for America.

Now, many believe that President Johnson's decision to send American combat forces to South Vietnam was wrong. And many others—I among them—have been strongly critical of the way the war has been conducted.

But the question facing us today is: Now that we are in the war, what is the best way to end it?

In January I could only conclude that the precipitate withdrawal of American forces from Vietnam would be a disaster not only for South Vietnam but for the United States and for the cause of peace.

For the South Vietnamese, our precipitate withdrawal would inevitably allow the Communists to repeat the massacres which followed their takeover in the North 15 years before.

- They then murdered more than 50,000 people and hundreds of thousands more died in slave labor camps.
- We saw a prelude of what would happen in South Vietnam when the Communists entered the city of Hue last year. During their brief rule there, there was a bloody reign of terror in which 3,000 civilians were clubbed, shot to death, and buried in mass graves.

- With the sudden collapse of our support, these atrocities of Hue would become the nightmare of the entire nation—and particularly for the million and a half Catholic refugees who fled to South Vietnam when the Communists took over in the North.
- For the United States, this first defeat in our Nation's history would result in a collapse of confidence in American leadership, not only in Asia but throughout the world.

Three American Presidents have recognized the great stakes involved in Vietnam and understood what had to be done.

In 1963, President Kennedy, with his characteristic eloquence and clarity, said: "we want to see a stable government there, carrying on a struggle to maintain its national independence.

"We believe strongly in that. We are not going to withdraw from that effort. In my opinion, for us to withdraw from that effort would mean a collapse not only of South Viet-Nam, but Southeast Asia. So we are going to stay there."

Many people believe that the Vietnam War was the brainchild of Presidents Johnson and Nixon. However, as Nixon points out here, Presidents Eisenhower and Kennedy started the ball rolling in getting America involved in Vietnam by inserting military advisers, providing tactical support, and opening the door for escalation and full-scale regular U.S. Army troop involvement, which occurred under Johnson and then Nixon.

President Eisenhower and President Johnson expressed the same conclusion during their terms of office.

A favorite and ironic theme of Nixon in defending his decision to keep American troops fighting in Vietnam was peace. In a real sense, he was trying to get America to buy into the idea that peace would only come through war; that if America withdrew its troops prematurely, it would send a signal to other enemies of America that they could continue their dreams of international conquest without fear of America. He painted this view of America as one that would be abandoning its "friends." It was a hard sell not only at home but also to those in South Vietnam who had perceived America as having supported the dictator Ngo Dinh Diem.

For the future of peace, precipitate withdrawal would thus be a disaster of immense magnitude.

- **A nation cannot remain great if it betrays its allies and lets down its friends.**
- **Our defeat and humiliation in South Vietnam without question would promote recklessness in the councils of those great powers who have not yet abandoned their goals of world conquest.**
- **This would spark violence wherever our commitments help maintain the peace—in the Middle East, in Berlin, eventually even in the Western Hemisphere.**

Ultimately, this would cost more lives. It would not bring peace; it would bring more war.

For these reasons, I rejected the recommendation that I should end the war by immediately withdrawing all of our forces. I chose instead to change American policy on both the negotiating front and battlefront. In order to end a war fought on many fronts, I initiated a pursuit for peace on many fronts.

In a television speech on May 14, in a speech before the United Nations, and on a number of other occasions I set forth our peace proposals in great detail.

- **We have offered the complete withdrawal of all outside forces within 1 year.**
- **We have proposed a cease-fire under international supervision.**
- **We have offered free elections under international supervision with the Communists participating in the organization and conduct of the elections as an organized political force. And the Saigon Government has pledged to accept the result of the elections.**

We have not put forth our proposals on a take-it-or-leave-it basis. We have indicated that we are willing to discuss the proposals that have been put forth by the other side. We have declared that anything is negotiable except the right of the people of South Vietnam to determine their own future. At the Paris peace conference, Ambassador Lodge has demonstrated our flexibility and good faith in 40 public meetings.

Hanoi has refused even to discuss our proposals. They demand our unconditional acceptance of their terms, which are that we withdraw all American forces immediately and unconditionally and that we overthrow the Government of South Vietnam as we leave.

We have not limited our peace initiatives to public forums and public statements. I recognized, in January, that a long and bitter war like this usually cannot be settled in a public forum. That is why in addition to the public statements and negotiations I have explored every possible private avenue that might lead to a settlement.

It is highly doubtful that Nixon's call for complete withdrawal of U.S. troops would have taken place in a year. The May 1969 speech he cites came 16 months after the bloody Tet Offensive, which surprised America and showed that its enemy was much stronger and had deeper resolve than previously thought. Although U.S. troops had been fighting in Vietnam since 1965, most of the fights had been small skirmishes where the enemy used guerrilla tactics. But on January 30, 1968, North Vietnam staged a well-coordinated and comprehensive attack on 100 cities and villages in South Vietnam. Combined forces of North Vietnamese regulars and the South Vietnamese rebels known as the Viet Cong struck early in the morning and kept coming in numbers previously thought impossible. Although the attacks were ultimately repelled by American and South Vietnamese forces, it took a while to do so and wakened America to the ferocity and resolve of its enemy in North Vietnam. It also showed that cease-fires, such as Nixon had proposed, meant little because the Tet Offensive occurred during a cease-fire. Finally, as for proposing free elections in which communists would participate, many found this hard to believe. After all, it had been a U.S.-backed Diem regime that had rejected the idea of national elections years before and imprisoned some 100,000 political dissidents instead.

Tonight I am taking the unprecedented step of disclosing to you some of our other initiatives for peace—initiatives we undertook privately and secretly because we thought we thereby might open a door which publicly would be closed.

"I did not wait for my inauguration to begin my quest for peace."

I did not wait for my inauguration to begin my quest for peace.

- Soon after my election, through an individual who is directly in contact on a personal basis with the leaders of North Vietnam, I made two private offers for a rapid, comprehensive settlement. Hanoi's replies called in effect for our surrender before negotiations.
- Since the Soviet Union furnishes most of the military equipment for North Vietnam, Secretary of State Rogers, my Assistant for National Security Affairs, Dr. Kissinger, Ambassador Lodge, and I, personally, have met on a number of occasions with representatives of the Soviet Government to enlist their assistance in getting meaningful negotiations started. In addition, we have had extended discussions directed toward that same end with representatives of other governments which have diplomatic relations with North Vietnam. None of these initiatives have to date produced results.
- In mid-July, I became convinced that it was necessary to make a major move to break the deadlock in the Paris talks. I spoke directly in this office, where I am now sitting, with an individual who had known Ho Chi Minh [President, Democratic Republic of Vietnam] on a personal basis for 25 years. Through him I sent a letter to Ho Chi Minh. I did this outside of the usual diplomatic channels with the hope that with the necessity of making statements for propaganda removed, there might be constructive progress toward bringing the war to an end. Let me read from that letter to you now.

"Dear Mr. President:

"I realize that it is difficult to communicate meaningfully across the gulf of four years of war. But precisely because of this gulf, I wanted to take this opportunity to reaffirm in all solemnity my desire to work for a just peace. I deeply believe that the war in Vietnam has gone on too long and delay in bringing it to an end can benefit no one—least of all the people of Vietnam. . . .

"The time has come to move forward at the conference table toward an early resolution of this tragic war. You will find us forthcoming and open-minded in a common effort to bring the blessings of peace to the brave people of Vietnam. Let history record that at this critical juncture, both sides turned their face toward peace rather than toward conflict and war."

I received Ho Chi Minh's reply on August 30, 3 days before his death. It simply reiterated the public position North Vietnam had taken at Paris and flatly rejected my initiative. The full text of both letters is being released to the press.

In addition to the public meetings that I have referred to, Ambassador Lodge has met with Vietnam's chief negotiator in Paris in 11 private sessions

We have taken other significant initiatives which must remain secret to keep open some channels of communication which may still prove to be productive.

But the effect of all the public, private, and secret negotiations which have been undertaken since the bombing halt a year ago and since this administration came into office on January 20, can be summed up in one sentence: No progress whatever has been made except agreement on the shape of the bargaining table. Well now, who is at fault?

It has become clear that the obstacle in negotiating an end to the war is not the President of the United States. It is not the South Vietnamese Government.

The obstacle is the other side's absolute refusal to show the least willingness to join us in seeking a just peace. And it will not do so while it is convinced that all it has to do is to wait for our next concession, and our next concession after that one, until it gets everything it wants.

Although Nixon relates at least a portion of his letter to Ho Chi Minh, he does not include a response from the communist leader. And Nixon waited 70 days to let the American public know he had even received a response. In that response, Ho accused America of waging a "war of aggression" against the Vietnamese people, violating their "fundamental national rights" in the process. He warned that the longer the war continued, the harder it would be to achieve a peaceful settlement. Ho called for Nixon to accept the NLF's 10-point peace initiative, withdraw its troops, and allow the people of Vietnam to determine their own future.[6] It is interesting that both leaders called for an end to the war that was severely damaging to the people of Vietnam. Given that Nixon had also been promoting self-determination for the Vietnamese people, it could be argued that both leaders had the same goals in mind. As is always the case in international politics, however, face-saving becomes important on both sides, and the means to the commonly stated ends are hardly ever the same.

There can now be no longer any question that progress in negotiation depends only on Hanoi's deciding to negotiate, to negotiate seriously.

I realize that this report on our efforts on the diplomatic front is discouraging to the American people, but the American people are entitled to know the truth—the bad news as well as the good news—where the lives of our young men are involved.

Now let me turn, however, to a more encouraging report on another front.

At the time we launched our search for peace I recognized we might not succeed in bringing an end to the war through negotiation. I, therefore, put into effect another plan to bring peace—a plan which will bring the war to an end regardless of what happens on the negotiating front.

It is in line with a major shift in U.S. foreign policy which I described in my press conference at Guam on July 25. Let me briefly explain what has been described as the Nixon Doctrine—a policy which not only will help end the war in Vietnam, but which is an essential element of our program to prevent future Vietnams.

"We Americans are a do-it-yourself people. We are an impatient people."

We Americans are a do-it-yourself people. We are an impatient people. Instead of teaching someone else to do a job, we like to do it ourselves. And this trait has been carried over into our foreign policy. In Korea and again in Vietnam, the United States furnished most of the money, most of the arms, and most of the men to help the people of those countries defend their freedom against Communist aggression.

Before any American troops were committed to Vietnam, a leader of another Asian country expressed this opinion to me when I was traveling in Asia as a private citizen. He said: "When you are trying to assist another nation defend its freedom, U.S. policy should be to help them fight the war but not to fight the war for them."

Well, in accordance with this wise counsel, I laid down in Guam three principles as guidelines for future American policy toward Asia:

- First, the United States will keep all of its treaty commitments.
- Second, we shall provide a shield if a nuclear power threatens the freedom of a nation allied with us or of a nation whose survival we consider vital to our security.
- Third, in cases involving other types of aggression, we shall furnish military and economic assistance when requested in accordance with our treaty commitments. But we shall look to the nation directly threatened to assume the primary responsibility of providing the manpower for its defense.

After I announced this policy, I found that the leaders of the Philippines, Thailand, Vietnam, South Korea, and other nations which might be threatened by Communist aggression, welcomed this new direction in American foreign policy.

The defense of freedom is everybody's business—not just America's business. And it is particularly the responsibility of the people whose freedom is threatened.

"The defense of … everybody's business— not just America's business."

In the previous administration, we Americanized the war in Vietnam. In this administration, we are Vietnamizing the search for peace.

The policy of the previous administration not only resulted in our assuming the primary responsibility for fighting the war, but even more significantly did not adequately stress the goal of strengthening the South Vietnamese so that they could defend themselves when we left.

The Vietnamization plan was launched following Secretary Laird's visit to Vietnam in March. Under the plan, I ordered first a substantial increase in the training and equipment of South Vietnamese forces.

In July, on my visit to Vietnam, I changed General Abrams' orders so that they were consistent with the objectives of our new policies. Under the new orders, the primary mission of our troops is to enable the South Vietnamese forces to assume the full responsibility for the security of South Vietnam.

Our air operations have been reduced by over 20 percent.

And now we have begun to see the results of this long overdue change in American policy in Vietnam.

After 5 years of Americans going into Vietnam, we are finally bringing American men home. By December 15, over 60,000 men will have been withdrawn from South Vietnam including 20 percent of all of our combat forces.

The South Vietnamese have continued to gain in strength. As a result they have been able to take over combat responsibilities from our American troops.

The way Nixon frames his policy is interesting. Although he continued to press American troops into more fighting, he envisioned them as assisting South Vietnamese forces and strengthening those forces to be able to handle their own war: hence the term "Vietnamization." If that framing sounds familiar, it is the same perception that Americans were asked to accept decades later in the Iraq War: first American troops were used as the main fighting force to subdue Saddam Hussein and Al Qaeda, then they were depicted by the White House as strengthening Iraqi forces to handle their own war. So, as the American public was growing more and more upset over the war, the president was asking the public to view America's involvement in a different way: we were paving the way for our withdrawal by strengthening South Vietnamese forces against the invading communists. This framing did not appease the war protestors and ultimately did not prevent the communist takeover of South Vietnam after American forces left four years later. Nevertheless, Nixon did begin the process of withdrawing American troops from Vietnam. When he took office in 1968, there were 536,100 American troops in Vietnam, the largest number during the entire American involvement there. Nixon pulled 60,000 out in 1969, another 140,000 in 1970, another 180,000 in 1971, and 130,000 in 1972. By 1973 only 50 American soldiers were left, and they were evacuated as America finally withdrew from its long ordeal.

Two other significant developments have occurred since this administration took office.

Enemy infiltration, infiltration which is essential if they are to launch a major attack, over the last 3 months is less than 20 percent of what it was over the same period last year.

Most important—United States casualties have declined during the last 2 months to the lowest point in 3 years.

Let me now turn to our program for the future.

We have adopted a plan which we have worked out in cooperation with the South Vietnamese for the complete withdrawal of all U.S. combat ground forces, and their replacement by South Vietnamese forces on an orderly scheduled timetable. This withdrawal will be made from strength and not from weakness. As South Vietnamese forces become stronger, the rate of American withdrawal can become greater.

I have not and do not intend to announce the timetable for our program. And there are obvious reasons for this decision which I am sure you will understand. As I have indicated on several occasions, the rate of withdrawal will depend on developments on three fronts.

One of these is the progress which can be or might be made in the Paris talks. An announcement of a fixed timetable for our withdrawal would completely remove any incentive for the enemy to negotiate an agreement. They would simply wait until our forces had withdrawn and then move in.

The other two factors on which we will base our withdrawal decisions are the level of enemy activity and the progress of the training programs of the South Vietnamese forces. And I am glad to be able to report tonight progress on both of these fronts has been greater than we anticipated when we started the program in June for withdrawal. As a result, our timetable for withdrawal is more optimistic now than when we made our first estimates in June. Now, this clearly demonstrates why it is not wise to be frozen in on a fixed timetable.

We must retain the flexibility to base each withdrawal decision on the situation as it is at that time rather than on estimates that are no longer valid.

Along with this optimistic estimate, I must—in all candor—leave one note of caution.

If the level of enemy activity significantly increases we might have to adjust our timetable accordingly.

However, I want the record to be completely clear on one point.

At the time of the bombing halt just a year ago, there was some confusion as to whether there was an understanding on the part of the enemy that if we stopped the bombing of North Vietnam they would stop the shelling of cities in South Vietnam. I want to be sure that there is no misunderstanding on the part of the enemy with regard to our withdrawal program.

We have noted the reduced level of infiltration, the reduction of our casualties, and are basing our withdrawal decisions partially on those factors.

If the level of infiltration or our casualties increase while we are trying to scale down the fighting, it will be the result of a conscious decision by the enemy.

Hanoi could make no greater mistake than to assume that an increase in violence will be to its advantage. If I conclude that increased enemy action jeopardizes our remaining forces in Vietnam, I shall not hesitate to take strong and effective measures to deal with that situation.

"Hanoi could make no greater mistake than to assume that an increase in violence will be to its advantage."

This is not a threat. This is a statement of policy, which as Commander in Chief of our Armed Forces, I am making in meeting my responsibility for the protection of American fighting men wherever they may be.

My fellow Americans, I am sure you can recognize from what I have said that we really only have two choices open to us if we want to end this war.

—I can order an immediate, precipitate withdrawal of all Americans from Vietnam without regard to the effects of that action.

—Or we can persist in our search for a just peace through a negotiated settlement if possible, or through continued implementation of our plan for Vietnamization if necessary—a plan in which we will withdraw all of our forces from Vietnam on a schedule in accordance with our program, as the South Vietnamese become strong enough to defend their own freedom. I have chosen this second course. It is not the easy way. It is the right way.

It is a plan which will end the war and serve the cause of peace—not just in Vietnam but in the Pacific and in the world.

In speaking of the consequences of a precipitate withdrawal, I mentioned that our allies would lose confidence in America.

Far more dangerous, we would lose confidence in ourselves. Oh, the immediate reaction would be a sense of relief that our men were coming home. But as we saw the consequences of what we had done, inevitable remorse and divisive recrimination would scar our spirit as a people.

"We have faced other crises in our history and have become stronger by rejecting the easy way out and taking the right way in meeting our challenges."

We have faced other crises in our history and have become stronger by rejecting the easy way out and taking the right way in meeting our challenges. Our greatness as a nation has been our capacity to do what had to be done when we knew our course was right.

I recognize that some of my fellow citizens disagree with the plan for peace I have chosen. Honest and patriotic Americans have reached different conclusions as to how peace should be achieved.

In San Francisco a few weeks ago, I saw demonstrators carrying signs reading: "Lose in Vietnam, bring the boys home." Well, one of the strengths of our free society is that any American has a right to reach that conclusion and to advocate that point of view. But as President of the United States, I would be untrue to my oath of office if I allowed the policy of this Nation to be dictated by the minority who hold that point of view and who try to impose it on the Nation by mounting demonstrations in the street.

Here Nixon lays the groundwork for his belief that only a vocal minority of Americans were against the U.S. involvement in Vietnam and that he would not give into a minority in a country where the majority rules. He offered no evidence or statistics for war protestors constituting only a minority of the population, however, but he used this rhetorical framing to lay a foundation for his final appeal, which comes at the end of this speech.

For almost 200 years, the policy of this Nation has been made under our Constitution by those leaders in the Congress and the White House elected by all of the people. If a vocal minority, however fervent its cause, prevails over reason and the will of the majority, this Nation has no future as a free society.

And now I would like to address a word, if I may, to the young people of this Nation who are particularly concerned, and I understand why they are concerned, about this war.

I respect your idealism.

I share your concern for peace. I want peace as much as you do. There are powerful personal reasons I want to end this war. This week I will have to sign 83 letters to mothers, fathers, wives, and loved ones of men who have given their lives for America in Vietnam. It is very little satisfaction to me that this is only one-third as many letters as I signed the first week in office. There is nothing I want more than to see the day come when I do not have to write any of those letters.

I want to end the war to save the lives of those brave young men in Vietnam. But I want to end it in a way which will increase the chance that their younger brothers and their sons will not have to fight in some future Vietnam someplace in the world. And I want to end the war for another reason. I want to end it so that the energy and dedication of you, our young people, now too often directed into bitter hatred against those responsible for the war, can be turned to the great challenges of peace, a better life for all Americans, a better life for all people on this earth.

I have chosen a plan for peace. I believe it will succeed. If it does succeed, what the critics say now won't matter. If it does not succeed, anything I say then won't matter.

"I have chosen a plan for peace. I believe it will succeed."

I know it may not be fashionable to speak of patriotism or national destiny these days. But I feel it is appropriate to do so on this occasion

Two hundred years ago this Nation was weak and poor. But even then, America was the hope of millions in the world. Today we have become the strongest and richest nation in the world. And the wheel of destiny has turned so that any hope the world has for the survival of peace and freedom will be determined by whether the American people have the moral stamina and the courage to meet the challenge of free world leadership.

Let historians not record that when America was the most powerful nation in the world we passed on the other side of the road and allowed the last hopes for peace and freedom of millions of people to be suffocated by the forces of totalitarianism.

And so tonight—to you, the great silent majority of my fellow Americans—I ask for your support.

I pledged in my campaign for the Presidency to end the war in a way that we could win the peace. I have initiated a plan of action which will enable me to keep that pledge.

So here is the final appeal: one made to the "great silent majority" of Americans whom Nixon frames as supporting his plan for ultimately ending the Vietnam War and bringing American troops home. Again, he offers no statistics for supporters as being in the majority, but he uses the concept to remind the public that America is a country where the Constitution rules and is governed by the will of the majority, not the minority.

The more support I can have from the American people, the sooner that pledge can be redeemed; for the more divided we are at home, the less likely the enemy is to negotiate at Paris.

Let us be united for peace. Let us also be united against defeat. Because let us understand: North Vietnam cannot defeat or humiliate the United States. Only Americans can do that.

Fifty years ago, in this room and at this very desk, President Woodrow Wilson spoke words which caught the imagination of a war-weary world. He said: "This is the war to end war." His dream for peace after World War I was shattered on the hard realities of great power politics and Woodrow Wilson died a broken man.

Tonight I do not tell you that the war in Vietnam is the war to end wars. But I do say this: I have initiated a plan which will end this war in a way that will bring us closer to that great goal to which Woodrow Wilson and every American President in our history has been dedicated—the goal of a just and lasting peace.

As President I hold the responsibility for choosing the best path to that goal and then leading the Nation along it.

I pledge to you tonight that I shall meet this responsibility with all of the strength and wisdom I can command in accordance with your hopes, mindful of your concerns, sustained by your prayers.

Thank you and goodnight.

Source: Richard M. Nixon, *Public Papers of the Presidents of the United States: Richard Nixon, 1969* (Washington, DC: U.S. Government Printing Office, 1971), 901–909.

"As President I hold the responsibility for choosing a path to that goal and then leading the nation along it."

Notes

1. John Simpkin, "Ngo Dinh Diem," Spartacus Educational, September 1997 (updated August 2014), http://www.spartacus.schoolnet.co.uk/VNngo.htm.

2. Ibid.

3. Ibid.

4. Robert K. Brigham, "Battlefield Vietnam: A Brief History, PBS," http://www.pbs.org/battlefieldvietnam/history/.

5. Ibid.

6. "Ho Chi Minh Responds to Nixon Letter" (August 30, 1969), History.com, http://www.history.com/this-day-in-history/ho-chi-minh-responds-to-nixon-letter.

Chapter 4

We Shall Overcome: Protesting Racial Discrimination

Introduction

Alongside the national unrest over the Vietnam War and the many daily demonstrations that arose to protest that war was the national debate over civil rights, particularly the rights of black Americans. Although a century had passed since the end of the Civil War, blacks were still suffering from segregationist policies, especially in southern states. Was the time at hand for a national civil rights bill? Congress and even the John F. Kennedy administration were uncertain. Advisers to President Kennedy told him that such legislation might well fail in Congress. Still, the trouble in southern states continued as blacks were increasingly conducting an organized fight for equal rights under the law.

"A Moral Crisis"

John F. Kennedy's Address on Civil Rights
June 11, 1963

INTRODUCTION

On June 11, 1963, the fight came to a head in the state of Alabama when two black teenagers presented themselves to register as students at the University of Alabama in Tuscaloosa. Alabama was the only state still not desegregating its educational system. Governor George Wallace, long a staunch supporter of segregation, went to the university along with a cadre of Alabama state troopers. Their mission was to prevent the students from registering in this all-white university. President John F. Kennedy had exhausted measures to negotiate with Wallace. The governor refused to budge as he stood, flanked by the troopers, on the steps of the campus administration building. As a last resort, President Kennedy issued Presidential Proclamation 3542, ordering Wallace to stand down and let the students register. Kennedy also stood ready with Executive Order 11111, which would have called up and federalized the Alabama National Guard to arrest the governor, should he refuse.[1] Ultimately Wallace backed down and let the students register.

As historians point out, Kennedy decided that this night would be a great time to go on national television with a speech about racial discrimination in America. Although most of his advisers—with the exception of his brother Attorney General Robert Kennedy—said that there was no reason for such a speech now that Wallace had backed down, the president disagreed. He said that the country would only listen on a day like this, when the issue had reached a boiling point on the University of Alabama campus. So, Kennedy ordered his speech writer Ted Sorensen—at 2:00 p.m.—to draft the speech that he would deliver at 8:00 p.m.[2]

Robert Schlesinger, whose father was Arthur Schlesinger Jr., a top aide to Kennedy, writes in *U.S. News & World Report* that this speech almost had to be delivered extemporaneously by Kennedy because Sorensen didn't finish it until five minutes before airtime. President Kennedy and his brother Robert were working up an extemporaneous draft of their own. The final delivered version of the speech was an amalgam of the two drafts, although most of it was Sorensen's, using his intimate knowledge of Kennedy and of the things Kennedy had been saying all day long. The result was this landmark speech stating that a "moral crisis" exists in America and calling for Congress to expedite passage of national civil rights legislation to ensure equal rights for all Americans.

Good evening, my fellow citizens:

This afternoon, following a series of threats and defiant statements, the presence of Alabama National Guardsmen was required on the University of Alabama to carry out the final and unequivocal order of the United States District Court of the Northern District of Alabama. That

order called for the admission of two clearly qualified young Alabama residents who happened to have been born Negro.

The president begins by referencing the day's critical incident as a means of connecting the larger issue of civil rights reform to a current event that showed the need for such legislation. This was his purpose in delivering the speech on this day. The term "Negro" was the accepted description of blacks or African Americans at the time and was not seen as perjorative.

That they were admitted peacefully on the campus is due in good measure to the conduct of the students of the University of Alabama, who met their responsibilities in a constructive way.

I hope that every American, regardless of where he lives, will stop and examine his conscience about this and other related incidents. This nation was founded by men of many nations and backgrounds. It was founded on the principle that all men are created equal, and that the rights of every man are diminished when the rights of one man are threatened.

The reference to Vietnam and West Berlin here point to the controversial conflict in which the United States was becoming involved in Southeast Asia and to the capital city in Germany that had just been divided into communist and free sectors by the construction of the Berlin Wall. It was unknown at the time how explosive either of these situations would become, but Kennedy was noting that equal dangers came to rest on both whites and blacks in the military, so they should both have equal access to opportunities at home in America.

Today we are committed to a worldwide struggle to promote and protect the rights of all who wish to be free. And when Americans are sent to Viet-Nam or West Berlin, we do not ask for whites only. It ought to be possible, therefore, for American students of any color to attend any public institution they select without having to be backed up by troops.

All of these battles were being fought in the southern states, as equal opportunity was being denied African Americans on a regular basis in many places. Kennedy uses these references to lay the justification for national civil rights legislation.

It ought to be possible for American consumers of any color to receive equal service in places of public accommodation, such as hotels and restaurants and theaters and retail stores, without being forced to resort to demonstrations in the street, and it ought to be possible for American citizens of any color to register and to vote in a free election without interference or fear of reprisal.

It ought to be possible, in short, for every American to enjoy the privileges of being American without regard to his race or his color. In short, every American ought to have the right to be treated as he would wish to be treated, as one would wish his children to be treated. But this is not the case.

Here Kennedy moves from the general conditions of discrimination to the specific statistics to show, on an individual basis, how discrimination is blocking an equal path to success for African Americans. The term "Negro" was the generally accepted form of referring to African Americans in the early 1960s. It would give way to the use of "blacks," especially after the black power movement later in the decade.

The Negro baby born in America today, regardless of the section of the nation in which he is born, has about

one-half as much chance of completing a high school as a white baby born in the same place on the same day, one-third as much chance of completing college, one-third as much chance of becoming a professional man, twice as much chance of becoming unemployed, about one-seventh as much chance of earning $10,000 a year, a life expectancy which is 7 years shorter, and the prospects of earning only half as much.

This is not a sectional issue. Difficulties over segregation and discrimination exist in every city, in every State of the Union, producing in many cities a rising tide of discontent that threatens the public safety. Nor is this a partisan issue. In a time of domestic crisis men of good will and generosity should be able to unite regardless of party or politics. This is not even a legal or legislative issue alone. It is better to settle these matters in the courts than on the streets, and new laws are needed at every level, but law alone cannot make men see right.

We are confronted primarily with a moral issue. It is as old as the scriptures and is as clear as the American Constitution.

Kennedy discards the idea that this is a regional issue and lays it out as a moral one confronting the whole country.

The heart of the question is whether all Americans are to be afforded equal rights and equal opportunities, whether we are going to treat our fellow Americans as we want to be treated. If an American, because his skin is dark, cannot eat lunch in a restaurant open to the public, if he cannot send his children to the best public school available, if he cannot vote for the public officials who represent him, if, in short, he cannot enjoy the full and free life which all of us want, then who among us would be content to have the color of his skin changed and stand in his place? Who among us would then be content with the counsels of patience and delay?

This was the age before gender consciousness in rhetoric reached the level it has today, when not much thought was given to using the masculine pronouns "he," "him," and "his" to stand generically for both genders. There was no disrespect of the female gender intended; the language used had just not become an issue of public debate by then.

One hundred years of delay have passed since President Lincoln freed the slaves, yet their heirs, their grandsons, are not fully free. They are not yet freed from the bonds of injustice. They are not yet freed from social and economic oppression. And this Nation, for all its hopes and all its boasts, will not be fully free until all its citizens are free.

Kennedy continues to sound the theme that national unity calls for equal rights for citizens of all colors. He adds that America cannot call itself a free nation to the world unless all its citizens are free to pursue equal opportunities.

We preach freedom around the world, and we mean it, and we cherish our freedom here at home, but are we to say to the world, and much more importantly, to each other that this is a land of the free except for the Negroes; that we have no second-class citizens except Negroes; that we have no class or caste system, no ghettoes, no master race except with respect to Negroes?

Now the time has come for this Nation to fulfill its promise. The events in Birmingham and elsewhere have so increased the cries for equality that no city or State or legislative body can prudently choose to ignore them.

The fires of frustration and discord are burning in every city, North and South, where legal remedies are not at hand. Redress is sought in the streets, in demonstrations, parades, and protests which create tensions and threaten violence and threaten lives.

This may well have been the part of the speech that resonated so much with many Americans but that others found so controversial: the notion that we have created a moral crisis that is not being handled well by local authorities and needs federal regulation to resolve in favor of equality. To many Americans it was welcome rhetoric from the president—and overdue. To others it produced the often-heard response "You can't legislate morality."

We face, therefore, a moral crisis as a country and as a people. It cannot be met by repressive police action. It cannot be left to increased demonstrations in the streets. It cannot be quieted by token moves or talk. It is a time to act in the Congress, in your State and local legislative body and, above all, in all of our daily lives.

It is not enough to pin the blame on others, to say this is a problem of one section of the country or another, or deplore the fact that we face. A great change is at hand, and our task, our obligation, is to make that revolution, that change, peaceful and constructive for all.

Those who do nothing are inviting shame as well as violence. Those who act boldly are recognizing right as well as reality.

Next week I shall ask the Congress of the United States to act, to make a commitment it has not fully made in this century to the proposition that race has no place in American life or law. The Federal judiciary has upheld that proposition in a series of forthright cases. The executive branch has adopted that proposition in the conduct of its affairs, including the employment of Federal personnel, the use of Federal facilities, and the sale of federally financed housing.

But there are other necessary measures which only the Congress can provide, and they must be provided at this session. The old code of equity law under which we live commands for every wrong a remedy, but in too many communities, in too many parts of the country, wrongs are inflicted on Negro citizens and there are no remedies at law. Unless the Congress acts, their only remedy is in the street.

I am, therefore, asking the Congress to enact legislation giving all Americans the right to be served in facilities which are open to the public—hotels, restaurants, theaters, retail stores, and similar establishments.

Having set up the justification for federal intervention and congressional legislation, the president now specifically shows his hand to the American public: he will seek such a needed act from Congress. He states that such action is needed or else the issue will produce more turbulence in the streets of the states refusing to allow equal access for all citizens. In a very real way, Kennedy is laying down the gauntlet to Congress: Act or face the consequences.

This seems to me to be an elementary right. Its denial is an arbitrary indignity that no American in 1963 should have to endure, but many do.

I have recently met with scores of business leaders urging them to take voluntary action to end this discrimination and I have been encouraged by their response, and in the last 2 weeks over 75 cities have seen progress made in desegregating these kinds of facilities. But many are unwilling to act alone, and for this reason, nationwide legislation is needed if we are to move this problem from the streets to the courts.

I am also asking Congress to authorize the Federal Government to participate more fully in lawsuits designed to end segregation in public education. We have succeeded in persuading many districts to de-segregate voluntarily. Dozens have admitted Negroes without violence. Today a Negro is attending a State-supported institution in every one of our 50 States, but the pace is very slow.

Too many Negro children entering segregated grade schools at the time of the Supreme Court's decision 9 years ago will enter segregated high schools this fall,

Kennedy here extends his call for equal rights to the world of education as well, showing that the movement for change is not progressing quickly enough without such federal legislation. Media reports of African Americans denied school entry in cities from Little Rock to Tuscaloosa had been beamed regularly into America's living rooms through television, so Kennedy knew that viewers understood what he was talking about.

having suffered a loss which can never be restored. The lack of an adequate education denies the Negro a chance to get a decent job.

The orderly implementation of the Supreme Court decision, therefore, cannot be left solely to those who may not have the economic resources to carry the legal action or who may be subject to harassment.

Other features will be also requested, including greater protection for the right to vote. But legislation, I repeat, cannot solve this problem alone. It must be solved in the homes of every American in every community across our country.

In this respect, I want to pay tribute to those citizens North and South who have been working in their communities to make life better for all. They are acting not out of a sense of legal duty but out of a sense of human decency.

There is a lot in this section of the speech: a quick extension of the requested rights into the voting arena and acknowledgment that individual Americans need to buy into this idea of freedom for all Americans. Kennedy here expresses gratitude to those who have already adopted the changes themselves and worked in groups to convince others of the need for such change.

Like our soldiers and sailors in all parts of the world they are meeting freedom's challenge on the firing line, and I salute them for their honor and their courage.

My fellow Americans, this is a problem which faces us all—in every city of the North as well as the South. Today there are Negroes unemployed, two or three times as many compared to whites, inadequate in education, moving into the large cities, unable to find work, young people particularly out of work without hope, denied equal rights, denied the opportunity to eat at a restaurant or lunch counter or go to a movie theater, denied the right to a decent education, denied almost today the right to attend a State university even though qualified. It seems to me that these are matters which concern us all, not merely Presidents or Congressmen or Governors, but every citizen of the United States.

This is one country. It has become one country because all of us and all the people who came here had an equal chance to develop their talents.

We cannot say to 10 percent of the population that you can't have that right; that your children can't have the chance to develop whatever talents they have; that the only way that they are going to get their rights is to go into the streets and demonstrate. I think we owe them and we owe ourselves a better country than that.

Therefore, I am asking for your help in making it easier for us to move ahead and to provide the kind of equality of treatment which we would want ourselves; to give a chance for every child to be educated to the limit of his talents.

According to Robert Schlesinger, this was the portion of the speech that Kennedy and his brother Robert developed themselves when crafting an extemporaneous version of the speech before Ted Sorensen's draft was finished. Everyone involved knew that this speech was risky, and they had to walk a tightrope to produce the desired effect of civil rights legislation without polarizing the country even further or being the catalyst for more violent confrontations. Then, of course, there were the political considerations and associated risks that went along with making such a bold move on the controversial issue of race relations at a time when it was boiling over in parts of the country.

As I have said before, not every child has an equal talent or an equal ability or an equal motivation, but they should have the equal right to develop their talent and their ability and their motivation, to make something of themselves.

We have a right to expect that the Negro community will be responsible, will uphold the law, but they have a right to expect that the law will be fair, that the Constitution will be color blind, as Justice Harlan said at the turn of the century.

This is what we are talking about and this is a matter which concerns this country and what it stands for, and in meeting it I ask the support of all our citizens.

Thank you very much.

Source: *Congressional Record,* 88 Cong., 1 Sess., pp. 10965–10966.

"We Shall Overcome"

Lyndon B. Johnson's Voting Rights Speech
March 15, 1965

INTRODUCTION

On March 15, 1965, President Lyndon B. Johnson delivered what most rhetorical scholars consider one of the great speeches in American history, despite the fact that Johnson was never considered among the most eloquent of American presidents and certainly not one of the more charismatic. Still, the speech resonated with Americans and went a long way toward paving the road for the Voting Rights Act, which would be passed by Congress and become effective five months later on August 6, one year and four days after the landmark Civil Rights Act became effective on July 2, 1964. The Voting Rights Act would result in a guarantee that the privileges of the Fourteenth and Fifteenth Amendments would be enforced and applied for all African American voters in the South, many of whom had been disenfranchised by their states over the years. Johnson's speech, often called the "We Shall Overcome" speech, came on the heels of civil rights demonstrations and violent reaction by local authorities in Selma, Alabama.

As Garth E. Pauley of Calvin College has said, "In an uncharacteristically eloquent way, the president interpreted the meaning of the Selma demonstrations for a nation awakened to the problem of voter discrimination: His interpretation focused on the very meaning of the nation, what he called 'the American Promise.' Out of that interpretation, he crafted a compelling rationale for immediate passage of a strong federal voting rights law. His language effectively framed public and congressional deliberations. His appeals helped cement equal voting rights as a fundamental American principle."[3]

Mr. Speaker, Mr. President, Members of the Congress:

I speak tonight for the dignity of man and the destiny of democracy. I urge every member of both parties, Americans of all religions and of all colors, from every section of this country, to join me in that cause.

Johnson begins by drawing parallels between moments in American history valued by all Americans and the recent civil rights protest in Selma, Alabama. The purpose of such analogies is to explain and interpret what the audience is unclear about by comparing it to something they do know about. This is an effective writing and rhetorical tool that helps ensure the points being made by the speaker will resonate with contemporary audiences. Johnson had some of the most effective speech writers of any president in history. But his ability to deliver and sell those speeches was not as strong. This speech was an exception to that norm.

At times, history and fate meet at a single time in a single place to shape a turning point in man's unending search for freedom. So it was at Lexington and Concord. So it was a century ago at Appomattox. So it was last week in Selma, Alabama. There, long-suffering men and women peacefully protested the denial of their rights as Americans. Many were brutally assaulted. One good man, a man of God, was killed.

There is no cause for pride in what has happened in Selma. There is no cause for self-satisfaction in the long denial of equal rights of millions of Americans. But there is cause for hope and for faith in our democracy in what is happening here tonight. For the cries of pain and the hymns and protests of oppressed people have summoned into convocation all the majesty of this great government—the government of the greatest nation on earth. Our mission is at once the oldest and the most basic of this country: to right wrong, to do justice, to serve man.

In our time we have come to live with the moments of great crisis. Our lives have been marked with debate about great issues—issues of war and peace, issues of prosperity and depression. But rarely in any time does an issue lay bare the secret heart of America itself. Rarely are we met with a challenge, not to our growth or abundance, or our welfare or our security, but rather to the values, and the purposes, and the meaning of our beloved nation.

The issue of equal rights for American Negroes is such an issue.

So here it is: a clear statement that the nation is in a state of crisis. To many, it summoned up President Kennedy's phrase of "moral crisis" given in his own civil rights speech two years earlier. Johnson underscores the moment by calling the treatment of African Americans a "rare moment" that threatens American values. He underscores the urgency of action in suggesting that this opportunity may not arise again in the near future. Certainly the televised violence in Selma, beamed across the nation, was a visual expression of that threat to the millions of Americans who were still seeing film of that event.

And should we defeat every enemy, and should we double our wealth and conquer the stars, and still be unequal to this issue, then we will have failed as a people and as a nation.

For with a country as with a person, "What is a man profited, if he shall gain the whole world, and lose his own soul?"

Johnson here invokes Mark 8:36 from the New Testament, seemingly not only to add weight to his point about meeting the voting rights challenge but also to resonate with southern audiences of the Bible Belt states where voting discrimination was being practiced.

There is no Negro problem. There is no Southern problem. There is no Northern problem. There is only an American problem. And we are met here tonight as Americans—not as Democrats or Republicans. We are met here as Americans to solve that problem.

The president summons up a theme from John F. Kennedy's 1963 address on civil rights: the assertion that this is not a regional problem but a national one.

This was the first nation in the history of the world to be founded with a purpose. The great phrases of that purpose still sound in every American heart, North and South: "All men are created equal," "government by consent of the governed," "give me liberty or give me death." Well, those are not just clever words, or those are not just empty theories. In their name Americans have fought and died for two centuries, and tonight around the world they stand there as guardians of our liberty, risking their lives.

Those words are a promise to every citizen that he shall share in the dignity of man. This dignity cannot be found in a man's possessions; it cannot be found in his power, or in his position. It really rests on his right to be treated as a man equal in opportunity to all others. It says that he shall share in freedom, he shall choose his leaders, educate his children, provide for his family according to his ability and his merits as a human being.

Here the president links another cherished idea—the sacrifices made for freedom by Americans on the battlefields—to the freedoms sought by African Americans in the South. Johnson understood that in the South, pride in the military and its veterans was very strong.

To apply any other test—to deny a man his hopes because of his color, or race, or his religion, or the place of his birth is not only to do injustice, it is to deny America and to dishonor the dead who gave their lives for American freedom.

Our fathers believed that if this noble view of the rights of man was to flourish, it must be rooted in democracy. The most basic right of all was the right to choose your own leaders. The history of this country, in large measure, is the history of the expansion of that right to all of our people. Many of the issues of civil rights are very complex and most difficult. But about this there can and should be no argument.

It doesn't get any more straightforward and simple in Johnson's speech than this. This one sentence gave clarity to his entire message.

Every American citizen must have an equal right to vote.

There is no reason which can excuse the denial of that right. There is no duty which weighs more heavily on us than the duty we have to ensure that right.

In his speech, Johnson moves back and forth between the abstract and the specific. Here he breaks down the overall fact of voting discrimination in the South into the specific ways in which that discrimination is being practiced.

Yet the harsh fact is that in many places in this country men and women are kept from voting simply because they are Negroes. Every device of which human ingenuity is capable has been used to deny this right. The Negro citizen may go to register only to be told that the day is wrong, or the hour is late, or the official in charge is absent. And if he persists, and if he manages to present himself to the registrar, he may be disqualified because he did not spell out his middle name or because he abbreviated a word on the application. And if he manages to fill

out an application, he is given a test. The registrar is the sole judge of whether he passes this test. He may be asked to recite the entire Constitution, or explain the most complex provisions of State law. And even a college degree cannot be used to prove that he can read and write.

For the fact is that the only way to pass these barriers is to show a white skin. Experience has clearly shown that the existing process of law cannot overcome systematic and ingenious discrimination. No law that we now have on the books—and I have helped to put three of them there—can ensure the right to vote when local officials are determined to deny it. In such a case our duty must be clear to all of us. The Constitution says that no person shall be kept from voting because of his race or his color. We have all sworn an oath before God to support and to defend that Constitution. We must now act in obedience to that oath.

Wednesday, I will send to Congress a law designed to eliminate illegal barriers to the right to vote.

In this section, Johnson lays the justification for a federal law to enforce constitutional rights that state and local authorities in the South are denying their African American citizens. And he follows that justification with the direct statement of what he plans to do about it the very next day: lay the challenge before Congress.

The broad principles of that bill will be in the hands of the Democratic and Republican leaders tomorrow. After they have reviewed it, it will come here formally as a bill. I am grateful for this opportunity to come here tonight at the invitation of the leadership to reason with my friends, to give them my views, and to visit with my former colleagues. I've had prepared a more comprehensive analysis of the legislation which I had intended to transmit to the clerk tomorrow, but which I will submit to the clerks tonight. But I want to really discuss with you now, briefly, the main proposals of this legislation.

This bill will strike down restrictions to voting in all elections—Federal, State, and local—which have been used to deny Negroes the right to vote. This bill will establish a simple, uniform standard which cannot be used, however ingenious the effort, to flout our Constitution. It will provide for citizens to be registered by officials of the United States Government, if the State officials refuse to register them. It will eliminate tedious, unnecessary lawsuits

In a simple summary interpretation, Johnson presents what the bill is designed to do and how it will do it. He is using his position as president and the time he has on national television to give a prime definition (first definition) to the Voting Rights Act. Communication experts have often pointed out the importance of this priming function in planting a definition in the minds of those hearing or reading it.

which delay the right to vote. Finally, this legislation will ensure that properly registered individuals are not prohibited from voting.

I will welcome the suggestions from all of the Members of Congress—I have no doubt that I will get some—on ways and means to strengthen this law and to make it effective. But experience has plainly shown that this is the only path to carry out the command of the Constitution.

To those who seek to avoid action by their National Government in their own communities, who want to and who seek to maintain purely local control over elections, the answer is simple: open your polling places to all your people.

Allow men and women to register and vote whatever the color of their skin. Extend the rights of citizenship to every citizen of this land.

There is no constitutional issue here. The command of the Constitution is plain. There is no moral issue. It is wrong—deadly wrong—to deny any of your fellow Americans the right to vote in this country. There is no issue of States' rights or national rights. There is only the struggle for human rights. I have not the slightest doubt what will be your answer.

Johnson cites recent legislative history here to put this Voting Rights Bill into context: it would not have been a necessary bill if the Civil Rights Act had emerged from its long debate in Congress with its own voting rights provision intact. Now he takes aim at that eliminated provision with this separate act and insists—a few days after the bloody violence in Selma—that it be passed quickly.

But the last time a President sent a civil rights bill to the Congress, it contained a provision to protect voting rights in Federal elections. That civil rights bill was passed after eight *long* months of debate. And when that bill came to my desk from the Congress for my signature, the heart of the voting provision had been eliminated. This time, on this issue, there must be no delay, or no hesitation, or no compromise with our purpose.

We cannot, we must not, refuse to protect the right of every American to vote in every election that he may desire to participate in. And we ought not, and we cannot, and we must not wait another eight months before we get a bill. We have already waited a hundred years and more, and the time for waiting is gone.

So I ask you to join me in working long hours—nights and weekends, if necessary—to pass this bill. And I don't make that request lightly. For from the window where I sit with the problems of our country, I recognize that from outside this chamber is the outraged conscience of a nation, the grave concern of many nations, and the harsh judgment of history on our acts.

But even if we pass this bill, the battle will not be over. What happened in Selma is part of a far larger movement which reaches into every section and State of America. It is the effort of American Negroes to secure for themselves the full blessings of American life. Their cause must be our cause too. Because it's not just Negroes, but really it's all of us, who must overcome the crippling legacy of bigotry and injustice.

"But even if we pass this bill, the battle will not be over."

And we shall overcome.

As a man whose roots go deeply into Southern soil, I know how agonizing racial feelings are. I know how difficult it is to reshape the attitudes and the structure of our society. But a century has passed, more than a hundred years since the Negro was freed. And he is not fully free tonight.

It was more than a hundred years ago that Abraham Lincoln, a great President of another party, signed the Emancipation Proclamation; but emancipation is a proclamation, and not a fact. A century has passed, more than a hundred years, since equality was promised. And yet the Negro is not equal. A century has passed since the day of promise. And the promise is unkept.

There is a lot packed into this section of the speech. First, Johnson reminds Americans that he is a southerner himself (from Texas) who understands how southerners feel and how hard it is to change those attitudes. Second, he invokes a Republican president (Abraham Lincoln) and his Emancipation Proclamation to show that this is not a party issue. Third, he reiterates his theme that although 100 years have passed since African Americans were freed in the United States, they still do not have access to equal rights promised in the Constitution for all Americans. In so stating, Johnson is showing that voting rights is not a new idea or one that just arose two years ago in the debate over the Civil Rights Act. Fourth, he invokes the mantra of the civil rights movement and its leader Dr. Martin Luther King Jr. in the statement "And we shall overcome."

The time of justice has now come. I tell you that I believe sincerely that no force can hold it back. It is right in the eyes of man and God that it should come. And when it does, I think that day will brighten the lives of every American. For Negroes are not the only victims. How many white children have gone uneducated? How many white families have lived in stark poverty? How many white lives have been scarred by fear, because we've wasted our energy and our substance to maintain the barriers of hatred and terror?

And so I say to all of you here, and to all in the nation tonight, that those who appeal to you to hold on to the past do so at the cost of denying you your future.

This great, rich, restless country can offer opportunity and education and hope to all, all black and white, all North and South, sharecropper and city dweller. These are the enemies: poverty, ignorance, disease. They're our enemies, not our fellow man, not our neighbor. And these enemies too—poverty, disease, and ignorance: we shall overcome.

Now let none of us in any section look with prideful righteousness on the troubles in another section, or the problems of our neighbors. There's really no part of America where the promise of equality has been fully kept. In Buffalo as well as in Birmingham, in Philadelphia as well as Selma, Americans are struggling for the fruits of freedom. This is one nation. What happens in Selma or in Cincinnati is a matter of legitimate concern to every American. But let each of us look within our own hearts and our own communities, and let each of us put our shoulder to the wheel to root out injustice wherever it exists.

As we meet here in this peaceful, historic chamber tonight, men from the South, some of whom were at Iwo Jima, men from the North who have carried Old Glory to far corners of the world and brought it back without a stain on it, men from the East and from the West, are all fighting together without regard to religion, or color, or region, in Vietnam. Men from every region fought for us across the world twenty years ago.

And now in these common dangers and these common sacrifices, the South made its contribution of honor and gallantry no less than any other region in the Great Republic—and in some instances, a great many of them, more.

And I have not the slightest doubt that good men from everywhere in this country, from the Great Lakes to the Gulf of Mexico, from the Golden Gate to the harbors along the Atlantic, will rally now together in this cause to vindicate the freedom of all Americans.

For all of us owe this duty; and I believe that all of us will respond to it. Your President makes that request of every American.

"And I have not the slightest doubt that good men from everywhere in this country . . . will rally now in this cause to vindicate the freedom for all Americans."

Johnson reminds America that African Americans, especially those in the Deep South, have risked their lives to demonstrate, protest, and break the local laws that perpetuate segregation and discrimination. Because television news had hit its stride by the early 1960s, all Americans had witnessed these bloody sacrifices each night in the comfort of their own homes via the network newscasts of NBC, CBS, and ABC.

The real hero of this struggle is the American Negro. His actions and protests, his courage to risk safety and even to risk his life, have awakened the conscience of this nation. His demonstrations have been designed to call attention

to injustice, designed to provoke change, designed to stir reform. He has called upon us to make good the promise of America. And who among us can say that we would have made the same progress were it not for his persistent bravery, and *his* faith in American democracy.

For at the real heart of battle for equality is a deep-seated belief in the democratic process. Equality depends not on the force of arms or tear gas but depends upon the force of moral right; not on recourse to violence but on respect for law and order.

And there have been many pressures upon your President and there will be others as the days come and go. But I pledge you tonight that we intend to fight this battle where it should be fought—in the courts, and in the Congress, and in the hearts of men.

We must preserve the right of free speech and the right of free assembly. But the right of free speech does not carry with it, as has been said, the right to holler fire in a crowded theater. We must preserve the right to free assembly. But free assembly does not carry with it the right to block public thoroughfares to traffic.

We do have a right to protest, and a right to march under conditions that do not infringe the constitutional rights of our neighbors. And I intend to protect all those rights as long as I am permitted to serve in this office.

We will guard against violence, knowing it strikes from our hands the very weapons which we seek: progress, obedience to law, and belief in American values.

In this section, Johnson seems to be balancing the scales a bit by sending a message to those white southerners worried about the impact of the demonstrations and protests on the order of daily life in the targeted communities and by the fear of infringement on other people's rights during these protests.

In Selma, as elsewhere, we seek and pray for peace. We seek order. We seek unity. But we will not accept the peace of stifled rights, or the order imposed by fear, or the unity that stifles protest. For peace cannot be purchased at the cost of liberty.

In Selma tonight—and we had a good day there—as in every city, we are working for a just and peaceful settlement. And we must all remember that after this speech I am making tonight, after the police and the FBI and the Marshals have all gone, and after you have promptly passed this bill, the people of Selma and the other cities of the Nation must still live and work together. And when the attention of the nation has gone elsewhere, they must try to heal the wounds and to build a new community.

This cannot be easily done on a battleground of violence, as the history of the South itself shows. It is in recognition of this that men of both races have shown such an outstandingly impressive responsibility in recent days—last Tuesday, again today.

Two things about this section: First, the bill will be known by a common name (civil rights bill) that will be hard for opponents to speak against, because everyone is for civil rights, correct? But all bills—especially controversial ones such as today's Affordable Care Act (Obamacare)—are given such agreeable names, and that hasn't thwarted opposition to them. The same was true with the Civil Rights Act. Second, Johnson's use of the "city of hope" metaphor was a great framing, encapsulating the idea of a black person's equal right to such hope.

The bill that I am presenting to you will be known as a civil rights bill. But, in a larger sense, most of the program I am recommending is a civil rights program. Its object is to open the city of hope to all people of all races. Because all Americans just must have the right to vote. And we are going to give them that right.

All Americans must have the privileges of citizenship—regardless of race. And they are going to have those privileges of citizenship—regardless of race.

But I would like to caution you and remind you that to exercise these privileges takes much more than just legal right. It requires a trained mind and a healthy body. It requires a decent home, and the chance to find a job, and the opportunity to escape from the clutches of poverty.

Johnson begins to enlarge the importance of the voting rights issue to the bigger issue of poverty and equal access to good jobs, two themes that buttressed his "war on poverty" during his term as president. Limited civil rights and poverty have been seen to go hand in hand in all parts of the country, and Johnson realized this.

Of course, people cannot contribute to the nation if they are never taught to read or write, if their bodies are stunted from hunger, if their sickness goes untended, if their life is spent in hopeless poverty just drawing a welfare check. So we want to open the gates to opportunity. But we're also going to give all our people, black and white, the help that they need to walk through those gates.

My first job after college was as a teacher in Cotulla, Texas, in a small Mexican-American school. Few of

them could speak English, and I couldn't speak much Spanish. My students were poor and they often came to class without breakfast, hungry. And they knew, even in their youth, the pain of prejudice. They never seemed to know why people disliked them. But they knew it was so, because I saw it in their eyes. I often walked home late in the afternoon, after the classes were finished, wishing there was more that I could do. But all I knew was to teach them the little that I knew, hoping that it might help them against the hardships that lay ahead.

And somehow you never forget what poverty and hatred can do when you see its scars on the hopeful face of a young child. I never thought then, in 1928, that I would be standing here in 1965. It never even occurred to me in my fondest dreams that I might have the chance to help the sons and daughters of those students and to help people like them all over this country.

In this passage, Johnson is able to take the need for this civil rights bill and personalize it in a much-needed way, also offering a rare glimpse into the human side of this president that the public had rarely seen. Many did not even know that this man, known for his political intimidation tactics and overt use of power, had even been a schoolteacher, let alone a teacher in a Mexican American school. Johnson uses that chapter of his life effectively in letting America know that he is not just treating civil rights as an abstract issue; it is a personal one. He has seen the human face of poverty and injustice in the eyes of schoolchildren, and he intends now to use his power to do something about fixing the problem.

But now I do have that chance—and I'll let you in on a secret—I mean to use it.

And I hope that you will use it with me.

This is the richest and the most powerful country which ever occupied this globe. The might of past empires is little compared to ours. But I do not want to be the President who built empires, or sought grandeur, or extended dominion.

I want to be the President who educated young children to the wonders of their world.

I want to be the President who helped to feed the hungry and to prepare them to be tax-payers instead of tax-eaters.

I want to be the President who helped the poor to find their own way and who protected the right of every citizen to vote in every election.

I want to be the President who helped to end hatred among his fellow men, and who promoted love among the people of all races and all regions and all parties.

Johnson uses the rhetorical device of repetition ("I want to be the President who . . .") to drive home key summary points and goals of equality to all Americans as he draws his speech to a close. It is an effective tool for spotlighting individual aspects of the civil rights issue and giving them equal importance.

I want to be the President who helped to end war among the brothers of this earth.

And so, at the request of your beloved Speaker, and the Senator from Montana, the majority leader, the Senator from Illinois, the minority leader, Mr. McCulloch, and other Members of both parties, I came here tonight—not as President Roosevelt came down one time, in person, to veto a bonus bill, not as President Truman came down one time to urge the passage of a railroad bill—but I came down here to ask you to share this task with me, and to share it with the people that we both work for. I want this to be the Congress, Republicans and Democrats alike, which did all these things for all these people.

"Who can tell what deep and unspoken hopes are in their hearts tonight as they sit there and listen."

Beyond this great chamber, out yonder in fifty States, are the people that we serve. Who can tell what deep and unspoken hopes are in their hearts tonight as they sit there and listen. We all can guess, from our own lives, how difficult they often find their own pursuit of happiness, how many problems each little family has. They look most of all to themselves for their futures. But I think that they also look to each of us.

Above the pyramid on the great seal of the United States it says in Latin: "God has favored our undertaking." God will not favor everything that we do. It is rather our duty to divine His will.

But I cannot help believing that He truly understands and that He really favors the undertaking that we begin here tonight.

Source: Lyndon B. Johnson, *Public Papers of the Presidents of the United States: Lyndon B. Johnson, 1965,* Vol. 1, entry 107 (Washington, DC: US. Government Printing Office, 1966), 281–287.

"Black Power"

Stokely Carmichael's Speech to the SNCC
October 29, 1966

INTRODUCTION

Stokely Carmichael was a Trinidad-born American who engaged in civil rights protests in the South, was jailed in 1961 for 53 days in Mississippi for riding in a whites-only section of a train, and rose to become president of the Student Nonviolent Coordinating Committee (SNCC), replacing John Lewis in that office. Carmichael later joined the more militant Black Panther Party. In the following speech, delivered on the campus of the University of California at Berkeley, he introduced the phrase "black power" into the civil rights movement. It was a speech he delivered after spending time in a Mississippi jail in 1966.

Thank you very much. It's a privilege and an honor to be in the white intellectual ghetto of the West. We wanted to do a couple of things before we started. The first is, that, based on the fact that SNCC, through the articulation of its program by its chairman, has been able to win elections in Georgia, Alabama, Maryland, and by our appearance here will win an election in California. In 1968 I'm goin' to run for President of the United States. I just can't make it, 'cause I wasn't born in the United States. That's the only thing holding me back.

We wanted to say that this is a student conference, as it should be, held on a campus and that we're not ever to be caught up in the intellectual masturbation of the question of Black Power. That's a function of people who are advertisers that call themselves reporters. Oh, for my members and friends of the press, my self-appointed white critics, I was reading Mr. Bernard Shaw two days ago, and I came across a very important quote which I think is most apropos for you. He says, "All criticism is a [sic] autobiography." Dig yourself. Okay.

The philosophers Camus and Sartre raise the question whether or not a man can condemn himself. The black existentialist philosopher who is pragmatic, Frantz Fanon, answered the question. He said that man could not. Camus and Sartre was [sic] not. We in SNCC tend to agree with Camus and Sartre that a man cannot condemn

Carmichael was not grammatically correct in all of his rhetoric, and at times his meaning was obfuscated by his language and syntax. Nevertheless, the Howard University graduate was astute and forceful in the passion in his speech that was delivered to a friendly and receptive audience at this SNCC conference in Berkeley. The speech would prove effective in coalescing the black power movement in America.

100

himself. Were he to condemn himself, he would then have to inflict punishment upon himself. An example would be the Nazis. Any prisoner who any of the Nazi prisoners who admitted, after he was caught and incarcerated, that he committed crimes, that he killed all the many people that he killed, he committed suicide. The only ones who were able to stay alive were the ones who never admitted that they committed a crime against people—that is, the ones who rationalized that Jews were not human beings and deserved to be killed, or that they were only following orders.

Carmichael alludes to Lawrence Rainey, who was the 41-year-old sheriff of Neshoba County in 1964. Rainey was sheriff when three young civil rights workers came to Philadelphia, Mississippi, and were killed. Rainey was arrested, along with 18 other persons, on charges that they conspired to deprive the three men of their civil rights. These were federal charges that stemmed from the murders of the civil rights workers on June 21. Rainey was acquitted at trial of the charges.

On a more immediate scene, the officials and the population—the white population—in Neshoba County, Mississippi—that's where Philadelphia is—could not, could not condemn [Sheriff] Rainey, his deputies, and the other fourteen men that killed three human beings. They could not because they elected Mr. Rainey to do precisely what he did, and that for them to condemn him will be for them to condemn themselves.

"[I]nstitutions that function in this country are clearly racist . . ."

In a much larger view, SNCC says that white America cannot condemn herself. And since we are liberal, we have done it: You stand condemned. Now, a number of things that arises from that answer of how do you condemn yourselves. Seems to me that the institutions that function in this country are clearly racist, and that they're built upon racism. And the question, then, is how can black people inside of this country move? And then how can white people who say they're not a part of those institutions begin to move? And how then do we begin to clear away the obstacles that we have in this society, that make us live like human beings? How can we begin to build institutions that will allow people to relate with each other as human beings? This country has never done that, especially around the country of white or black.

Now, several people have been upset because we've said that integration was irrelevant when initiated by blacks, and that in fact it was a subterfuge, an insidious subterfuge, for the maintenance of white supremacy. Now we maintain that in the past six years or so, this country has been feeding us a "thalidomide drug of integration," and that some Negroes have been walking down a dream street talking about sitting next to white people; and that that does not begin to solve the problem.

> **That when we went to Mississippi we did not go to sit next to Ross Barnett; we did not go to sit next to Jim Clark; we went to get them out of our way; and that people ought to understand that; that we were never fighting for the right to integrate, we were fighting against white supremacy.**

Now, then, in order to understand white supremacy we must dismiss the fallacious notion that white people can give anybody their freedom. No man can give anybody his freedom. A man is born free. You may enslave a man after he is born free, and that is in fact what this country does. It enslaves black people after they're born, so that the only acts that white people can do is to stop denying black people their freedom; that is, they must stop denying freedom. They never give it to anyone.

> **Now we want to take that to its logical extension, so that we could understand, then, what its relevancy would be in terms of new civil rights bills. I maintain that every civil rights bill in this country was passed for white people, not for black people. For example, I am black. I know that. I also know that while I am black I am a human being, and therefore I have the right to go into any public place. White people didn't know that. Every time I tried to go into a place they stopped me. So some boys had to write a bill to tell that white man, "He's a human being; don't stop him." That bill was for that white man, not for me. I knew it all the time. I knew it all the time.**

I knew that I could vote and that that wasn't a privilege; it was my right. Every time I tried I was shot, killed or jailed, beaten or economically deprived. So somebody had to write a bill for white people to tell them, "When a black man comes to vote, don't bother him." That bill, again, was for white people, not for black people. So that when you talk about open occupancy, I know I can live anyplace I want to live. It is white people across this country who are incapable of allowing me to live where I want to live. You need a civil rights bill, not me. I know I can live where I want to live.

Ross Barnett was the segregationist governor of Mississippi, and Jim Clark was sheriff of Dallas County, Alabama, during the Selma protests. He was one of the officials who directed the brutal response to the civil rights marchers there. Both men became symbols, at least to black America, of the oppression that white leadership was exerting on people of color, especially in the South.

Carmichael advances the theme begun earlier about the insufficiency of integration laws, the Civil Rights Act, and the Voting Rights Act. These acts, he says, are the work of white men and have not actually made life better for most blacks. He continues to lay the foundation for the need of black America to stand up for itself and not depend on white men or be deceived by laws that are attempts to manipulate blacks into submission. While much of black America was supportive—many enthusiastically so—of the civil rights bill, Carmichael and his followers were clearly not.

This is the first time the phrase "Black Power" appears in Carmichael's speech. It will appear several more times before he is finished. The inspiration that many African Americans drew from that phrase has lasted even to today.

So that the failures to pass a civil rights bill isn't because of Black Power, isn't because of the Student Nonviolent Coordinating Committee; it's not because of the rebellions that are occurring in the major cities. It is incapability of whites to deal with their own problems inside their own communities. That is the problem of the failure of the civil rights bill.

And so in a larger sense we must then ask, how is it that black people move? And what do we do? But the question in a greater sense is, how can white people who are the majority—and who are responsible for making democracy work—make it work? They have miserably failed to this point. They have never made democracy work, be it inside the United States, Vietnam, South Africa, Philippines, South America, Puerto Rico. Wherever America has been, she has not been able to make democracy work. So that in a larger sense, we not only condemn the country for what it's done internally, but we must condemn it for what it does externally. We see this country trying to rule the world, and someone must stand up and start articulating that this country is not God, and cannot rule the world.

"Wherever America has been [in the world], she has not been able to make democracy work."

Now then, before we move on we ought to develop the white supremacy attitudes that were either conscious or subconscious thought and how they run rampant through the society today. For example, the missionaries were sent to Africa. They went with the attitude that blacks were automatically inferior. As a matter of fact, the first act the missionaries did, you know, when they get [*sic*] to Africa was to make us cover up our bodies, because they said it got them excited. We couldn't go bare-breasted any more because they got excited.

Here is a fascinating interpretation of why many African Americans distrusted white Americans, especially those who said they were going to help the blacks. The "price" he talks about of swapping the Bible for the land is an interesting one and shows how the black distrust of whites extended to those whites who called themselves Christians. The same distrust held true, obviously, of white lawmakers who said they were crafting laws such as the Civil Rights Act for African Americans. To Carmichael, it wasn't so much the provisions of the Civil Rights Act he distrusted; his skepticism was directed at the fact that it was whites who were drawing up the legislation in the first place. He asks rhetorically in his speech, in many ways, when blacks ever benefited from something that whites gave them.

Now when the missionaries came to civilize us because we were uncivilized, educate us because we were uneducated, and give us some—some literate studies because we were illiterate—they charged a price. The missionaries came with the Bible, and we had the land. When they left, they had the land, and we still have the Bible. And that has been the rationalization for Western civilization as it moves across the world and stealing and plundering and raping everybody in its path. Their one rationalization is that the rest of the world is uncivilized and they are in fact civilized. And they are uncivilized.

And that runs on today, you see, because what we have today is we have what we call "modern-day Peace Corps missionaries," and they come into our ghettos and they Head Start, Upward Lift, Bootstrap, and Upward Bound us into white society, 'cause they don't want to face the real problem which is a man is poor for one reason and one reason only: 'cause he does not have money—period. If you want to get rid of poverty, you give people money—period.

And you ought not to tell me about people who don't work, and you can't give people money without working, 'cause if that were true, you'd have to start stopping Rockefeller, Bobby Kennedy, Lyndon Baines Johnson, Lady Bird Johnson, the whole of Standard Oil, the Gulf Corp, all of them, including probably a large number of the Board of Trustees of this university.

So the question, then, clearly is not whether or not one can work, it's who has power? Who has power to make his or her acts legitimate? That is all. And that this country, that power is invested in the hands of white people, and they make their acts legitimate. It is now, therefore, for black people to make our acts legitimate.

Having argued the case that power in America rests with whites, Carmichael argues that true equality now calls for blacks to obtain power, too. And along with that is the insistence that blacks have a role to play in developing any laws that are going to affect their own civil liberties.

Now we are now engaged in a psychological struggle in this country, and that is whether or not black people will have the right to use the words they want to use without white people giving their sanction to it. And that we maintain, whether they like it or not, we gonna use the word "Black Power" and let them address themselves to that; but that we are not goin' to wait for white people to sanction Black Power. We are tired waiting; every time black people move in this country, they're forced to defend their position before they move. It's time that the people who are supposed to be defending their position do that. That's white people. They ought to start defending themselves as to why they have oppressed and exploited us.

Again the theme of black Americans fighting and achieving for themselves comes through. It is important to note that while he was head of the SNCC, Carmichael viewed nonviolence a little differently than others, such as Dr. Martin Luther King Jr. To King, nonviolence was a principle; to Carmichael, it was more of a tactic. And when he felt that the nonviolent movement was propelling blacks into integrating into white men's laws, Carmichael left the SNCC and moved to the more violence-prone Black Panther Party.

Now it is clear that when this country started to move in terms of slavery, the reason for a man being picked as a slave was one reason—because of the color of his skin. If one was black one was automatically inferior, inhuman, and therefore fit for slavery. So that the question of whether or not we are individually suppressed is nonsensical, and it's a downright lie. We are oppressed as a group because we are black, not because we are lazy, not because we're apathetic, not because we're stupid, not because we smell, not because we eat watermelon and have good rhythm.

We are oppressed because we are black. And in order to get out of that oppression one must wield the group power that one has, not the individual power which this country then sets the criteria under which a man may come into it. That is what is called in this country as integration: "You do what I tell you to do and then we'll let you sit at the table with us." And we are saying that we have to be opposed to that. We must now set up criteria and that if there's going to be any integration, it's going to be a two-way thing. If you believe in integration, you can come live in Watts. You can send your children to the ghetto schools. Let's talk about that. If you believe in integration, then we're going to start adopting us some white people to live in our neighborhood.

Here Carmichael strikes at the heart of why many African Americans were opposed to accepting the prevailing concept of integration: because white America said it is okay for blacks to come live in their neighborhoods. To Carmichael and his followers, no one but blacks themselves should give themselves permission to do whatever they want or live wherever they want. But for individual blacks to assert that right, they needed the force of a large black collective behind them, just as white America had behind individual whites. Hence the concept of—and need for—black power.

So it is clear that the question is not one of integration or segregation. Integration is a man's ability to want to move in there by himself. If someone wants to live in a white neighborhood and he is black, that is his choice. It should be his right. It is not because white people will not allow him. So vice versa: If a black man wants to live in the slums, that should be his right. Black people will let him. That is the difference. And it's a difference on which this country makes a number of logical mistakes when they begin to try to criticize the program articulated by SNCC.

Now we maintain that we cannot afford to be concerned about six percent of the children in this country, black children, who you allow to come into white schools. We have ninety-four percent who still live in shacks. We are going to be concerned about those ninety-four percent. You ought to be concerned about them, too. The question is, Are we willing to be concerned about those ninety-four percent? Are we willing to be concerned about the black people who will never get to Berkeley, who will never get to Harvard, and cannot get an education, so you'll never get a chance to rub shoulders with them and say, "Well, he's almost as good as we are; he's not like the others"?

The question is, how can white society begin to move to see black people as human beings? I am black, therefore I am; not that I am black and I must go to college to prove myself. I am black, therefore I am. And don't deprive me of anything and say to me that you must go to college before you gain access to X, Y, and Z. It is only a rationalization for one's oppression.

Blacks should not have to prove their value with their achievements, Carmichael says. Like everyone else, blacks are human beings who have intrinsic value. The color of their skin has nothing to do with that value.

The political parties in this country do not meet the needs of people on a day-to-day basis. The question is, how can we build new political institutions that will become the political expressions of people on a day-to-day basis? The question is, how can you build political institutions that will begin to meet the needs of Oakland, California? And the needs of Oakland, California, is not 1,000 policemen with submachine guns. They don't need that. They need that least of all.

The question is, how can we build institutions where those people can begin to function on a day-to-day basis, where they can get decent jobs, where they can get decent houses, and where they can begin to participate in the policy and major decisions that affect their lives? That's what they need, not Gestapo troops, because this is not 1942, and if you play like Nazis, we playin' back with you this time around. Get hip to that.

Carmichael calls for political institutions that function for people on a daily basis and provide for—and enforce laws requiring—equal opportunities for blacks. Without this there is oppression, which he likens to the ways the Nazis oppressed Jews in Germany in the 1930s and early 1940s.

The question then is, how can white people move to start making the major institutions that they have in this country function the way it is supposed to function? That is the real question. And can white people move inside their own community and start tearing down racism where in fact it does exist? Where it exists. It is you who live in Cicero and stop us from living there. It is white people who stop us from moving into Grenada. It is white people who make sure that we live in the ghettos of this country. It is white institutions that do that. They must change. In order . . . in order for America to really live on a basic principle of human relationships, a new society must be born. Racism must die, and the economic exploitation of this country of non-white peoples around the world must also die, must also die.

Now there are several programs that we have in the South, most in poor white communities. We're trying to organize poor whites on a base where they can begin to move around the question of economic exploitation and political disfranchisement. We know, we've heard the theory several times, but few people are willing to go into there. The question is, can the white activist not try to be a Pepsi generation who comes alive in the black community, but can he be a man who's willing to move into the white community and start organizing where the organization is needed? Can he do that? The question is, can the white society or the white activist disassociate himself with two clowns who waste time parrying with each other rather than talking about the problems that are facing people in this state? Can you disassociate yourself with those clowns and start to build new institutions that will eliminate all idiots like them.

Here he opens up the idea of black activists working in poor white communities in the South to try to get these whites to break away from what he feels is a prevailing white theory of oppression. This is interesting, because it reverses the concept of having white civil rights workers move into black areas to improve conditions; it has black civil rights workers moving into white communities to enlist the support of poor whites to push for equality of opportunity for everyone. He insists that this kind of movement—of reaching out to whites—is needed. And it is black leadership—and not white—that is the driver for change. This was welcome news for blacks who were so skeptical of white America that they didn't always trust whites deciding what changes were needed for blacks.

And the question is, if we are going to do that when and where do we start, and how do we start? We maintain that we must start doing that inside the white community. Our own personal position politically is that we don't think the Democratic Party represents the needs of black people. We know it don't. And that if, in fact, white people really believe that, the question is, if they're going to move inside that structure, how are they going to organize around a concept of whiteness based on true brotherhood and based on stopping exploitation, economic exploitation, so that there will be a coalition base for black people to hook up with? You cannot form a coalition based on national sentiment. That is not a coalition. If you need a coalition to redress itself to real changes in this country, white people must start building those institutions inside the white community. And that is the real

question, I think, facing the white activists today. Can they, in fact, begin to move into and tear down the institutions which have put us all in a trick bag that we've been into for the last hundred years?

I don't think that we should follow what many people say that we should fight to be leaders of tomorrow. Frederick Douglass said that the youth should fight to be leaders today. And God knows we need to be leaders today, 'cause the men who run this country are sick, are sick. So that can we on a larger sense begin now, today, to start building those institutions and to fight to articulate our position, to fight to be able to control our universities—we need to be able to do that— and to fight to control the basic institutions which perpetuate racism by destroying them and building new ones? That's the real question that face us today, and it is a dilemma because most of us do not know how to work, and that the excuse that most white activists find is to run into the black community.

Now we maintain that we cannot have white people working in the black community, and we mean it on a psychological ground. The fact is that all black people often question whether or not they are equal to whites, because every time they start to do something, white people are around showing them how to do it. If we are going to eliminate that for the generation that comes after us, then black people must be seen in positions of power, doing and articulating for themselves, for themselves.

That is not to say that one is a reverse racist; it is to say that one is moving in a healthy ground; it is to say what the philosopher Sartre says: One is becoming an "antiracist racist." And this country can't understand that. Maybe it's because it's all caught up in racism. But I think what you have in SNCC is an anti-racist racism. We are against racists. Now if everybody who is white see themself as a racist and then see us against him, they're speaking from their own guilt position, not ours, not ours.

Now then, the question is, How can we move to begin to change what's going on in this country. I maintain, as we have in SNCC, that the war in Vietnam is an illegal and immoral war. And the question is, what can we do to stop that war? What can we do to stop the people who, in the

Here Carmichael reiterates and adds depth and explanation to the theme begun a few paragraphs earlier: blacks should not trust whites to take the lead in pushing for civil rights; blacks need to take that leadership role as activists themselves. Again, black power.

Here Carmichael links the black power movement with opposition to the war in Vietnam, clearly and unabashedly. He encourages his followers to just say no when they are called to fight in that war. Although there were only 275,000 blacks among the 8.7 million personnel who were on duty during the decade-long Vietnam War and only 12.5 percent of the casualties were blacks,[4] there was a perception that blacks were more likely to be called into that fighting because many more whites than blacks were going to college (and thus getting deferments). Although the student deferment system was open to all races and technically did not discriminate, the hard part for poor blacks was paying for college, so only 5 percent of draft-eligible blacks in America were in college during the Vietnam War. Putting that into context, however, blacks made up only 11 percent of the draft-eligible population during those years and accounted for 16 percent of all draftees. Said another way, blacks had a higher percentage chance of being drafted (30 percent) than did whites (18 percent). By 1967, however, nearly 33 percent of whites had a chance of being drafted, while 64 percent of blacks were vulnerable to the draft. Michael Krenn notes that many blacks enlisted out of a sense of needing to prove their worth as men.[5] It was this kind of thinking that Carmichael was opposed to when he said that blacks should not have to prove their intrinsic value by achieving standards set by white men.

name of our country, are killing babies, women, and children? What can we do to stop that? And I maintain that we do not have the power in our hands to change that institution, to begin to re-create it, so that they learn to leave the Vietnamese people alone, and that the only power we have is the power to say, "Hell no!" to the draft. We have to say. We have to say to ourselves that there is a higher law than the law of a racist named McNamara. There is a higher law than the law of a fool named Rusk. And there's a higher law than the law of a buffoon named Johnson. It's the law of each of us. It's the law of each of us. It is the law . . . It is the law of each of us saying that we will not allow them to make us hired killers. We will stand pat. We will not kill anybody that they say kill. And if we decide to kill, we're going to decide who we gonna kill. And this country will only be able to stop the war in Vietnam when the young men who are made to fight it begin to say, "Hell, no, we ain't going."

Now then, there's a failure because the Peace Movement has been unable to get off the college campuses where everybody has a 2S and not gonna get drafted anyway. And the question is, how can you move out of that into the white ghettos of this country and begin to articulate a position for those white students who do not want to go. We cannot do that. It is something, sometimes ironic, that many of the peace groups have beginning to call us violent and say they can no longer support us, and we are in fact the most militant organization [for] peace or civil rights or human rights against the war in Vietnam in this country today. There isn't one organization that has begun to meet our stance on the war in Vietnam, 'cause we not only say we are against the war in Vietnam; we are against the draft! We are against the draft! No man has the right to take a man for two years and train him to be a killer. A man should decide what he wants to do with his life.

Carmichael gave people an added reason to protest the Vietnam War, and one that many had not thought about. It was the question of how a country that sees itself as founded upon the notion of equality could deny an individual certain basic civil liberties and then require that same person to go and fight, risking his life in the process, for others who are enjoying rights that he himself is cut off from. Carmichael frames this individual as a mercenary and not a patriot.

So the question then is it becomes crystal clear for black people because we can easily say that anyone fighting in the war in Vietnam is nothing but a black mercenary, and that's all he is. Any time a black man leaves a country where he can't vote to supposedly deliver the vote for somebody else, he's a black mercenary. Any time a . . . any

time a black man leaves this country, gets shot in Vietnam on foreign ground, and returns home and you won't give him a burial in his own homeland, he's a black mercenary, a black mercenary.

And that even if I were to believe the lies of Johnson, if I were to believe his lies that we're fighting to give democracy to the people in Vietnam, as a black man living in this country I wouldn't fight to give this to anybody! I wouldn't give it to anybody! So that we have to use our bodies and our minds in the only way that we see fit. We must begin like the like the philosopher Camus to come alive by saying "No!" That is the only act in which we begin to come alive, and we have to say "No!" to many, many things in this country. This country is a nation of thieves. It has stole everything it has, beginning with black people, beginning with black people. And that the question is, how can we move to start changing this country from what it is, a nation of thieves. This country cannot justify any longer its existence. We have become the policemen of the world. The marines are at our disposal to always bring democracy, and if the Vietnamese don't want democracy, well dammit, "We'll just wipe them the hell out, 'cause they don't deserve to live if they won't have our way of life."

There is then in a larger sense, what do you do on your university campus? Do you raise questions about the hundred black students who were kicked off campus a couple of weeks ago? Eight hundred? Eight hundred? And how does that question begin to move? Do you begin to relate to people outside of the ivory tower and university wall? Do you think you're capable of building those human relationships, as the country now stands? You're fooling yourself. It is impossible for white and black people to talk about building a relationship based on humanity when the country is the way it is, when the institutions are clearly against us.

"Do you begin to relate to people outside of the ivory tower and university wall?"

Carmichael here attacks the belief that all Americans see America in the same light. While white America might see the country as a land of equality and opportunity, black America had good reason to see it as something else: a place where the denial of rights and the limitations to one's self-actualization were commonplace.

We have taken all the myths of this country and we've found them to be nothing but downright lies. This country told us that if we worked hard we would succeed, and if that were true we would own this country lock, stock, and barrel—lock, stock, and barrel—lock, stock, and barrel. It is we who have picked the cotton for nothing. It is we who are the maids in the kitchens of liberal white people. It is we who are the janitors, the porters,

the elevator men. It is we who sweep up your college floors. Yes, it is we who are the hardest workers and the lowest paid, and the lowest paid.

And that it is nonsensical for people to start talking about human relationships until they're willing to build new institutions. Black people are economically insecure. White liberals are economically secure. Can you begin to build an economic coalition? Are the liberals willing to share their salaries with the economically insecure black people they so much love? Then if you're not, are you willing to start building new institutions that will provide economic security for black people? That's the question we want to deal with. That's the question we want to deal with.

"Are the liberals willing to share their salaries with the economically insecure black people they so much love?"

We have to seriously examine the histories that we have been told. But we have something more to do than that. American students are perhaps the most politically unsophisticated students in the world, in the world, in the world. Across every country in this world, while we were growing up, students were leading the major revolutions of their countries. We have not been able to do that. They have been politically aware of their existence. In South America our neighbors down below the border have one every twenty-four hours just to remind us that they're politically aware.

And we have been unable to grasp it because we've always moved in the field of morality and love while people have been politically jiving with our lives. And the question is, how do we now move politically and stop trying to move morally? You can't move morally against a man like Brown and Reagan. You've got to move politically to put 'em out of business. You've got to move politically.

You can't move morally against Lyndon Baines Johnson because he is an immoral man. He doesn't know what it's all about. So you've got to move politically. You've got to move politically. And that we have to begin to develop a political sophistication, which is not to be a parrot: "The two-party system is the best party in the world." There is a difference between being a parrot and being politically sophisticated. We have to raise questions about whether or not we do need new types of political institutions in this country, and we in SNCC maintain that we need them now. We need new political institutions in this country.

At any time, any time, Lyndon Baines Johnson can head a party which has in it Bobby Kennedy, Wayne Morse, Eastland, Wallace, and all those other supposed-to-be-liberal cats, there's something wrong with that party. They're moving politically, not morally. And that if that party refuses to seat black people from Mississippi and goes ahead and seats racists like Eastland and his clique, it is clear to me that they're moving politically, and that one cannot begin to talk morality to people like that.

We must begin to think politically and see if we can have the power to impose and keep the moral values that we hold high. We must question the values of this society, and I maintain that black people are the best people to do that because we have been excluded from that society. And the question is, we ought to think whether or not we want to become a part of that society. That's what we want to do.

And that that is precisely what it seems to me that the Student Nonviolent Coordinating Committee is doing. We are raising questions about this country. I do not want to be a part of the American pie! The American pie means raping South Africa, beating Vietnam, beating South America, raping the Philippines, raping every country you've been in. I don't want any of your blood money! I don't want it, don't want to be part of that system. And the question is, how do we raise those questions? How do we raise (inaudible). How do we begin to raise them?

Carmichael seems to be calling for a black separatist movement when he says that blacks should not want to be a part of the America that is being run and managed so badly by white leaders and white-controlled institutions. In fact, most historians believe that Carmichael was a voice for black separatism, at least in this stage of his life. Another key black leader calling for separatism was Malcom X, the chief spokesman of the Nation of Islam, a black Muslim organization led by Elijah Muhammad. Like Carmichael, Malcolm X insisted that America was too racist to offer any hope or help to black America. He went further than Carmichael, however, advocating a nation of Islam as a separate black nation where blacks could live among themselves, uncontaminated by the self-destructive nature of white America. Dr. Martin Luther King Jr. disagreed with separatism, however, offering love and nonviolent protest as a way of constructing a truly integrated white and black America. King retained a faith in America and believed that it would be possible for blacks and whites to live in harmony and equality.

We have grown up and we are the generation that has found this country to be a world power, that has found this country to be the wealthiest country in the world. We must question how she got her wealth? That's what we're questioning, and whether or not we want this country to continue being the wealthiest country in the world at the price of raping every, everybody else across the world. That's what we must begin to question. And that because black people are saying we do not now want to become a part of you, we are called reverse racists. Ain't that a gas?

With so much of Carmichael's rhetoric aimed at attacking white America as being racist and calling for blacks to forcefully exert their power, it is sometimes confusing to many as to how he was leading a group with the word "nonviolent" in its name (Student Nonviolent Coordinating Committee). In this passage, however, he lays out his belief that nonviolence works only if both whites and blacks are practicing it, and he asserts that whites are the ones who need to learn to be nonviolent; it is they who are causing the bloodshed in the South, he says. And, as noted earlier, he disagreed with King that nonviolence should be an overarching principle of the civil rights movement; Carmichael saw it only as a tactic to secure the goal of equality. As a tactic, it could be replaced with other tactics if it didn't work. Carmichael would leave the SNCC for the more militant Black Panther Party in the next stage of his activist career.

Now then, we want to touch on nonviolence because we see that again as the failure of white society to make nonviolence work. I was always surprised at Quakers who came to Alabama and counseled me to be nonviolent, but didn't have the guts to start talking to James Clark to be nonviolent. That is where nonviolence needs to be preached—to Jim Clark, not to black people. They have already been nonviolent too many years. The question is, can white people conduct their nonviolent schools in Cicero where they belong to be conducted, not among black people in Mississippi? Can they conduct it among the white people in Grenada? Six-foot-two men who kick little black children—can you conduct nonviolent schools there? That is the question that we must raise, not that you conduct nonviolence among black people. Can you name me one black man today who's killed anybody white and is still alive? Even after rebellion, when some black brothers throw some bricks and bottles, ten thousand of us has to pay the crime, 'cause when the white policeman comes in, anybody who's black is arrested, "'cause we all look alike."

So that we have to raise those questions. We, the youth of this country, must begin to raise those questions. And we must begin to move to build new institutions that's going to speak to the needs of people who need it. We are going to have to speak to change the foreign policy of this country. One of the problems with the peace movement is that it's just too caught up in Vietnam, and that if we pulled out the troops from Vietnam this week, next week you'd have to get another peace movement for Santo Domingo. And the question is, how do you begin to articulate needs to change the foreign policy of this country—a policy that is decided upon race, a policy on which decisions are made upon getting economic wealth at any price, at any price.

Now we articulate that we therefore have to hook up with black people around the world, and that that hookup is not only psychological, but becomes very real. If South America today were to rebel, and black people were to shoot the hell out of all the white people there—as they should, as they should—then Standard Oil would crumble tomorrow. If South Africa were to go today, Chase Manhattan Bank would crumble tomorrow. If Zimbabwe, which is called Rhodesia by white people, were to go tomorrow, General Electric would cave in on the East Coast. The question is, how do we stop those institutions that are so willing to fight against "Communist aggression" but closes their eyes to racist oppression? That is the question that you raise. Can this country do that?

Now, many people talk about pulling out of Vietnam. What will happen? If we pull out of Vietnam, there will be one less aggressor in there—we won't be there, we won't be there. And so the question is, how do we articulate those positions? And we cannot begin to articulate them from the same assumptions that the people in the country speak, 'cause they speak from different assumptions than I assume what the youth in this country are talking about. That we're not talking about a policy or aid or sending Peace Corps people in to teach people how to read and write and build houses while we steal their raw materials from them. Is that what we're talking about? 'Cause that's all we do. What underdeveloped countries need is information on how to become industrialized, so they can keep their raw materials where they have it, produce them and sell it to this country for the price it's supposed to pay; not that we produce it and sell it back to them for a profit and keep sending our modern day missionaries in, calling them the sons of Kennedy. And that if the youth are going to participate in that program, how do you raise those questions where you begin to control that Peace Corps program? How do you begin to raise them?

"What underdeveloped countries need is information on how to become industrialized . . ."

How do we raise the questions of poverty? The assumptions of this country is that if someone is poor, they are poor because of their own individual blight, or they weren't born on the right side of town; they had too many children; they went in the army too early; or their father was a drunk, or they didn't care about school, or they made a mistake. That's a lot of nonsense. Poverty is well calculated in this country. It is well calculated, and the reason why the poverty program won't work is because the calculators of poverty are administering it. That's why it won't work.

Here Carmichael articulates a popular belief among many Americans: that it is the fault of the unemployed or underemployed that they are not tapping into the American dream. It is not that America doesn't offer the opportunities to them; the problem is that they are too lazy or not intelligent or educated enough to take advantage of those opportunities. In fact, Carmichael says, having a poverty class is essential to the white power structure of America, because it keeps blacks and other minorities from becoming threats to white power.

So how can we, as the youth in the country, move to start tearing those things down? We must move into the white community. We are in the black community. We have developed a movement in the black community. The challenge is that the white activist has failed miserably to develop the movement inside of his community. And the question is, can we find white people who are going to have the courage to go into white communities and start organizing them? Can we find them? Are they here and are they willing to do that? Those are the questions that we must raise for the white activist. And we're never going to get caught up in questions about power. This country knows what power is. It knows it very well. And it knows what Black Power is 'cause it deprived black people of it for four hundred years. So it knows what Black Power is.

But the question of, why do black people, why do white people in this country associate Black Power with violence? And the question is because of their own inability to deal with "blackness." If we had said "Negro Power" nobody would get scared. Everybody would support it. Or if we said power for colored people, everybody'd be for that, but it is the word "Black," it is the word "Black" that bothers people in this country, and that's their problem, not mine—their problem, their problem.

"Now there's one modern day lie that we want to attack . . . the lie that says anything all black is bad."

Now there's one modern day lie that we want to attack and then move on very quickly and that is the lie that says anything all black is bad. Now, you're all a college university crowd. You've taken your basic logic course. You know about a major premise and minor premise. So people have been telling me anything all black is bad. Let's make that our major premise.

Major premise: Anything all black is bad.

Minor premise or particular premise: I am all black.

Therefore . . .

I'm never going to be put in that trick bag; I am all black and I'm all good. Anything all black is not necessarily bad. Anything all black is only bad when you use force to keep whites out. Now that's what white people have done in this country, and they're projecting their same fears and guilt on us, and we won't have it, we won't have it. Let them handle their own fears and their own guilt. Let them find their own psychologists. We refuse to be the therapy for white society any longer. We have gone mad trying to do it. We have gone stark raving mad trying to do it.

I look at Dr. King on television every single day, and I say to myself: "Now there is a man who's desperately needed in this country. There is a man full of love. There is a man full of mercy. There is a man full of compassion." But every time I see Lyndon on television, I said, "Martin, baby, you've got a long way to go."

This is the first time that Carmichael mentions King, and he does so in admiration. But Carmichael also infers that the love which King preaches may not be enough of a match for the power of President Johnson.

So that the question stands as to what we are willing to do, how we are willing to say "no" to withdraw from that system and begin within our community to start to function and to build new institutions that will speak to our needs. In Lowndes County, we developed something called the Lowndes County Freedom Organization. It is a political party. The Alabama law says that if you have a Party you must have an emblem. We chose for the emblem a black panther, a beautiful black animal which symbolizes the strength and dignity of black people, an animal that never strikes back until he's backed so far into the wall, he's got nothing to do but spring out. Yeah. And when he springs he does not stop.

Now there is a party in Alabama called the Alabama Democratic Party. It is all white. It has as its emblem a white rooster and the words "white supremacy" for the white. Now the gentlemen of the press, because they're advertisers, and because most of them are white, and because they're produced by that white institution, never called the Lowndes Country Freedom Organization by its name, but rather they call it the Black Panther Party. . . . It's fair to us, it's fair to us. It is clear to me that that just points out America's problem with sex and color, not our problem, not our problem. And it is now white America that is going to deal with those problems of sex and color.

If we were to be real and to be honest, we would have to admit that most people in this country see things black and white. We have to do that. All of us do. We live in a country that's geared that way. White people would have to admit that they are afraid to go into a black ghetto at night. They are afraid. That's a fact. They're afraid because they'd be "beat up," "lynched," "looted," "cut up," etcetera, etcetera. It happens to black people inside the ghetto every day, incidentally, and white people are afraid of that. So you get a man to do it for you—a policeman. And now you figure his mentality, when he's afraid of black people. The first time a black man jumps, that white man gonna shoot him. He's gonna shoot him.

"If we were to be real and honest, we would have to admit that most people in this country see things black and white."

So police brutality is going to exist on that level because of the incapability of that white man to see black people come together and to live in the conditions. This country is too hypocritical and we cannot adjust ourselves to its hypocrisy.

The only time I hear people talk about nonviolence is when black people move to defend themselves against white people. Black people cut themselves every night in the ghetto—don't anybody talk about nonviolence. Lyndon Baines Johnson is busy bombing the hell of out Vietnam—don't nobody talk about nonviolence. White people beat up black people every day—don't nobody talk about nonviolence. But as soon as black people start to move, the double standard comes into being.

Carmichael brings up another way that whites and blacks looked at the demonstrations and protest movements in the South. White America, he notes, fears the violence that may erupt from blacks, while blacks see themselves as defending themselves against violence perpetrated on them by whites. But, he says, whites don't promote nonviolence when dealing with black protestors. It's an unequal playing field, he says: whites can be violent, but not blacks.

You can't defend yourself. That's what you're saying, 'cause you show me a man who, who would advocate aggressive violence that would be able to live in this country. Show him to me. The double standards again come into itself. Isn't it ludicrous and hypocritical for the political chameleon who calls himself a vice president in this country to—to stand up before this country and say, "Looting never got anybody anywhere"? Isn't it hypocritical for Lyndon to talk about looting, that you can't accomplish anything by looting and you must accomplish it by the legal ways? What does he know about legality? Ask Ho Chi Minh, he'll tell you.

So that in conclusion we want to say that number one, it is clear to me that we have to wage a psychological battle on the right for black people to define their own terms, define themselves as they see fit, and organize themselves as they see it.

Now the question is, how is the white community going to begin to allow for that organizing, because once they start to do that, they will also allow for the organizing that they want to do inside their community. It doesn't make a difference, 'cause we're going to organize our way anyway. We're goin' to do it. The question is, how are we goin' to facilitate those matters, whether it's going to be done with a thousand policemen with submachine guns, or whether or not it's goin' to be done in a context where it is allowed to be done by white people warding off those policemen. That is the question.

And the question is, how are white people who call themselves activists ready to start [to] move into the white communities on two counts: on building new political institutions to destroy the old ones that we have, and to move around the concept of white youth refusing to go into the army? So that we can start, then, to build a new world. It is ironic to talk about civilization in this country. This country is uncivilized. It needs to be civilized. It needs to be civilized.

And that we must begin to raise those questions of civilization: What it is? And who do it? And so we must urge you to fight now to be the leaders of today, not tomorrow. We've got to be the leaders of today. This country, this country is a nation of thieves. It stands on the brink of becoming a nation of murderers. We must stop it. We must stop it. We must stop it. We must stop it.

And then, therefore, in a larger sense there's the question of black people. We are on the move for our liberation. We have been tired of trying to prove things to white people. We are tired of trying to explain to white people that we're not going to hurt them. We are concerned with getting the things we want, the things that we have to have to be able to function. The question is, can white people allow for that in this country?

The question is, will white people overcome their racism and allow for that to happen in this country? If that does not happen, brothers and sisters, we have no choice but to say very clearly, "Move over, or we goin' to move on over you." Thank you.

"We are on the move for our liberation. We have been tired of trying to prove things to white people."

Source: "Stokely Carmichael: Black Power," Voices of Democracy, October, 29, 1966, http://voicesofdemocracy.umd.edu/carmichael-black-power-speech-text/.

Notes

1. "JFK Faces Down Defiant Governor" (June 11, 1963), History .com, http://www.history.com/this-day-in-history/jfk-faces-down -defiant-governor.

2. Robert Schlesinger, "The Story behind JFK's 1963 Landmark Civil Rights Speech," *U.S. News & World Report,* June 11, 2013, http://www.usnews.com/opinion/blogs/robert-schlesinger/2013/ 06/11/the-story-behind-jfks-1963-landmark-civil-rights-speech.

3. Garth E. Pauley, "Lyndon Baines Johnson, 'We Shall Overcome Speech' (15 March 1965)," Voices of Democracy: The U.S. Oratory Project, http://archive.vod.umd.edu/citizen/lbj1965int.htm.

4. "Vietnam War Statistics," Mobile Riverine Force Association, http://www.mrfa.org/vnstats.htm.

5. Michael Krenn, *The African American Voice in U.S. Foreign Policy since World War II* (New York: Routledge, 1999), 211.

Chapter 5

I Am a Woman: Protesting Gender Discrimination

Introduction

The Equal Rights Amendment (ERA) was written in 1923 by women's rights activist Alice Paul. Every year between 1923 and 1972, the ERA was introduced in Congress as an extension of the Nineteenth Amendment, which gave women the right to vote. Largely because of the support received during the protest era of the 1960s for equal rights for women, the ERA finally passed Congress in 1972 and was sent to the states for ratification. The speech to Congress by Representative Shirley Chisholm, which follows this introduction, gave the ERA a big boost in 1970. Even though the deadline for that ratification was extended, the amendment ultimately fell 3 states short (35 ratified, but 38 were needed) in 1982 to have it become part of the Constitution. Negotiations are still ongoing between ERA supporters and members of Congress to try to get the bill to become law. The ERA is brief and reads as follows:

> Section 1. Equality of rights under the law shall not be denied or abridged by the United States or by any state on account of sex.
> Section 2. The Congress shall have the power to enforce, by appropriate legislation, the provisions of this article.
> Section 3. This amendment shall take effect two years after the date of ratification.

Indeed, part of the protest era of the 1960s came from the voices raised over equal rights for women. America had just emerged from the postwar decade of the 1950s, when soldiers returned home from World War II and reasserted their male dominance in the workplace. Women had taken over some of the jobs traditionally reserved for men during the 1940s, but society had seen that as an emergency. The understanding was that men would resume their "rightful" place in the workforce once the war was over. The late 1940s and early 1950s were also the start of the baby boomer generation, when families were started at an increasingly high rate after the troops came home. So, the place of women as being in the home was a widespread view held in America. Clearly there were exceptions and many women who asserted themselves professionally, but the norm was the woman as the wife, mother, and homemaker.

As America began to raise questions in the 1960s about the Vietnam War and especially civil rights, however, it came to question the prevailing views toward women: Why should women be relegated to the home? Why should women be paid less than men when they did enter the workplace? And why should women confront a discriminatory glass ceiling when trying to rise into the executive ranks? Can a woman have it all by being a good wife, mother, and professional? The 1960s was the decade when modern America began asking that question about women in earnest.

Equal Rights for Women

Shirley Chisholm's Speech in the House of Representatives
May 21, 1969

INTRODUCTION

In this address, Shirley Anita St. Hill Chisholm was in her second year as a congresswoman and was already a strong advocate for women's equality. Altogether, she served a total of 14 years in Congress, retiring in 1982. During her tenure she would be the first black female candidate for president, seeking the Democratic nomination in 1972 but losing to Senator George McGovern. Chisholm was one of the four founders of the National Women's Political Caucus and the National Political Congress of Black Women, which represented black women's concerns. When asked how she wanted to be remembered, Chisholm is quoted as saying, "When I die, I want to be remembered as a woman who lived in the 20th century and who dared to be a catalyst of change."[1] She passed away in 2005.

Mr. Speaker, when a young woman graduates from college and starts looking for a job, she is likely to have a frustrating and even demeaning experience ahead of her. If she walks into an office for an interview, the first question she will be asked is, "Do you type?"

There is a calculated system of prejudice that lies unspoken behind that question. Why is it acceptable for women to be secretaries, librarians, and teachers, but totally unacceptable for them to be managers, administrators, doctors, lawyers, and Members of Congress.

The unspoken assumption is that women are different. They do not have executive ability orderly minds, stability, leadership skills, and they are too emotional.

Chisholm begins with the same theme that black activists, such as Stokely Carmichael, had used: that there should be no inherent difference in abilities attributed to a person just because of one's gender, just as there should be no inherent difference because of one's skin color. Chisholm can speak to both of these well, since she is both black and female.

It has been observed before, that society for a long time, discriminated against another minority, the blacks, on the same basis—that they were different and inferior. The happy little homemaker and the contented "old darkey" on the plantation were both produced by prejudice.

123

As a black person, I am no stranger to race prejudice. But the truth is that, in the political world, I have been far oftener discriminated against because I am a woman than because I am black.

Prejudice against blacks is becoming unacceptable although it will take years to eliminate it. But it is doomed because, slowly, white America is beginning to admit that it exists. Prejudice against women is still acceptable.

There is very little understanding yet of the immorality involved in double pay scales and the classification of most of the better jobs as "for men only." More than half of the population of the United States is female. But women occupy only 2 percent of the managerial positions. They have not even reached the level of tokenism yet. No women sit on the AFL-CIO council or Supreme Court. There have been only two women who have held Cabinet rank, and at present there are none. Only two women now hold ambassadorial rank in the diplomatic corps. In Congress, we are down to one Senator and 10 Representatives.

Considering that there are about 3½ million more women in the United States than men, this situation is outrageous.

Unlike many other speakers of the protest era, Chisholm is brief and to the point in her remarks. She presents the overall issue, then quickly backs up her arguments with specific figures indicating that discrimination against females does, in fact, exist in America. One could make the strong case, as Chisholm alludes to in the opening sentence of the next section, that most women in America had not yet woken up to the need for demanding greater rights. Putting this into historical context, two things seemed to happen in the 1960s that began alerting American women to their unequal status in the workplace. The first was that more women were coming out of the placid 1950s and deciding to assert themselves as career women. The second was the rising crescendo of voices from female college students who were joining the growing women's liberation movement in the latter part of the decade. Once again, the importance of the university asserted itself for a group seeking greater equality, in this case an entire gender.

It is true that part of the problem has been that women have not been aggressive in demanding their rights. This was also true of the black population for many years. They submitted to oppression and even cooperated with it. Women have done the same thing. But now there is an awareness of this situation particularly among the younger segment of the population.

As in the field of equal rights for blacks, Spanish-Americans, the Indians, and other groups, laws will not change such deep-seated problems overnight. But they can be used to provide protection for those who are most

Here Chisholm ties equal rights for women to the larger context of the era when so many groups were voicing the need for equality and for questioning the policies and assumptions undergirding a status quo situation where many Americans were feeling disenfranchised from equal rights.

abused, and to begin the process of evolutionary change by compelling the insensitive majority to reexamine it's unconscious attitudes.

Her purpose here is not simply to advocate for women's rights but to specifically introduce—once again—the proposed Equal Rights Amendment.

It is for this reason that I wish to introduce today a proposal that has been before every Congress for the last 40 years and that sooner or later must become part of the basic law of the land—the equal rights amendment.

Let me note and try to refute two of the commonest arguments that are offered against this amendment. One is that women are already protected under the law and do not need legislation. Existing laws are not adequate to secure equal rights for women. Sufficient proof of this is the concentration of women in lower paying, menial, unrewarding jobs and their incredible scarcity in the upper level jobs. If women are already equal, why is it such an event whenever one happens to be elected to Congress?

It is obvious that discrimination exists. Women do not have the opportunities that men do. And women that do not conform to the system, who try to break with the accepted patterns, are stigmatized as "odd" and "unfeminine." The fact is that a woman who aspires to be chairman of the board, or a Member of the House, does so for exactly the same reasons as any man. Basically, these are that she thinks she can do the job and she wants to try.

Again, with no flowery rhetoric preceding it, Chisholm moves right to the two main arguments that had been used consistently against the need for the ERA: (1) that it would be a redundant and unnecessary law and (b) that it would throw existing marriage and divorce laws into chaos. Raising those opposing issues, she then refutes them. The thinking that often goes "We'd better keep things the way they are, because who knows what damage would come from changing the current system?" has been a part of congressional debates since the beginning of America. It is often—but not always—offered by conservatives and traditionalists in Congress and is argued against by those lawmakers who believe that the current system is so bad that the risk posed by change is worthwhile.

A second argument often heard against the equal rights amendment is that it would eliminate legislation that many States and the Federal Government have enacted giving special protection to women and that it would throw the marriage and divorce laws into chaos.

As for the marriage laws, they are due for a sweeping reform, and an excellent beginning would be to wipe the

existing ones off the books. Regarding special protection for working women, I cannot understand why it should be needed. Women need no protection that men do not need.

What we need are laws to protect working people, to guarantee them fair pay, safe working conditions, protection against sickness and layoffs, and provision for dignified, comfortable retirement. Men and women need these things equally. That one sex needs protection more than the other is a male supremacist myth as ridiculous and unworthy of respect as the white supremacist myths that society is trying to cure itself of at this time.

Source: "Address to the United States House Of Representatives, Washington, DC: May 21, 1969," *Congressional Record,* Extensions of Remarks E4165–E4166.

Judge Carswell and the "Sex Plus" Doctrine

Betty Friedan's Testimony before the Senate Judicial Committee
January 29, 1970

INTRODUCTION

Betty Friedan was one of the most influential leaders in the women's rights movement in the 1960s and beyond. Her popular 1963 book *The Feminine Mystique* ignited a new wave of feminism in America and helped catapult her to the first presidency of the National Organization for Women in 1966. She would later organize the Women's Strike for Equality on the 50th anniversary of the passage of the Nineteenth Amendment, which gave women the right to vote.

Judge G. Harrold Carswell was one of President Richard Nixon's nominations to the U.S. Supreme Court in 1970 who failed to garner the approval of Congress and so never became an associate justice on the Court. Carswell was from Georgia and had voiced support for segregation and even white supremacy when he ran unsuccessfully for the Georgia legislature in 1948. He was criticized by civil rights groups for his rulings as a judge on desegregation. But he was also criticized by women's rights advocates, including Friedan in her testimony to the Senate Judicial Committee below. This testimony came in hearings over Carswell's nomination to the Supreme Court. This, and the testimony from other critics, eventually contributed to his nomination being defeated, which was a setback for Nixon.

I am here to testify before this committee to oppose Judge Carswell's appointment to Supreme Court Justice on the basis of his proven insensitivity to the problems of the 53 percent of United States citizens who are women, and specifically on the basis of his explicit discrimination in a circuit court decision in 1969 against working mothers.

I speak in my capacity as national president of the National Organization for Women, which has led the exploding new movement in this country for "full equality for women in truly equal partnership with men," and which was organized in 1966 to take action to break through discrimination against women in employment, education, government and in all fields of American life.

On October 13, 1969, in the Fifth Circuit Court of Appeals, Judge Carswell was party to a most unusual judiciary action which would permit employers, in defiance of the law of the land as embodied in Title VII of the 1964 Civil Rights Act, to refuse to hire women who have children.

The case involved Mrs. Ida Phillips, who was refused employment by Martin Marietta Corporation as an aircraft assembler because she had pre-school aged children, although the company said it would hire a man with pre-school aged children. This case was considered a clear-cut violation of the law which forbids job discrimination on the grounds of sex as well as race. The E.E.O.C., empowered to administer Title VII, filed an amicus brief on behalf of Mrs. Phillips; an earlier opinion of the Fifth Circuit filed in May upholding the company was considered such a clear violation of the Civil Rights Act by Chief Judge John Brown that he vacated the opinion and asked to convene the full court to consider the case.

Judge Carswell voted to deny a rehearing of the case, an action which in effect would have permitted employers to fire the 4.1 million working mothers in the U.S. today who have children under 6. They comprise 38.9 percent of the nearly 10.6 million mothers in the labor force today.

While such a situation today would seem unthinkable, the country's attitude toward women's role in society was still in transition in the 1960s, as was the attitude toward forcing businesses to abide by the newly passed civil rights legislation. It was because of voices such as Friedan's and Steinem's that the country transitioned more quickly into recognizing the need for equal treatment of genders than it otherwise might have.

In his dissent to this ruling in which Judge Carswell claimed no sex discrimination was involved, Chief Judge Brown said: "The case is simple. A woman with pre-school aged children may not be employed, a man with pre-school children may. The distinguishing factor seems to be motherhood versus fatherhood. The question then arises: Is this sex related? To the simple query, the answer is just as simple: Nobody—and this includes judges, Solomonic or life-tenured—has yet seen a male mother. A mother, to over-simplify the simplest biology, must then be a woman.

"It is the fact of the person being a mother—i.e., a woman—not the age of the children, which denies employment opportunity to a woman which is open to men."

It is important for this committee to understand the dangerous insensitivity of Judge Carswell to sex discrimination, when the desire and indeed the necessity of women to take a fully equal place in American society has already emerged as one of the most explosive issues in the 1970's, entailing many new problems which will ultimately have to be decided by the Supreme Court.

According to government figures, over 25 percent of mothers who have children under 6 are in the labor force today. Over 85 percent of them work for economic reasons. Over half a million are widowed, divorced or separated. Their incomes are vitally important to their children. Perhaps even more important, as a portent of the future, is the fact that there has been an astronomical increase in the last three decades in the number of working mothers. Between 1950 and the most recent compilation of government statistics, the number of working mothers in the United States nearly doubled. For every mother of children who worked in 1940, ten mothers are working today, an increase from slightly over 1.5 million to nearly 11 million.

Here Friedan uses an ingenious argument and points out how the Nixon administration is at odds with itself. The argument is that if you deny a mother the right to work, then you put her on welfare, although the stated goal of the Nixon administration was to reduce welfare. In fact, it had gone to great lengths to expand day care centers to give women the opportunity to work. Yet now Nixon had nominated to the highest court in the land a judge who had a record of voting against some mothers' right to work.

In his pernicious action, Judge Carswell not only flauted the Civil Rights Act, designed to end the job discrimination which denied women, along with other minority groups, equal opportunity in employment, but specifically defied the policy of this administration to encourage women in poverty, who have children, to work by expanding day-care centers, rather than having them depend on the current medieval welfare system which perpetuates the cycle of poverty from generation to generation. Mothers and children today comprise 80 percent of the welfare load in major cities.

Judge Carswell justified discrimination against such women by a peculiar doctrine of "sex plus," which claimed that discrimination which did not apply to all women but only to women who did not meet special standards—standards not applied to men—was not sex discrimination.

Once again, we see the parallels drawn—in this case by a federal judge—between discriminatory practices targeted at blacks and similar practices targeted at women. During the 1960s and 1970s, the equal rights status of women and blacks were often compared as similar, if not identical.

In his dissent, Chief Judge Brown said, "the sex plus rule in this case sows the seed for future discrimination against black workers through making them meet extra standards not imposed on whites." The "sex plus" doctrine would also penalize the very women who most need jobs.

Chief Judge Brown said, "Even if the 'sex plus' rule is not expanded, in its application to mothers of pre-school children, it will deal a serious blow to the objectives of Title VII. If the law against sex discrimination means anything, it must protect employment opportunities for those groups of women who most need jobs because of economic necessity. Working mothers of pre-schoolers are such a group. Studies show that, as compared to women with older children or no children, these mothers of pre-school children were much more likely to have gone to work because of pressing need . . . because of financial necessity and because their husbands are unable to work. Frequently, these women are a key or only source of income for their families. Sixty-eight percent of working women do not have husbands present in the household, and two-thirds of these women are raising children in poverty. Moreover, a barrier to jobs for mothers of pre-schoolers tends to harm non-white mothers more then white mothers."

I am not a lawyer, but the wording of Title VII of the Civil Rights Act so clearly conveys its intention to provide equal job opportunity to all oppressed groups, including women—who today in America earn on the average less than half the earnings of men—that only outright sex discrimination or sexism, as we new feminists call it, can explain Judge Carswell's ruling.

Human rights are indivisible, and I, and those for whom I speak, would oppose equally the appointment to the Supreme Court of a racist judge who had been totally blind to the humanity of black men and women since 1948, as the appointment of a sexist judge totally blind to the humanity of women in 1969.

To countenance outright sexism, not only in words, but by judicial flaunting of the law in an appointee to the Supreme Court in 1970, when American women—not in the hundreds or thousands but in the millions—are finally beginning to assert their human rights, is unconscionable.

I trust that you gentlemen of the committee do not share Judge Carswell's inability to see women as human beings, too. I will, however, put these questions to you.

How would you feel if in the event you were not reelected, you applied for a job at some company or law firm or university, and were told you weren't eligible because you had a child?

How would you feel if your sons were told explicitly or implicitly that they could not get or keep certain jobs if they had children?

"I trust that you gentlemen of the committee do not share Judge Carswell's inability to see women as human beings, too."

In this series of questions, Friedan takes the practices she sees as discriminatory toward women and asks the male committee members to consider how they would feel if they were practices directed at men, specifically men (such as their sons) whom have they love. It was an effective argument.

Then how do you feel about appointing to the Supreme Court a man who has said your daughters may not hold a job if they have children?

The economic misery and psychological conflicts entailed for untold numbers of American women, and their children and husbands, by Judge Carswell's denial of the protection of a law that was enacted for their benefit suggest only a faint hint of the harm that would be done in appointing such a sexually backward judge to the Supreme Court. For during the next decade I can assure you that the emerging revolution of the no-longer-quite-so-silent majority will pose many pressing new problems to our society, problems which will inevitably come before the courts and which indeed will probably preoccupy the Supreme Court of the 1970's as did questions arising from the civil rights movement in the 1960's.

It is already apparent from decisions made by judges in other circuit courts that Judge Carswell is unusually blind in the matter of sex prejudice and that his blindness will make it impossible for him to judge fairly the cases of sex prejudice that will surely come up.

Recently, courts have begun to outlaw forms of discrimination against women long accepted in society. The Fifth Circuit Court of Appeals (convened as a three-judge court without Judge Carswell), on March 4, 1969, in *Weeks v. Southern Bell Telephone* ruled that weight-lifting limitations barring women, but not men, from jobs, were illegal under Title VII. The Seventh Circuit Court of Appeals, on September 26, 1969, in *Bowe v. Colgate Palmolive Co.* ruled that, if retained, a weight-lifting test must apply to ALL employees, male and female, and that each individual must be permitted to "bid on and fill any job which his or her seniority entitled him or her." Separate seniority lists for men and women were forbidden.

Here and in the seven examples to follow, Friedan enlarges the discussion—and its importance on America—to many other discriminatory situations existing against women. This made it difficult for committee members to treat the one ruling by Judge Carswell as an isolated case and also increased the pressure on them to rule accordingly on his nomination.

Here are a few existing instances of discrimination against women, that are or will be before the courts:

1. In New York City, male, but not female, teachers are paid for their time spent on jury duty.

2. In Syracuse, New York, male, but not female, teachers are paid for athletic coaching.

3. In Syracuse, an employer wants to challenge the rule that forbids her to hire female employees at night in violation of New York State restrictive laws.

4. In Pennsylvania, a woman has requested help in obtaining a tax deduction for household help necessary for her to work.

5. In Arizona, a female law professor is fighting a rule that forbids her to be hired by the same university that employs her husband in another department.

6. In California, a wife is challenging a community property law which makes it obligatory for a husband to control their joint property.

7. And all over the country the E.E.O.C. regulation, which made it illegal to have separate want ads for males and females, have not been followed by most newspapers.

The Honorable Shirley Chisholm, a national board member of NOW, has summed it all up in her statement that she has been more discriminated against as a woman than as a black.

It would show enormous contempt for every woman of this country and contempt for every black American, as well as contempt for the Supreme Court itself, if you confirm Judge Carswell's appointment.

Source: *Nomination of George Harrold Carswell of Florida, Hearings before the Committee on the Judiciary, United States Senate, 91st Congress, 2nd Session, January 27, 28, 29, and Feburary 2 and 3, 1970* (Washington, DC: U.S. Government Printing Office, 1970), 88–101, http://www.loc.gov/law/find/nominations/carswell/hearing.pdf.

"It would show enormous contempt for every woman of this country and contempt for every black American . . . if you confirm Judge Carswell's appointment."

"We Won't Be Silent Anymore"

Gloria Steinem's Testimony on the Equal Rights Amendment
May 6, 1970

INTRODUCTION

The next two documents represent the thinking of another leader in the women's rights movement, Gloria Steinem. She became a household name in the late 1960s and the 1970s, forever identified as one of the leading spokeswomen of the women's liberation movement. As a journalist, she used her talents and aggressive nature as an activist to push for equal rights for women and for women to be seen fundamentally differently than they had been seen traditionally. A columnist for *New York* magazine, Steinem cofounded, with several other women, the leading magazine for women's rights, *Ms.*, a publication that initially appeared as an insert to *New York* magazine in 1971 but became a stand-alone national magazine in 1972. Her reasoning, she said later, for starting the magazine was to produce a magazine advocating for women that would be controlled by women. The ideological basis of the magazine eventually ran afoul of commercial interests. Since 2001, *Ms.* has been owned and published by the Feminist Majority Foundation, based in Los Angeles and the Washington, D.C., area. Since her *New York* article "After Black Power, Women's Liberation" appeared in 1969, Steinem has been a leader for women's rights, joining hands with Jane Fonda and Robin Morgan in 2005 to cofound the Women's Media Center.

My name is Gloria Steinem. I am a writer and editor, and I am currently a member of the Policy Council of the Democratic National Committee. And, I work regularly with the lowest-paid workers in the country, the migrant workers, men, women, and children both in California and in my own State of New York.

The "Wolfgang" Steinem refers to is Mrs. Myra Wolfgang, an officer in the Restaurant Workers Union in Detroit. Mrs. Wolfgang was not a fan of the Equal Rights Amendment and called it "The Tonkin Gulf Resolution of the American woman's struggle for equality."[2] She and others believed that it would place added burdens on women—such as making them subject to the military draft of the day—instead of liberating them.

I am here in support of the equal rights amendment. Before I get on with the statement I would like to point out that Mrs. Wolfgang does not disavow the principle of equality; only disagrees on the matter of tactic. I believe that she is giving up a long-term gain for a short-term holding action. Some protective legislation is gradually proving to be unenforceable or contrary to title VII. It gives poor women jobs but serves to keep them poor. Restrictions on working hours, for instance, may keep women in the assembly line from becoming foremen. No one is trying to say that there is no difference between men and women, only as I will discuss more in my

statement that the differences between, the differences within the groups, male and female, are much, much greater than the differences between the two groups. Therefore, requirements can only be sensibly suited to the requirements of the job itself.

During twelve years of working for a living, I have experienced much of the legal and social discrimination reserved for women in this country. I have been refused service in public restaurants, ordered out of public gathering places, and turned away from apartment rentals; all for the clearly-stated, sole reason that I am a woman. And all without the legal remedies available to blacks and other minorities. I have been excluded from professional groups, writing assignments on so-called "unfeminine" subjects such as politics, full participation in the Democratic Party, jury duty, and even from such small male privileges as discounts on airline fares. Most important to me, I have been denied a society in which women are encouraged, or even allowed to think of themselves as first-class citizens and responsible human beings.

However, after 2 years of researching the status of American women, I have discovered that in reality, I am very, very lucky. Most women, both wage-earners and housewives, routinely suffer more humiliation and injustice than I do.

As a freelance writer, I don't work in the male-dominated hierarchy of an office. (Women, like blacks and other visibly-different minorities, do better in individual professions such as the arts, sports, or domestic work; anything in which they don't have authority over white males.) I am not one of the millions of women who must support a family. Therefore, I haven't had to go on welfare because there are no day-care centers for my children while I work, and I haven't had to submit to the humiliating welfare inquiries about my private and sexual life, inquiries from which men are exempt. I haven't had to brave the sex bias of labor unions and employers, only to see my family subsist on a median salary 40 percent less than the male median salary.

I hope this committee will hear the personal, daily injustices suffered by many women—professionals and day laborers, women housebound by welfare as well as suburbia. We have all been silent for too long. But we won't be silent anymore.

"I have been refused service in public restaurants, ordered out of public gathering places, and turned away from apartment rentals . . ."

Indeed, the voices for women's rights were becoming louder by 1970, and activists such as Steinem, Betty Friedan, and Shirley Chisholm were leading the charge. Voices were also being raised in the entertainment world, and vocalist Helen Reddy would soon have a top musical hit with the song she wrote with Ray Burton called "I Am Woman." The first line of that song goes "I am woman, hear me roar."

The truth is that all our problems stem from the same sex based myths. We may appear before you as white radicals or the middle-aged middleclass or black soul sisters, but we are all sisters in fighting against these outdated myths. Like racial myths, they have been reflected in our laws. Let me list a few.

Steinem starts her list of myths with powerful evidence that the reverse is true here: women are indeed good at surviving and have been shown to often be cooler heads in times of crisis than men. Such was not the popular understanding in the 1960s, however. It was the job of Steinem and her allies in the cause of women's rights to change this understanding.

That women are biologically inferior to men. In fact, an equally good case can be made for the reverse. Women live longer than men, even when the men are not subject to business pressures. Women survived Nazi concentration camps better, keep cooler heads in emergencies currently studied by disaster-researchers, are protected against heart attacks by their female sex hormones, and are so much more durable at every stage of life that nature must conceive 20 to 50 percent more males in order to keep some balance going.

Man's hunting activities are forever being pointed to as tribal proof of superiority. But while he was hunting, women built houses, tilled the fields, developed animal husbandry, and perfected language. Men, being all alone in the bush, often developed into a creature as strong as women, fleeter of foot, but not very bright.

However, I don't want to prove the superiority of one sex to another. That would only be repeating a male mistake. English scientists once definitively proved, after all, that the English were descended from the angels, while the Irish were descended from the apes: it was the rationale for England's domination of Ireland for more than a century. The point is that science is used to support current myth and economics almost as much as the church was.

Stein refers to Dr. Sigmund Freud, who lived from 1856 to 1939 and is considered one of the most influential psychotherapists who ever lived. Despite his fame and importance to psychiatry, Freud is often criticized for his belief that women were inferior beings to men. Female sexuality, according to his early theories, is exactly the same as male sexuality up until the phallic stage of psychosexual development. That's when problems set in. Since females do not have a penis, they experience "penis envy." This is the jealousy that little girls feel toward boys and the resentment toward their mothers, whom, Freud says, they blame for not having a penis. So, he continues, girls transfer their affection from their mothers to their fathers. This is an attempt to "gain" a penis. But since the girls are female and not male, they cannot identify with their father. When they come to understand they cannot "gain" a penis, these daughters seek to have children instead.[3]

What we do know is that the difference between two races or two sexes is much smaller than the differences to be found within each group. Therefore, in spite of the slide show on female inferiorities that I understand was shown to you yesterday, the law makes much more sense when it treats individuals, not groups bundled together by some condition of birth.

A word should be said about Dr. Freud, the great 19th century perpetuator of female inferiority. Many of the differences he assumed to be biological, and therefore changeless, have turned out to be societal, and have

already changed. Penis Envy, for instance, is clinically disappearing. Just as black people envied white skins, 19th century women envied penises. A second-class group envies whatever it is that makes the first-class group first class.

Another myth, that women are already treated equally in this society. I am sure there has been ample testimony to prove that equal pay for equal work, equal chance for advancement, and equal training or encouragement is obscenely scarce in every field, even those—like food and fashion industries—that are supposedly "feminine."

A deeper result of social and legal injustice, however, is what sociologists refer to as "Internalized Aggression." Victims of aggression absorb the myth of their own inferiority, and come to believe that their group is in fact second class. Even when they themselves realize they are not second class, they may still think their group is, thus the tendency to be the only Jew in the club, the only black woman on the block, the only woman in the office.

Women suffer this second class treatment from the moment they are born. They are expected to be, rather than achieve, to function biologically rather than learn. A brother, whatever his intellect, is more likely to get the family's encouragement and education money, while girls are often pressured to conceal ambition and intelligence, to "Uncle Tom."

"Women suffer this second class treatment from the moment they are born. They are expected to be, rather than achieve, to function biologically rather than learn."

I interviewed a New York public school teacher who told me about a black teenager's desire to be a doctor. With all the barriers in mind, she suggested kindly that he be a veterinarian instead.

The same day, a high school teacher mentioned a girl who wanted to be a doctor. The teacher said, "How about a nurse?"

Teachers, parents, and the Supreme Court may exude a protective, well-meaning rationale, but limiting the individual's ambition is doing no one a favor. Certainly not this country; it needs all the talent it can get.

Another myth, that American women hold great economic power. Fifty-one percent of all shareholders in this country are women. That is a favorite male-chauvinist statistic.

Ten thousand dollars in 1970 would be the equivalent of approximately $60,000 in 2014 and—like today—would be considered a good salary for the time. This statistic was obviously meant to show the poor and unequal earning power of women compared to men, and the disparity in economic power between the sexes.

"American mothers spend more time with their homes and children than those of any other society we know about."

However, the number of shares they hold is so small that the total is only 18 percent of all shares. Even those holdings are often controlled by men.

Similarly, only 5 percent of all the people in the country who receive $10,000 a year or more, earned or otherwise, are women. And that includes the famous rich widows.

The constantly repeated myth of our economic power seems less testimony to our real power than to the resentment of what little power we do have.

Another myth, that children must have full-time mothers. American mothers spend more time with their homes and children than those of any other society we know about. In the past, joint families, servants, a prevalent system in which grandparents raised the children, or family field work in the agrarian systems—all these factors contributed more to child care than the labor-saving devices of which we are so proud.

The truth is that most American children seem to be suffering from too much mother, and too little father. Part of the program of Women's Liberation is a return of fathers to their children. If laws permit women equal work and pay opportunities, men will then be relieved of their role as sole breadwinner. Fewer ulcers, fewer hours of meaningless work, equal responsibility for his own children: these are a few of the reasons that Women's Liberation is Men's Liberation, too.

As for the psychic health of the children, studies show that the quality of time spent by parents is more important than the quantity. The most damaged children were not those whose mothers worked, but those whose mothers preferred to work but stayed home out of role-playing desire to be a "good mother."

Another myth, that the women's movement is not political, won't last, or is somehow not "serious."

When black people leave their 19th century roles, they are feared. When women dare to leave theirs, they are ridiculed. We understand this: we accept the burden of ridicule. It won't keep us quiet anymore.

Similarly, it shouldn't deceive male observers into thinking that this is somehow a joke. We are 51 percent of the population; we are essentially united on these issues across boundaries of class or race or age; and we may well end by changing this society more than the civil rights movement. That is an apt parallel. We, too, have our right wing and left wing, our separatists, gradualists, and Uncle Toms. But we are changing our own consciousness, and that of the country. Engels noted the relationship of the authoritarian, nuclear family to capitalism: the father as capitalist, the mother as means of production, and the children as labor. He said the family would change as the economic system did, and that seems to have happened, whether we want to admit it or not. Women's bodies will no longer be owned by the state for the production of workers and soldiers; birth control and abortion are facts of everyday life. The new family is an egalitarian family.

Gunnar Myrdal noted 30 years ago the parallel between women and Negroes in this country. Both suffered from such restricting social myths as: smaller brains, passive natures, inability to govern themselves (and certainly not white men), sex objects only, childlike natures, special skills, and the like. When evaluating a general statement about women, it might be valuable to substitute "black people" for "women"—just to test the prejudice at work.

Gunnar Myrdal was a Swedish Nobel Prize laureate in the 20th century who wrote an influential book, *An American Dilemma: The Negro Problem and Modern Democracy*. The book was published in 1944 as the culmination of a comprehensive study of race relations in the United States, funded by the Carnegie Corporation. *An American Dilemma* became an influential force in the 1954 landmark Supreme Court decision *Brown vs. Board of Education* that made segregation in public schools illegal.

And it might be valuable to do this constitutionally as well. Neither group is going to be content as a cheap labor pool anymore. And neither is going to be content without full constitutional rights.

Finally, I would like to say one thing about this time in which I am testifying. I had deep misgivings about discussing this topic when National Guardsmen are occupying our campuses, the country is being turned against itself in a terrible polarization, and America is enlarging an already inhuman and unjustifiable war. But it seems to me that much of the trouble in this country has to do with the "masculine mystique"; with the myth that masculinity somehow depends on the subjugation of other people. It is a bipartisan problem; both our past and current Presidents seem to be victims of this myth, and to behave accordingly.

Women are not more moral than men. We are only uncorrupted by power. But we do not want to imitate men, to join this country as it is, and I think our very participation will change it. Perhaps women elected leaders—and there will be many more of them—will not be so likely to dominate black people or yellow people or men; anybody who looks different from us.

After all, we won't have our masculinity to prove.

Source: "The Equal Rights Amendment," Hearings before the Subcommittee on Constitutional Amendments of the Committee on the Judiciary, United States Senate, 91st Congress, 2nd session, on S.J. Res. 61, May 5, 6, and 7, 1970, pp. 331–334.

"Living the Revolution"

Gloria Steinem's Commencement Speech at Vassar College

May 31, 1970

INTRODUCTION

The speech that follows is a commencement speech that Gloria Steinem gave to graduates of Vassar College before the launching of her famous magazine. The fact she was asked to do this, even in the 1960s before *Ms.* began publication, shows that Steinem had already achieved notoriety as a leading women's rights advocate. This speech came 25 days after Steinem testified before Congress on behalf of the Equal Rights Amendment.

President Simpson, members of the faculty, families and friends, first brave and courageous male graduates of Vassar, and Sisters.

You may be surprised that I am a commencement speaker. You can possibly be as surprised as I am. In my experience, commencement speakers are gray-haired, respected creatures, heavy with the experience of power in the world and with Establishment honors. Which means, of course, that they are almost always men.

But this is the year of Women's Liberation. Or at least, it is the year the press has discovered a movement that has been strong for several years now, and reported it as a small, privileged, rather lunatic event instead of the major revolution in consciousness—in everyone's consciousness—male or female that I believe it truly is.

It may have been part of that revolution that caused the senior class to invite me here—and I am grateful. It is certainly a part of that revolution that I, a devout non-speaker, am managing to stand before you at all: I don't know whether you will be grateful or not. The important thing is that we are spending this time together, considering the larger implications of a movement that some call "feminist" but should more accurately be called humanist; a movement that is an integral part of rescuing this country from its old, expensive patterns of elitism, racism, and violence.

The women's liberation movement had no exact launch date, although the movement for women's rights certainly extends back into the 19th century when the push began for women's suffrage. It took almost 100 years for that movement to produce the constitutional right for women to vote, which came with the passage of the Nineteenth Amendment in 1920. The women's rights movement ebbed and flowed from that time, interrupted by two world wars, and coalesced in the 1960s, when various forms of protest and questioning of cultural traditions found fertile ground in America.

The first problem for all of us, men and women, is not to learn, but to un-learn. We are filled with the Popular Wisdom of several centuries just past, and we are terrified to give it up. Patriotism means obedience, age means wisdom, woman means submission, black means inferior—these are preconceptions imbedded so deeply in our thinking that we honestly may not know that they are there.

Unfortunately, authorities who write textbooks are sometimes subject to the same Popular Wisdom as the rest of us. They gather their proof around it, and end by becoming the theoreticians of the status quo. Using the most respectable of scholarly methods, for instance, English scientists proved definitively that the English were descended from the angels, while the Irish were descended from the apes. It was beautifully done, complete with comparative skull-measurements, and it was a rationale for the English domination of the Irish for more than 100 years. I try to remember that when I'm reading Arthur Jensen's current and very impressive work on the limitations of black intelligence. Or when I'm reading Lionel Tiger on the inability of women to act in groups.

Here Steinem goes beyond simply saying we are being guided by unconscious stereotypes into showing the so-called scientific and rational bases for such stereotypes. In so doing, she seems to echo what journalist and philosopher Walter Lippmann wrote in his classic book *Public Opinion* in 1922. Writing about the impact of stereotypes in American culture, Lippmann defined a stereotype as a thing a person focuses on because of her or his own personal cultural experience and that is defined by that culture. He noted that because we get most of our view of the world from the media, we are often given the media's stereotypes of that world. Those stereotypes then go on to form the basis of public opinion.[4]

The apes-and-angels example is an extreme one, but so may some of our recent assumptions be. There are a few psychologists who believe that anti-Communism may eventually be looked upon as a mental disease.

It wasn't easy for the English to give up their mythic superiority. Indeed, there are quite a few Irish who doubt that they have done it yet. Clearing our minds and government policies of outdated myths is proving to be at least difficult. But it is also inevitable. Whether it's woman's secondary role in society or the paternalistic role of the United States in the world, the old assumptions just don't work anymore.

Rollo May was a 20th-century American psychologist and author who helped introduce the concept of existential psychology to the country in the late 1950s. His chief goal was to probe the dynamics behind human crises and suffering. Joining a long line of other psychologists and psychiatrists, he believed that the human psyche developed by going through different challenges or crises, including innocence, rebellion, decision, conformity, and creativity. He, and others such as Steinem here, adapted and extrapolated this development from the individual to the society as a whole.[5]

Rollo May has a theory that I find comforting. There are three periods in history, he says—one in which myths are built up, one in which they obtain, and one in which they are torn down.

Clearly, we are living in a time of myths being torn down. We look at the more stable period just past, and we think that such basic and terrifying change has never happened before. But, relatively, it has. Clinging to the comfortable beliefs of the past serves no purpose, and only slows down the growth of new forms to suit a new reality.

Part of living this revolution is having the scales fall from our eyes. Everyday we see small obvious truths that we had missed before. Our histories, for instance, have generally been written for and about white men. Inhabited countries were "discovered" when the first white male set foot there, and most of us learned more about any one European country than we did about Africa and Asia combined.

I confess that, before some consciousness-changing of my own, I would have thought the Women History courses springing up around the country belonged in the same cultural ghetto as home economics. The truth is that we need Women's Studies almost as much as we need Black Studies, and for exactly the same reason: too many of us have been allowed from a "good" education believing that everything from political power to scientific discovery was the province of white males. I don't know about Vassar, but at Smith we learned almost nothing about women.

Steinem warns not only that we are taking stereotypes as truth but also that these stereotypes come almost entirely from men, and white males at that. Today this hardly sounds like a groundbreaking idea, but it certainly was in 1970.

We believed, for instance, that the vote had been "given" to women in some whimsical, benevolent fashion. We never learned about the long desperation of women's struggle, or about the strength and wisdom of the women who led it. We heard about the men who risked their lives in the Abolitionist Movement, but seldom about the women; even though women, as in many movements of social reform, had played the major role. We knew a great deal more about the outdated, male-supremacist theories of Sigmund Freud than we did about societies in which women had equal responsibility, or even ruled.

"Anonymous," Virginia Woolf once said sadly, "was a woman."

I don't mean to equate our problems of identity with those that flowed from slavery. But, as Gunnar Myrdal pointed out in his classic study, An American Dilemma,

Steinem may in fact not be trying to "equate" the struggles of women with the struggles of blacks, but she certainly did connect the two struggles and used these examples to do so. Whether this was an attempt to garner larger support for the women's movement by empathizing with blacks or not, this strategy did work to elevate the need for equal treatment for women in the years shortly after civil rights legislation was enacted for black America.

"In drawing a parallel between the position of, and the feeling toward, women and Negroes, we are uncovering a fundamental basis of our culture." Blacks and women suffer from the same myths of childlike natures; smaller brains; inability to govern themselves, much less white men; limited job skills; identity as sex objects—and so on. Ever since slaves arrived on these shores and were given the legal status of wives—that is, chattel—our legal reforms have followed on each other's heels. (With women, I might add, still lagging considerably behind. Nixon's Commission on Women concluded that the Supreme Court was sanctioning discrimination against women—discrimination that it had long ago ruled unconstitutional in the case of blacks—but the Commission report remains mysteriously unreleased by the White House. An Equal Rights Amendment, now up again before the Senate, has been delayed by a male-chauvinist Congress for 47 years.) Neither blacks nor women have role-models in history: models of individuals who have been honored in authority outside the home.

I remember when I was interviewing Mrs. Nixon just before the 1968 election, I asked her what woman in history she most admired and would want to be like. She said, "Mrs. Eisenhower." When I asked her why, she thought for a moment, and said, "Because she meant so much to young people."

It was the last and most quizzical straw in a long, difficult interview, so I ventured a reply. I was in college during the Eisenhower years, I told her, and I didn't notice any special influence that Mrs. Eisenhower had on youth. Mrs. Nixon just looked at me warily, and said, "You didn't?" But afterwards, I decided I had been unfair. After all, neither one of us had that many people to choose from. As Margaret Mead has noted, the only women allowed to be dominant and respectable at the same time are widows. You have to do what society wants you to do, have a husband who dies, and then have power thrust upon you through no fault of your own. The whole thing seems very hard on the men.

"[T]he only women allowed to be dominant and respectable at the same time are widows."

Before we go on to other reasons why Women's Liberation is Man's Liberation, too—and why this incarnation of the women's movement is inseparable from the larger revolution—perhaps we should clear the air of a few more myths.

The myth that women are biologically inferior, for instance. In fact, an equally good case could be made for the reverse. Women live longer than men. That's always being cited as proof that we work them to death, but the truth is: women live longer than men even when groups being studied are monks and nuns. We survived Nazi concentration camps better, are protected against heart attacks by our female hormones, are less subject to many diseases, withstand surgery better, and are so much more durable at every stage of life that nature conceives 20 to 50 percent more males just to keep the balance going.

The Auto Safety Committee of the American Medical Association has come to the conclusion that women are better drivers because they are less emotional than men. I never thought I would hear myself quoting the AMA, hut that one was too good to resist.

Here Steinem comes up with a good source of refutation for a popular argument of the day posed by men: that women are too emotional to be put into leadership positions. One personal memory I have of hearing this assertion was at a gathering in the lobby of a sorority house in college. It was a meeting of a campus group of Christian students, and an older male leader actually made the statement (to a large mixed-gender group of students) that "Women are a speck of intellect on a sea of emotion." It drew laughter, but no protest, from both male and female students in the room. The speaker felt that he was simply uttering a well-established truth. That was in 1967, three years before Steinem made the speech we are analyzing here.

Men's hunting activities are forever being pointed to as proof of Tribal Superiority. But while they were out hunting, women built houses, tilled the fields, developed animal husbandry, and perfected language. Men, isolated from each other out there in the bush, often developed into creatures that were fleet of foot, but not very bright.

I don't want to prove the superiority of one sex to another. That would only be repeating a male mistake. The truth is that we're just not sure how many of our differences are biological, and how many are societal. In spite of all the books written on the subject, there is almost no such thing as a culture-free test. What we do know is that the differences between the two sexes, like the differences between races, are much less great than the differences to be found within each group. Therefore, requirements of a job can only be sensibly suited to the job itself. It deprives the country of talent to bundle any group of workers together by condition of birth.

A second myth is that women are already being treated equally in this society. We ourselves have been guilty of perpetuating this myth, especially at upper economic levels where women have grown fond of being lavishly maintained as ornaments and children. The chains may be made of mink and wall-to-wall carpeting, but they are still chains.

The truth is that a woman with a college degree working full-time makes less than a black man with a high school degree working full-time. And black women make least of all. In many parts of the country[,] New York City, for instance, woman has no legally-guaranteed right to rent an apartment, buy a house, get accommodations in a hotel, or be served in a public restaurant. She can be refused simply because of her sex. In some states, women cannot own property, and get longer jail sentences for the same crime. Women on welfare must routinely answer humiliating personal questions; male welfare recipients do not. A woman is the last to be hired, the first to be fired. Equal pay for equal work is the exception. Equal chance for advancement, especially at upper levels or at any level with authority over men, is rare enough to be displayed in a museum.

Seventy percent of families in America had a stay-at-home mom in 1960, and when women did enter the workforce, they often faced an uphill battle competing with men. One professor at the University of Southern California looked at the subject in an essay titled "What Does It Take for a Woman to Make It in Management?" She listed 10 qualities that woman must have, and one of them was "the support of an influential man." Another was "femininity." The professor quoted an unnamed male Equal Employment Opportunity director as saying that "For a woman to succeed, there must be a man in her life who believed it's the right thing to do."[6]

As for our much-touted economic power, we make up only 5 percent of all the people in the country receiving $10,000 a year or more. And that includes all the famous rich widows. We are 51 percent of all stockholders, a dubious honor these days, but we hold only 18 percent of the stock—and that is generally controlled by men. The power women have as consumers is comparable to that power all of us currently have as voters: we can choose among items presented to us, but we have little chance to influence the presentation. Women's greatest power to date is her nuisance value. The civil rights, peace, and consumer movements are impressive examples of that.

In fact, the myth of economic matriarchy in this country is less testimony to our power than to the resentment of the little power we do have.

You may wonder why we have submitted to such humiliations all these years; why, indeed, women will sometimes deny that they are second-class citizens at all.

The "uncle Tomming" reference is to the title character of Uncle Tom in Harriett Beecher Stowe's 1852 novel Uncle Tom's Cabin. The phrase is an epithet to anyone who is slavish and excessively obedient to authority figures, even if those figures are wrongheaded or oppressive individuals or groups.

The answer lies in the psychology of second-classness. Like all such groups, we come to accept what society says about us. And that is the most terrible punishment of all. We believe that we can only make it in the world by "uncle Tomming," by a real or pretended subservience to white males.

Even when we come to understand that we, as individuals, are not second-class, we still accept society's assessment of our group—a phenomenon psychologists refer to as Internalized Aggression. From this stems the desire to be the only woman in an office, an academic department, or any other part of the man's world. From this also stems women who put down their sisters—and my own profession of journalism has some of them. By writing or speaking of their non-conformist sisters in a disapproving, conformist way, they are essentially saying, "See what a real woman I am," and expecting to be rewarded by ruling-class approval and favors. That is only beginning to change.

It shouldn't be surprising that women behave this way, too. After all, Internalized Aggression has for years been evident in black people who criticized each other ("See what a good Nigger I am"), or in Jews who ridiculed Jewishness ("See how I am different from other Jews"). It has been responsible for the phenomenon of wanting to be the only black family in the block, or the only Jew in the club.

Steinem seems to be equating the idea of "Internalized Aggression" with a theory of second-classness, although that's not what psychologists seem to mean by internalized aggression. This is when a person who has been exposed to aggression takes that inside himself/herself and must find a way of dealing with it. Certainly subservience and passive-aggressive behavior is one way, but so is acting out that aggression. While there is no actual psychological syndrome called "second-classness," there is a body of literature—and studies behind it—that look at individuals' need for social acceptance. Psychologist Mark Leary has written that "People have realized just how much our concern with social acceptance spreads its fingers into almost everything we do. . . . [T]he pain of being excluded is not so different from the pain of physical injury. . . . Social rejection can influence emotion, cognition, and even physical health."[7] Other studies show that this need for acceptance is one reason why individuals wind up accepting how others might frame them.

Again Steinem draws a comparison between not only the struggles of women and blacks but also of women and Jews as she makes her point about these groups falling prey to others' stereotypes of them.

With women, the whole system reinforces this feeling of being a mere appendage. It's hard for a man to realize just how full of self-doubt we become as a result. Locked into suburban homes with the intellectual companionship of three-year-olds; locked into bad jobs, watching less-qualified men get promoted above us; trapped into poverty by a system that supposes our only identity is motherhood—no wonder we become pathetically grateful for small favors.

I don't want to give the impression, though, that we want to join society exactly as it is. I don't think most women want to pick up slimline briefcases and march off to meaningless, de-personalized jobs. Nor do we want to be drafted—and women certainly should be drafted: even the readers of *Seventeen* magazine were recently polled as being overwhelmingly in favor of women in National Service—to serve in an unconstitutional, racist, body-count war like the one in Indochina.

We want to liberate men from those inhuman roles as well. We want to share the work and responsibility, and to have men share equal responsibility for the children.

Here Steinem takes on one of the most controversial questions, that of whether a woman somehow abdicates her role as a nurturing mother by going out to work full-time. It was—and still is—controversial not only among many men but also among many women too and has often been a polarizing issue in the argument over the pros and cons of two-career marriages. Steinem asserts her belief that it is possible for women to be both caring mothers and working professionals, and she calls upon husbands to partner with their wives in being real parents.

Probably the ultimate myth is that children must have fulltime mothers, and that liberated women make bad ones. The truth is that most American children seem to be suffering from too much mother and too little father. Women now spend more time with their homes and families than in any past or present society we know about. To get back to the sanity of the agrarian or joint-family system, we need free universal daycare. With that aid, as in Scandinavian countries, and with laws that permit women equal work and equal pay, men will be relieved of their role as sole breadwinner and stranger to his own children.

No more alimony. Fewer boring wives, fewer child-like wives. No more so-called "Jewish mothers," who are simply normal ambitious human beings with all their ambitions confined to the house. No more wives who fall apart with the first wrinkle, because they've been taught their total identity depends on their outsides. No more responsibility for another adult human being who has never been told she is responsible for her own life, and who sooner or later comes up with some version of, "If I hadn't married you, I could have been a star." And let's say it one more time because it such a great organizing tool, no more alimony. Women Liberation really is Men's Liberation, too.

The family system that will emerge is a great subject of anxiety. Probably there will be a variety of choice. Colleague marriages, such as young people have now, with both partners going to law school or the Peace Corps together: that's one alternative. At least they share more than the kitchen and the bedroom. Communes, marriages that are valid for the child-rearing years only . . . there are many possibilities, but they can't be predicted. The growth of new forms must be organic.

The point is that Women's Liberation is not destroying the American family; it is trying to build a human, compassionate alternative out of its ruins. Engels said that the paternalistic, 19th Century family system was the prototype of capitalism—with man, the capitalist; woman, the means of production; children the labor—and that the family would only change as the economic system did. Well, capitalism and the mythical American family seem to be in about the same shape.

Here Steinem alludes to Frederich Engels, the 19th-century social scientist and activist who is generally seen as the father of Marxist thought, which lay at the foundation of communism. Steinem was taking a risk in invoking a communist as an expert source to buttress her point, given that the United States was in a state of cold war with European communism at the time.

Of course, there are factors other than economic ones. As Margaret Mead says: No wonder marriage worked so well in the 19th century; people only lived to be fifty years old.

Margaret Mead was a 20th-century cultural anthropologist—possibly the best known in this century—who provided revelatory insight into the American culture and psyche.

And there are factors other than social reform that will influence women's work success. "No wonder women do less well in business," says a woman-executive. "They don't have wives." But the family is the first political unit, and to change it is the most radical act of all.

Women have a special opportunity to live the revolution. By refusing to play their traditional role, they upset and displace the social structure around them. We may be subject to ridicule and suppression, just as men were when they refused to play their traditional role by going to war. But those refusals together are a hope for peace. Anthropologist Geoffrey Corer discovered that the few peaceful human tribes had a common characteristic: sex roles were not polarized, boys weren't taught that manhood depended on aggression (or short hair or military skills), and girls weren't taught that womanhood depended on submission (or working at home instead of the fields).

For those who still fear that Women Liberation involves some loss of manhood, let me quote from the Black Panther code. Certainly, if the fear with which they are being met is any standard, the Panthers are currently the most potent male symbol of all. In Seize The Time, Bobby Seale writes, "Where there's a Panther house, we try to live socialism. When there's cooking to be done, both brothers and sisters cook. Both wash the dishes. The sisters

Steinem was nothing if not a risk-taker. As she did in the previous section where she invoked the name of Frederich Engels as a source, now she is invoking the code of the Black Panthers, a militant activist organization for black power that was perceived by many white Americans as a violent and intimidating group. Bobby Seale cofounded the party along with Huey Newton. Seale was one of the original Chicago 8 defendants, charged with conspiracy, and was sentenced in 1969 to four years in prison on 16 counts of contempt of court.

don't just serve and wait on the brothers. A lot of black nationalist organizations have the idea of regulating women to the role of serving their men, and they relate this to black manhood. But a real manhood is based on humanism, and it is not based on any form of oppression."

One final myth: that women are more moral than men. We are not more moral, we are only uncorrupted by power. But until the leaders of our country put into action the philosophy that Bobby Seale has set down until the old generation of male chauvinists is out of office—women in positions of power can increase our chances of peace a great deal. I personally would rather have had Margaret Mead as president during the past six years of Vietnam than either Johnson or Nixon. At least, she wouldn't have had her masculinity to prove.

Much of the trouble this country is in has to do with the Masculine Mystique: the idea that manhood somehow depends on the subjugation of other people. It's a bipartisan problem.

The challenge to all of us, and to you men and women who are graduating today, is to live a revolution, not to die for one. There has been too much killing, and the weapons are now far too terrible. This revolution has to change consciousness, to upset the injustice of our current hierarchy by refusing to honor it, and to live a life that enforces a new social justice.

In her belief that no one can be free if all are not free, Steinem echoes the same thought expressed by both President Kennedy and President Johnson as they made their pleas for congressional passage of civil rights legislation. As she has done elsewhere in her speech, Steinem simply applies the same logic to the equal treatment of women.

Because the truth is none of us can be liberated if other groups are not. Women's Liberation is a bridge between black and white women, but also between the construction workers and the suburbanites, between Nixon's "silent majority" and the young people they hate and fear. Indeed, there's much more injustice and rage among working-class women than among the much-publicized white radicals.

Women are sisters, they have many of the same problems, and they can communicate with each other. "You only get radicalized," as black activists always told us, "on your own thing." Then we make the connection to other injustices in society. The Women's Movement is an important revolutionary bridge. And we are building it.

I know it's traditional on such an occasion to talk about "entering the world." But this is an untraditional generation: you have made the campus part of the world. I thank you for it.

I don't need to tell you what awaits you in this country. You know that much better than I. I will only say that my heart goes with you, and that I hope we will be working together. Divisions of age, race, class, and sex are old-fashioned and destructive.

"Divisions of age, race, class, and sex are old-fashioned and destructive."

One more thing, especially to the sisters, because I wish someone had said it to me; it would have saved me so much time. You don't have to play one role in this revolutionary age above all others. If you're willing to pay the price for it, you can do anything you want to do. And the price is worth it.

Source: Gloria Steinem, "Living the Revolution," *Vassar Quarterly* (Fall 1970): 12–15. Used by permission.

Notes

1. "Brooklyn College 'Catalyst for Change' Student Context Winners," The Shirley Chisholm Project, June 5, 2013, http://chisholmproject.com/2012/featured/1123.

2. Russell Kirk, "Equal Rights and Wrongs," *Milwaukee Journal,* May 16, 1971, 19, http://news.google.com/newspapers?nid=1499&dat=19720516&id=1zcdAAAAIBAJ&sjid=nSgEAAAAIBAJ&pg=5503,3684757.

3. "Sigmund Freud," Psychological History of Women, http://psychistofwomen.umwblogs.org/sexuality/pre-kinsey/freud/.

4. Walter Lippmann, *Public Opinion* (1922; reprint, Sioux Falls, SD: Greenbook, 2010).

5. "Rollo May (1909–1994)," Goodtherapy.org, http://www.goodtherapy.org/famous-psychologists/rollo-may.html#.

6. Susan G. Hauser, "The Women's Movement in the 1970s, Today: You've Come a Long Way, Baby, but . . .," *Workforce,* May 15, 2012, http://www.workforce.com/articles/the-women-s-movement-in-the-70s-today-you-ve-come-a-long-way-but.

7. Kirsten Weir, "The Pain of Social Rejection," *Science Watch* 43(4) (April 2012): 50, American Psychological Association, http://www.apa.org/monitor/2012/04/rejection.aspx.

Chapter 6

Embracing Differences:
Protesting GLBT Discrimination

Introduction

In the 1960s, voices promoting equal rights for gays and lesbians were starting to rise, but they had definitely not reached the crescendo stage they would in later years. Among the causes of protest in this era of protest, the cause of homosexuality was being drowned out by protests against the Vietnam War and for civil rights and women's rights. Still, there were straws in the wind that the movement supporting gay rights was gaining momentum. Underground organizations supporting homosexuals had been formed as early as 1950. One was the Mattachine Society in Los Angeles, founded by Harry Hay, a young musicologist. Hay was angry over the brutalization of gay people, even by local law enforcement agencies. The outing of gays and lesbians was likely to get them fired from their jobs and ostracized from their social groups and communities. President Dwight Eisenhower even signed an executive order allowing federal agencies to fire homosexuals. The U.S. Postal Service assisted in identifying homosexuals by tracking the mail of those suspected of having same-sex attractions.[1]

The homosexual rights movements, known as the homophile movement, picked up steam around 1965 as American cities—most notably San Francisco and New York—saw gays, lesbians, and transgender people form into more visible communities and neighborhoods. Threatened sometimes with eviction from their apartments for engaging in homosexual acts there, gays and lesbians would take to city parks at night to make love. This resulted in a large number of arrests, especially in San Francisco. These arrests and the brutality that sometimes accompanied them sparked reaction from the gay, lesbian, bisexual, and transgender (GLBT) communities who would take to the streets in protest. There was picketing and there were sit-ins as homosexuals came out into the public to fight for their rights. The East Coast Homophiles Organization (ECHO) was founded in New York City in 1963 as a kind of organizing group for smaller GLBT groups. On the West Coast, a similar group was formed the next year. This was the San Franciscan Society for Individual Rights (SIR), founded in that city in 1964. The organization would sponsor events for the GLBT community and in 1966 opened the first gay and lesbian bar in the nation. By 1968, SIR had more than 1,000 members and was the largest homophile group in the country.[2] The first gay bookstore had opened in New York, and Philadelphia was the site of a picket by gays, lesbians, and transgender people that was held right in front of Independence Hall. The name of the homophile movement gave way to the more generally accepted name of the gay liberation movement that came to be the GLBT movement.

"Under Conditions Other Than Honorable"

Fannie Mae Clackum v. United States

January 20, 1960

INTRODUCTION

In the courts, cases were being heard involving the question of how gay and lesbian people were being treated in the workplace. The following is one of the court cases heard that focused on the rights of a homosexual member of the U.S. Air Force, Fannie Mae Clackum, who was discharged from the service "under conditions other than honorable." Contrary to what some believe, the history of military policy on gay service members is a long one and goes back to 1778 when General George Washington ordered Lieutenant Gotthold Frederick Enslin to be dismissed from the U.S. military for homosexuality. Washington cited "an abhorance and detestation of such infamous crimes."[3] Enslin's was the first documented case of a member of the military being dismissed for homosexuality.

1 The plaintiff was separated from the United States Air Force on January 22, 1952, with a discharge "under conditions other than honorable." She asserts that the purported discharge was invalid, and sues for her pay from the date of the purported discharge. The following "Statement of Facts Alleged", contained in the following four paragraphs, is copied from the Government's brief.

2 "On February 2, 1951, plaintiff was a reservist in the United States Air Force, (WAF—Women in the Air Force) and was ordered to active duty as an airman. She was stationed thereafter at Barksdale Air Force Base, Louisiana, in the grade of corporal, with duty in Headquarters and Headquarters Squadron, 301st Air Base Group.

3 "On April 18, 1951, plaintiff, among others, was called before her commanding officer and a representative of the O.S.I. (Office of Special Intelligence) and interrogated on matters of homosexuality concerning which plaintiff alleges she had no knowledge. Thereafter, until January 1952, plaintiff was repeatedly interviewed by an officer of the O.S.I. concerning homosexual activities and informed that she was under investigation. She was never informed of any charges against her by the Air Force, although in October 1951 she was informed that some action was contemplated against her. Also in October 1951 plaintiff was called before her

commanding officer and was given an opportunity to resign under A.F.R. 35-66, (2). Upon being offered the opportunity to resign, plaintiff refused to resign and demanded in writing that she be tried by court-martial. The purpose of this demand was to require the Air Force to confront her with the basis of the accusations against her and to afford her an opportunity to present evidence in her own behalf.

4   **"Although charges were preferred against plaintiff under the Uniform Code of Military Justice, the charges were not referred for investigation under the provisions of the Code, they were not brought to her attention, and she had no knowledge of them until after her discharge. After plaintiff was given an opportunity to resign and refused, she was given a psychiatric examination but was not informed of the report of the psychiatrist. No sworn evidence against plaintiff was taken or received by the O.S.I. or by the Air Force, and prior to her discharge plaintiff was not confronted with the nature of the evidence against her. Plaintiff was demoted to the grade of private on January 22, 1952 and on that same day was discharged from the service under conditions other than honorable under A.F.R. 35-66 dated January 12, 1951.**

Historically, the U.S. Army was the first of the branches to declare homosexuality as a reason to consider a soldier unfit for military service. It was that year, 1940, when the army issued standards in which "stigmata of degeneration" such as feminine characteristics and "sexual perversion" could result in a male being dismissed from service. Later in 1941, the Selective Service System (the board that administered the military draft) cited homosexuality as a cause for denial of an individual into military service. The years 1950 and 1951 saw further codification of homosexuality as cause for dismissal. As part of these regulations, individuals considered active but nonaggressive were allowed to avoid a court-martial by resigning and accepting a dishonorable discharge, while those exhibiting homosexual tendencies but who were not active could be dismissed with a general or honorable discharge.[4]

5   "Plaintiff brought suit in this Court on June 8, 1956. By agreement of the parties, the Court suspended proceedings in this Court to permit plaintiff to file an application before the Air Force Board for the Correction of Military Records on the ground that plaintiff had failed to exhaust her administrative remedies. An application was filed and was denied by the Air Force Board for the Correction of Military Records. The suspension of proceedings in this Court was then removed."

6   Some of the effects upon a soldier of a discharge "under conditions other than honorable" are briefly stated in Air Force Regulations (A.F.R.) 35-66, dated January 12, 1951, 5(b) (1), which says that the person so discharged may be deprived of many rights as a veteran under both Federal and State legislation, and may expect to encounter substantial prejudice in civilian life in situations where the type of service rendered in any branch of the armed forces or the character of discharge received therefrom may have a bearing.

7   One's reaction to the foregoing narrative is "What's going on here?"

8   A woman soldier is interrogated about homosexual matters and is orally told that some action is contemplated against her. She is called before her commanding officer and is offered an opportunity to resign. She indignantly denies the implied charges involved in the situation and demands in writing that she be tried by a court-martial so that she can learn what the charges are, face her accusers, and present evidence in her own behalf. Although charges were preferred against her, they were not referred for investigation as the statutes governing courts-martial require, and neither the charges nor the evidence upon which they were based were ever made known to the soldier until after her discharge.

It was not until a half century later, in 2013, that the U.S. Supreme Court struck down portions of the 1996 Defense of Marriage Act that allowed gay couples entitlement to the same federal benefits (including GI benefits) that heterosexual couples enjoyed. Secretary of Defense Chuck Hagel said the armed forces would immediately begin honoring that ruling and called it "the right thing to do."[5]

She was summarily given a discharge "under conditions other than honorable", her reputation as a decent woman was officially destroyed, her rights to her accrued pay and accrued leave, and to the numerous and valuable benefits conferred by the nation and many of the states upon former soldiers were forfeited.

9   Air Force Regulations 35-66 5(b) (1) related to the handling of homosexual charges against enlisted personnel. They provided for a resignation agreeing to accept an undesirable discharge with all its damaging consequences. If the soldier refused to so resign, the regulations provided that a trial by general court-martial would be considered. If the evidence in the case indicated that conviction by a general court-martial was unlikely, then the Secretary of the Air Force was, by the regulations, authorized to "direct discharge and administratively determine whether an undesirable, general, or honorable type of discharge certificate will be furnished."

10   A dishonorable discharge is, for a soldier, one of the most severe penalties which may be imposed by a court-martial.

Elaborate provisions for review of court-martial sentences within the military hierarchy, and potentially by the Court of Military Appeals, are included in our military laws. Yet the Air Force regulations discussed above

provide that if the evidence at hand is so unsubstantial that a conviction by a court-martial would be unlikely, the executive officers of the Air Force may themselves convict the soldier and impose the penalty. It is as if a prosecuting attorney were authorized, in a case where he concluded that he didn't have enough evidence to obtain a conviction in court, to himself impose the fine or imprisonment which he thought the accused person deserved.

11   The Government defends this remarkable arrangement, and its operation in the instant case, on the ground that it is necessary in the interest of an efficient military establishment for our national defense. We see nothing in this argument. The plaintiff being a member of the Air Force Reserve, on active duty, the Air Force had the undoubted right to discharge her whenever it pleased, for any reason or for no reason, and by so doing preserve the Air Force from even the slightest suspicion of harboring undesirable characters. But it is unthinkable that it should have the raw power, without respect for even the most elementary notions of due process of law, to load her down with penalties. It is late in the day to argue that everything that the executives of the armed forces do in connection with the discharge of soldiers is beyond the reach of judicial scrutiny. Harmon v. Brucker, 355 U.S. 579, 78 S.Ct. 433, 2 L.Ed.2d 503.

> This court here appears to be pointing out ironic things in how the U.S. Air Force handled this case: (1) air force procedures were not followed; (2) the air force decided that if it couldn't win a court-martial, it would discharge Clackum anyway; (3) the air force has a right to discharge anyone from service for whatever reason; and (4) Clackum's due process rights should have been followed but were not. All of this apparently led the court to ask the earlier rhetorical question "What's going on here?"

12   After her discharge, the plaintiff appealed to the Air Force Discharge Review Board. Such an appeal is provided for in the Air Force Regulations. Her appeal and that of another female non-commissioned officer were heard together. They were represented by counsel. They had access to a brief which had been written by an investigator, and which summarized conversations which he had had with various persons. The plaintiff and the other appellant testified at length, directing their testimony to the incidents mentioned in the conversations summarized in the investigator's brief. Their testimony was, of course, entirely favorable to themselves. Some members of the Board asked some questions of the appellants. None of the answers to these

questions tended to show that the appellants were guilty. Testimonials of good character from Air Force superiors, civilian employers, clergymen and other acquaintances were placed in evidence.

13   No witnesses other than the two appellants testified. None of the persons mentioned in the investigator's brief as having made statements derogatory to the appellants were called to testify.

14   The appellants' counsel made an able argument on their behalf. Among other things, he pointed out the absurdity of the following oracular item in the investigator's brief:

15   "Psychiatric evaluation of appl. (appellant) 21 Nov. 51 reflected a diagnosis of sexual deviate manifested by homosexuality latent.,"

16   in view of the plaintiff's uncontradicted testimony that the only psychiatric interview to which she was subjected lasted from 20 to 30 minutes.

17   The hearing was closed and the Discharge Review Board made the following

18   "Findings

19   After consideration of the evidence of record, including the 201 file in the case, the Board finds:

20   "a. That the discharge of the applicants under the provisions of AFR 35-66 (discharge of homosexuals) was in accord with the regulations in force at the time.

21   "b. That the character of the discharges was amply supported by the evidence of record.

22   "c. That no additional evidence of sufficient weight and credibility as to warrant reversal of the prior action in these cases has been adduced before the Air Force Discharge Review Board.

23   "Conclusions

24   "The Board recommends that no change be made in the type of discharge certificates presently in effect."

"The Board recommends that no change be made in the type of discharge certificates presently in effect."

25   The "evidence of record" upon which the Board based its finding of guilt was obviously not the evidence received at the hearing. All of the evidence received at the hearing tended to prove the plaintiff's innocence. The "evidence of record" was a dossier of affidavits of persons, some of whom were not even mentioned in the investigator's brief which was made available to the plaintiff at the time of her hearing before the Discharge Review Board, although the statements made in their

"All of the evidence received at the hearing tended to prove the plaintiff's innocence."

affidavits, if believed, were extremely damaging to the plaintiff. None of the affidavits was seen by the plaintiff or her counsel until July 24, 1959, long after the plaintiff's case was pending in this court.

26   The "evidence of record" also contained the confidential reports of the Office of Special Investigations which were forwarded to the Air Force Personnel Counsel and the Secretary of the Air Force, and which have never been made available to the plaintiff or her counsel.

27   The so-called "hearing" before the Air Force Discharge Board was not a hearing at all, in the usual sense of that word. It was a meaningless formality, to comply with the regulations. The "evidence" upon which the case was going to be decided, and obviously was decided, was not present at the hearing, unless the undisclosed dossier which contained it was in the drawer of the table at which the Board sat. The appellant and her counsel were futilely tilting at shadows. However vulnerable the secret evidence may have been, there was no possible way to attack it.

28   The plaintiff was, after the proceeding before the Discharge Review Board, as before, a soldier dishonorably discharged, officially branded by her Government as an indecent woman, deprived of valuable rights and benefits which are given to other ex-soldiers. And all this without any semblance of an opportunity to know what

the evidence against her was, or to face her accusers in a trial or hearing.

The judge here lays down reason after reason why Clackum was not treated properly, nor was her air force hearing anything but a formality. That "formality" resulted in her being dismissed and stigmatized, although all the evidence presented at the hearing seemed to portray her as innocent. Some may find it difficult to fathom all this in a society where the constitutional right to due process under the law exists, but this case shows the degree to which homosexuality was feared, misunderstood, and seen as such perversion during this era of American history. And when it came to allowing homosexuals to be members of the military establishment, the issue became even more acute and controversial. Indeed, the issue of gays in the military remains a controversial issue even today. From the days of patently outlawing homosexuality in the ranks, the military moved in 1994 to a policy of "don't ask, don't tell," and it wasn't until the Barack Obama administration when that policy was abandoned in 2011 and gender status was to officially become irrelevant in the military.

29   As we have said, the plaintiff is suing for her pay as a soldier, on the theory that her purported discharge was illegal and invalid. The Government says that even if the discharge actually issued was invalid, the Air Force could have validly discharged her at the time it invalidly did so, and therefore she is not entitled to be paid. There are, of course, many situations in which, if a party had acted somewhat differently, he would not have violated the legal rights of the other person and would not be liable for damages.

30   In the instant case, the dishonorable nature of the discharge was its very essence, the most important thing about it. We feel no urge to dissect the discharge and discard its essence, retaining only its effect of getting the plaintiff out of the Air Force and off its payroll, thus leaving her to suffer, without compensation, all the other penalties which the discharge imposed upon her.

31   Our conclusion is that the purported discharge of the plaintiff was invalid, and did not effect the plaintiff's separation from the Air Force.

32   Since the parties have filed a stipulation of facts which the court has considered, the defendant's motion to dismiss the plaintiff's petition is, under our Rule 16(b), 28 U.S.C.A., treated as a motion for summary judgment. The motion is denied.

So, the court stated that Clackum's discharge from the air force was invalid and denied the motion by the air force to dismiss Clackum's petition that she receive her back pay and benefits from the air force. Although it took eight years to resolve, Clackum's was the first case where a member of the military successfully challenged her discharge from the armed forces. However, the court's ruling was based on the issue of due process and not on the question of homosexual rights.

33   It is so ordered.

34   JONES, Chief Judge, and LARAMORE and WHITAKER, Judges, concur.

Source: *Fannie Mae Clackum vs. The United States*, 296 F.2d 226.

"Raid on the Black Cat Bar"

Press Release from the Tavern Guild of Southern California
January 5, 1967

INTRODUCTION

Following the 1966 New Year's Eve raid on the Black Cat Bar in Los Angeles, a firestorm of reaction began arising from the gay, lesbian, bisexual, and transgender communities of southern California. The incident was seen as an assault on the civil liberties of individuals who were doing nothing other than choosing how they wanted to live their lives, without harming anyone else. The following press release, issued by the Tavern Guild of Southern California, is evidence of that reactionary protest.

Today 16 Los Angeles citizens appeared in court (Div. 59) to enter pleas to charges resulting from a police mass arrest at a bar located at 3909 Sunset Blvd. in Los Angeles.

The bar has been open approximately two months. The arrests took place New Year's eve (January 1, 1967) and were made by a large group of police officers.

About 12 vice-squad officers (plainclothesmen) started beating patrons to the floor about 5 minutes after midnight. They did not identify themselves except by their weapons. After beating the patrons, the 16 to be arrested were laid face down on the sidewalk outside the bar.

Five patrol cars, containing two uniformed officers each, were brought from a near-by side street where they had been parked for sometime and the individuals arrested were taken to the newly opened Rampart St. Police Station. Three bartenders were among those arrested.

Officers then went to a second bar, at 4001 Sunset Blvd., attacked the lady bar owner and the bar's manager and bartender, who came to her aid. The owner and manager

Police raids on gay bars were common in the 1950s and 1960s. Two years after this Los Angeles raid on the Black Cat Bar, police conducted what they thought would be a routine raid on a New York gay and lesbian bar, the Stonewall Inn. On the night of June 29, 1969, however, patrons of the bar decided that enough was enough. They resisted the police raid and entrapped the officers once they entered the building. This launched three days of rioting when area gays and gay supporters commandeered eight square blocks of New York City. News of the riot spread, and the gay support movement turned from its years of relative quiet protest to embrace supporters who took a more militant approach.[6]

were not arrested, although the manager was left on the sidewalk bleeding. The bartender was so badly beaten that he is still in County General Hospital, where he has undergone an operation to remove his ruptured spleen.

Four years after the violent confrontations described here, the gay support movement in America scored a major success when it succeeded in pressuring the American Psychiatric Association to remove homosexuality from its list of mental illnesses. This effectively eliminated one of the reasons that employers often used to fire homosexuals and one of the reasons that judges would often award custody of children to heterosexual couples rather than homosexuals.[7]

He had gone two hours before being sent to the hospital. He was finally booked on a felony charge of assaulting an officer.

Source: "Press Release regarding the Raid of the Black Cat Bar, New Year's Eve, 1966," Tavern Guild of Southern California, January 5, 1967, http://tangentgroup.org/mediawiki/index.php/Black_Cat_Bar_Raid.

"Unfitness to Teach"?

Morrison v. State Board of Education
November 20, 1969

INTRODUCTION

The following case appeared before the California Supreme Court on November 20, 1969, and dealt with the question of whether a teacher's proclivity toward homosexuality should result in stripping such persons of their "life diploma" or license to teach "exceptional children." The case throws a spotlight on the debate surrounding homosexuality as the decade of the 1960s drew to a close and on whether a teacher's inclination toward homosexuality was prima facie evidence of her or his unfitness to teach in the public schools.

For a number of years prior to 1965 petitioner held a General Secondary Life Diploma and a Life Diploma to Teach Exceptional Children, issued by the State Board of Education, which qualified petitioner for employment as a teacher in the public secondary schools of California. On August 5, 1965, an accusation was filed with the State Board of Education charging that petitioner's life diplomas should be revoked for cause.

On March 11, 1966, following a hearing, and pursuant to the recommendations of a hearing examiner, the board revoked petitioner's life diplomas because of immoral and unprofessional conduct and acts involving moral turpitude as authorized by section 13202 of the Education Code. This revocation rendered petitioner ineligible for employment as a teacher in any public school in the state.

Although this may seem hard to believe today, this extreme action shows the hostile climate that homosexuals faced in the 1960s, even though this was the decade that was so characterized by questioning of traditional societal values and the protests that were staged against the expressions of those values.

On February 14, 1967, petitioner sought a writ of mandate from the Superior Court of Los Angeles County to compel the board to set aside its decision and restore his life diplomas. After a hearing, the superior court denied the writ, and this appeal followed.

For the reasons hereinafter set forth we conclude (a) that section 13202 authorizes disciplinary measures only for conduct indicating unfitness to teach, (b) that properly

The California Supreme Court seemed to cut right to the heart of the issue: that this teacher's onetime expression of his homosexual leanings did not constitute any evidence that he was an unfit teacher. Lacking any other evidence, the court called for a reversal of the school board's ruling.

interpreted to this effect section 13202 is constitutional on its face and as here applied, and (c) that the record contains no evidence to support the conclusion that petitioner's conduct indicated his unfitness to teach. The judgment of the superior court must therefore be reversed.

I. The Facts

For a number of years prior to 1964 petitioner worked as a teacher for the Lowell Joint School District. During this period, so far as appears from the record, no one complained about, or so much as criticized, his performance as a teacher. Moreover, with the exception of a single incident, no one suggested that his conduct outside the classroom was other than beyond reproach.

Sometime before the spring of 1963 petitioner became friends with Mr. and Mrs. Fred Schneringer. Mr. Schneringer also worked as a teacher in the public school system. To the Schneringers, who were involved in grave marital and financial difficulties at the time, petitioner gave counsel and advice. In the course of such counseling Mr. Schneringer frequently visited petitioner's apartment to discuss his problems.

For a one-week period in April, during which petitioner and Mr. Schneringer experienced severe emotional stress, the two men engaged in a limited, non-criminal physical [1 Cal.3d 219] relationship which petitioner described as being of a homosexual nature.

Again, the court refers to the lack of evidence and states that one instance of overt homosexuality, away from school, does not constitute evidence of unfitness to teach. The court refuses to go along with popular opinion that all homosexuality should be evidence of deviant and damaging behavior.

Petitioner has never been accused or convicted of any criminal activity whatever, and the record contains no evidence of any abnormal activities or desires by petitioner since the Schneringer incident some six years in the past. Petitioner and Schneringer met on numerous occasions in the spring and summer after the incident and nothing untoward occurred. When Schneringer later obtained a separation from his wife, petitioner suggested a number of women whom Schneringer might consider dating.

Approximately one year after the April 1963 incident, Schneringer reported it to the Superintendent of the Lowell

Joint School District. As a result of that report petitioner resigned his teaching position on May 4, 1964. Some 19 months after the incident became known to the superintendent, the State Board of Education conducted a hearing concerning possible [1 Cal.3d 220] revocation of petitioner's life diplomas. Petitioner there testified that he had had some undefined homosexual problem at the age of 13, but that, with the sole exception of the Schneringer incident, he had not experienced the slightest homosexual urge or inclination for more than a dozen years.

Mr. Cavalier, an investigator testifying for the board, stated that the Schneringer incident "was the only time that [petitioner] ever engaged in a homosexual act with anyone." No evidence was presented that petitioner had ever committed any act of misconduct whatsoever while teaching.

The Board of Education finally revoked petitioner's life diplomas some three years after the Schneringer incident. The board concluded that that incident constituted immoral and unprofessional conduct, and an act involving moral turpitude, all of which warrant revocation of life diplomas under section 13202 of the Education Code.

Local school boards, made up of elected members, have often been known for acting in the interest of what they perceive as prevailing community opinion. The prevailing opinion during this era was highly skeptical of—if not hostile toward—homosexuality.

Petitioner's actions cannot constitute immoral or unprofessional conduct or conduct involving moral turpitude within the meaning of section 13202 unless those actions indicate his unfitness to teach. Section 13202 of the Education Code authorizes revocation of life diplomas for "immoral conduct," "unprofessional conduct," and "acts involving moral turpitude." Legislation authorizing disciplinary action against the holders of a variety of certificates, licenses and government jobs other than teaching also contain these rather general terms. This court has not attempted to formulate explicit definitions of those terms which would apply to all the statutes in which they are used. Rather, we have given those terms more precise meaning by referring in each case to the particular profession or the specific governmental position to which they were applicable. [1 Cal.3d 221]. . . .

In the instant case the terms denote immoral or unprofessional conduct or moral turpitude of the teacher which indicates unfitness to teach. Without such a reasonable interpretation the terms would be susceptible to so broad an application as possibly to subject to discipline virtually

The court points out that specific definitions are needed for causes of unfitness to teach instead of broad generalizations. Then it notes that there are several other abstract terms that could also be grounds for dismissal of any teacher who experienced times of laziness, gluttony, vanity, or selfishness. In so doing, it was pointing out the absurdity of classifying Morrison as being unfit to teach.

every teacher in the state. In the opinion of many people laziness, gluttony, vanity, selfishness, avarice, and cowardice constitute immoral conduct.

A recent study by the State Assembly reported that educators differed among themselves as to whether "unprofessional conduct" might include "imbibing alcoholic beverages, use of tobacco, signing petitions, revealing contents of school documents to legislative committees, appealing directly to one's legislative representative, and opposing majority opinions. . . ." (Report of the Subcommittee on Personnel Problems of the Assembly Interim Committee on Education, Appendix to the Journal of the Assembly, supra (1965) vol. 2, p. 25.)

Again, the court asks why other character issues wouldn't also be deemed as evidence of unfitness to teach. The example of a teacher having an extramarital heterosexual affair is an interesting one.

We cannot believe that the Legislature intended to compel disciplinary measures against teachers who committed such peccadillos if such passing conduct did not affect students or fellow teachers. Surely incidents of [1 Cal.3d 226] extramarital heterosexual conduct against a background of years of satisfactory teaching would not constitute "immoral conduct" sufficient justify revocation of a life diploma without any showing of an adverse effect on fitness to teach.

Nor is it likely that the Legislature intended by section 13202 to establish a standard for the conduct of teachers that might vary widely with time, location, and the popular mood. One could expect a reasonably stable consensus within the teaching profession as to what conduct adversely affects students and fellow teachers. No such consensus can be presumed about "morality."

Time has shown that this is a valid statement: the cultural standards of one generation are definitely not the cultural standards of another. For example, the segregation of whites and blacks prior to the Civil Rights Act gave way to integration and the acceptance of all races as equal under the law.

Today's morals may be tomorrow's ancient and absurd customs. (Note, supra, 14 U.C.L.A. L.Rev. 581, 587.) And conversely, conduct socially acceptable today may be anathema tomorrow.

Local boards of education, moreover, are authorized to revoke their own certificates and dismiss permanent teachers for immoral and unprofessional conduct (Ed. Code, §§ 13209, 13403); an overly broad interpretation of that authorization could result in disciplinary action in one county for conduct treated as permissible in another. What's more, constricted interpretation of "immoral," "unprofessional," [1 Cal.3d 227] and "moral turpitude" avoids these difficulties, enabling the State Board of Education to utilize its expertise in educational matters rather than having to act "as the prophet to which is revealed the state of morals of the people or the common conscience."

That the meaning of "immoral," "unprofessional," and "moral turpitude" must depend upon, and thus relate to, the occupation involved finds further confirmation in the fact that those terms are used in a wide variety of contexts. Along with public school teachers, all state college employees (Ed. Code, § 24306, subd. (a)), all state civil service workers (Gov. Code, § 19572, subd. (1)), and all barbers (Bus. & Prof. Code, § 6582) can be disciplined for "immoral conduct."

The prohibition against "acts involving [1 Cal.3d 228] moral turpitude" applies to attorneys (Bus. & Prof. Code, § 6106) and to technicians, bioanalysts and trainees employed in clinical laboratories (Bus. & Prof. Code, § 1320), as well as to teachers. The ban on "unprofessional conduct" is particularly common, covering not only teachers, but also dentists (Bus. & Prof. Code, § 1670), physicians (Bus. & Prof. Code, § 2361), vocational nurses (Bus. & Prof. Code, § 2878, subd. (a)), optometrists (Bus. & Prof. Code, § 3090), pharmacists (Bus. & Prof. Code, § 4350), psychiatric technicians (Bus. & Prof. Code, § 4521, subd. (a)), employment agency officials (Bus. & Prof. Code, § 9993), state college employees (Ed. Code, § 24306, subd. (b)), certified shorthand reporters (Bus. & Prof. Code, § 8025), and funeral directors and embalmers (Bus. & Prof. Code, § 7707).

Surely the Legislature did not intend that identical standards of probity should apply to more than half a million professionals and government employees in widely varying fields without regard to their differing duties, responsibilities, and degree of contact with the public.

> The court notes that nearly every profession and trade has its standards of conduct and that it doesn't make sense to apply one universal standard to all of these disciplines.

We therefore conclude that the Board of Education cannot abstractly characterize the conduct in this case as "immoral," "unprofessional," or "involving moral turpitude" within the meaning of section 13202 of the Education Code unless that conduct indicates that the petitioner is unfit to teach. In determining whether the teacher's

> The court simply reiterates its point that general accusations are not a cause for banning someone from teaching at public schools. Instead it lays out specific reasons why such a banning might be allowed, and they all are specific evidence of unfitness to teach.

conduct thus indicates unfitness to teach the board may consider such matters as the likelihood that the conduct may have adversely affected students or fellow teachers, the degree of such adversity anticipated, the proximity or remoteness in time of the conduct, the type of teaching certificate held by the party involved, the extenuating or aggravating circumstances, if any, surrounding the conduct, the praiseworthiness or blameworthiness of the motives resulting in the conduct, the likelihood of the recurrence of the questioned conduct, and the extent to which disciplinary action may inflict an adverse impact or chilling effect upon the constitutional rights of the teacher involved or other teachers.

These factors are relevant to the [1 Cal.3d 230] extent that they assist the board in determining whether the teacher's fitness to teach, i.e., in determining whether the teacher's future classroom performance and overall impact on his students are likely to meet the board's standards.

If interpreted in this manner section 13202 can be constitutionally applied to petitioner. Petitioner urges three substantive reasons to support his contention that section 13202 upon its face or as construed by the board deprived him of his constitutional rights. As we shall show, however, that section, as we have interpreted it, could constitutionally apply to petitioner. Petitioner first suggests that the terms "unprofessional," "moral turpitude," and particularly "immoral" are so vague as to constitute a denial of due process. [1 Cal.3d 231]

"Civil as well as criminal statutes must be sufficiently clear as to give a fair warning of the conduct prohibited . . ."

Civil as well as criminal statutes must be sufficiently clear as to give a fair warning of the conduct prohibited, and they must provide a standard or guide against which conduct can be uniformly judged by courts and administrative agencies. The knowledge that he has erred is of little value to the teacher when gained only upon the imposition of a disciplinary penalty that jeopardizes or eliminates his livelihood.

Courts and commentators have exposed and condemned the uncertainty of words such as "unprofessional," "immoral," and "moral turpitude." Indeed, in Orloff v. Los [1 Cal.3d 232] Angeles Turf Club, Inc., supra, 36 Cal.2d 734, 740, this court recognized that the term "immoral" might well be unconstitutionally vague.

Orloff also indicated, however, that such vagueness could be resolved by a more precise judicial construction and application of the statute in conformity with the legislative objectives. (Id at p. 740.) In this manner we upheld in Orloff a provision authorizing the exclusion from certain public accommodations of a person of immoral character.

We sustained in a similar way the term "unprofessional conduct" against a challenge of vagueness in Board of Education v. Swan, supra, 41 Cal.2d 546, 553–554.

As [1 Cal.3d 233] we have explained above, the prohibitions against immoral and unprofessional conduct and conduct involving moral turpitude by a teacher constitutes a general ban on conduct which would indicate his unfitness to teach. This construction gives section 13202 the required specificity. Teachers, particularly in the light of their professional expertise, will normally be able to determine what kind of conduct indicates unfitness to teach. Teachers are further protected by the fact that they cannot be disciplined merely because they made a reasonable, good faith, professional judgment in the course of their employment with which higher authorities later disagreed.

Petitioner secondly contends that the ban on immoral conduct in section 13202 violates his constitutionally protected right to privacy. It is true that an unqualified proscription against immoral conduct would raise serious constitutional problems. Conscientious school officials concerned with [1 Cal.3d 234] enforcing such a broad provision might be inclined to probe into the private life of each and every teacher, no matter how exemplary his classroom conduct. Such prying might all too readily lead school officials to search for "telltale signs" of immorality in violation of the teacher's constitutional rights. (Griswold v. Connecticut (1965) 381 U.S. 479, 485 [14 L.Ed.2d 510, 515, 85 S.Ct. 1678].)

The proper construction of section 13202, however, minimizes the danger of such sweeping inquiries. By limiting the application of that section to conduct shown to indicate unfitness to teach, we substantially reduce the incentive to inquire into the private lives of otherwise sound and competent teachers.

Finally, petitioner urges that the board cannot revoke his life diplomas because his questioned conduct does not rationally

"[T]he ban on immoral conduct . . . violates his constitutionally protected right to privacy."

relate to his duties as a teacher. [1c, 5] No person can be denied government employment because of factors unconnected with the responsibilities of that employment. Again, however, the proper construction of section 13202 avoids this problem, for that interpretation would bar disciplinary action against petitioner unless the record demonstrated that petitioner's conduct did indicate his unfitness to teach.

The record contains no evidence that petitioner's conduct indicated his unfitness to teach. As we have stated above, the statutes, properly interpreted, provide that the State Board of Education can revoke a life diploma or other document of certification and thus prohibit local school officials from hiring a particular teacher only if that individual has in some manner indicated that he is unfit to teach.

The court obviously found no "significant danger" just because a teacher had a dalliance with—or proclivity toward—homosexuality in his private life. In this opinion, which keeps coming back to the lack of evidence and the assumption of unfitness to teach, the court seems to be asking incredulously why the school board issued its ruling against Morrison in the first place.

Thus an individual can be removed from the teaching profession only upon a showing that his retention in the profession poses a significant danger of harm to either students, school employees, or others who might be affected by his actions as a teacher. Such a showing may be based on testimony (Gov. Code, § 11513), on official notice (Gov. Code, § 11515), or on both. Petitioner's conduct in this case is not disputed.

Accordingly, we must inquire whether any adverse inferences can be drawn from that past conduct as to petitioner's teaching ability, or as to the possibility that publicity surrounding past conduct may in and of itself substantially impair his function as a teacher. [1 Cal.3d 236]

As to this crucial issue, the record before the board and before this court contains no evidence whatsoever. The board called no medical, psychological, or psychiatric experts to testify as to whether a man who had had a single, isolated, and limited homosexual contact would be likely to repeat such conduct in the future. The board offered no evidence that a man of petitioner's background was any more likely than the average adult male to engage in any untoward conduct with a student. The board produced no testimony from school officials or others to indicate whether a man such as petitioner might publicly advocate improper conduct. The board did not attempt to invoke the provisions of the Government Code authorizing official notice of matters within the special competence of the board.

This lack of evidence is particularly significant because the board failed to show that petitioner's conduct in any manner affected his performance as a teacher. There was not the slightest suggestion that petitioner had ever attempted, sought, or even considered any form of physical or otherwise improper relationship with any student. There was no evidence that petitioner had failed to impress upon the minds of his pupils the principles of morality as required by section 13556.5 of the Education Code. There is no reason to believe that the Schneringer incident affected petitioner's apparently satisfactory relationship with his co-workers. [1 Cal.3d 237]

The board revoked petitioner's license three years after the Schneringer incident; that incident has now receded six years into the past. Petitioner's motives at the time of the incident involved neither dishonesty nor viciousness, and the emotional pressures on both petitioner and Schneringer suggest the presence of extenuating circumstances. Finally, the record contains no evidence that the events of April 1963 have become so notorious as to impair petitioner's ability to command the respect and confidence of students and fellow teachers in schools within or without the Lowell Joint School District. . . .

Respondent relies heavily on **Sarac v. Board of Education** (1967) 249 Cal.App.2d 58 [57 Cal.Rptr. 69]. The facts involved in *Sarac* are clearly distinguishable from the instant case; the teacher disciplined in that case had pleaded guilty to a criminal charge of disorderly conduct arising from his homosexual advances toward a police officer at a public beach; the teacher admitted a recent history of homosexual activities. The court's discussion in that case includes unnecessarily broad language suggesting that all homosexual conduct, even though not shown to relate to fitness to teach, warrants disciplinary action. (Id. at pp. 63–64.) The proper construction of section 13202, however, as we have demonstrated, is more restricted than indicated by this dicta in *Sarac*, and to the extent that *Sarac* conflicts with this opinion it must be disapproved.

Although the superior court in the instant case rendered a conclusion of law that petitioner had demonstrated his

"This lack of evidence is particularly significant because the board failed to show the petitioner's conduct in any manner affected his performance as a teacher."

Here the court points out the significant differences between the main case used by the school board as precedent for its ruling against Morrison. But in the *Sarac* case, the defendant was issued a citation for making homosexual advances to a police officer on a public beach and also admitted to other recent homosexual activity. Morrison made no such advances, however, nor was his expression of his homosexuality recent at all.

unfitness to teach, we cannot ascertain with certainty whether or not the court in so ruling relied upon this erroneous dicta in Sarac. In any event, "the ultimate conclusion to be drawn from undisputed facts is a question of law for an appellate court [citations]." (Yakov v. Board of Medical Examiners, supra, 68 Cal.2d 67, 74, fn.7. [7b]) Even if the trial court's statement were to be construed as a finding of fact it would not permit us to affirm the board's action, since, as indicated, no "credible, competent evidence" supports any such inference of petitioner's unfitness to teach.

Conclusion

In deciding this case we are not unmindful of the public interest in the elimination of unfit elementary and secondary school teachers. But petitioner is entitled to a careful and reasoned inquiry into his [1 Cal.3d 239] fitness to teach by the Board of Education before he is deprived of his right to pursue his profession. "The right to practice one's profession is sufficiently precious to surround it with a panoply of legal protection" (Yakov v. Board of Medical Examiners, supra, 68 Cal.2d 67, 75), and terms such as "immoral," "unprofessional," and "moral turpitude" constitute only lingual abstractions until applied to a specific occupation and given content by reference to fitness for the performance of that vocation.

The court does not discount the need to protect children from unfit teachers but asserts that a baseless accusation of such unfitness wrongly interferes with an individual's—in this case teacher's—right to due process under the law. The court also notes that the effect of stripping a teacher of the license to teach will have a serious impact on the teacher's ability to get a job in any profession.

The power of the state to regulate professions and conditions of government employment must not arbitrarily impair the right of the individual to live his private life, apart from his job, as he deems fit. Moreover, since modern hiring practices purport to rest on scientific judgments of fitness for the job involved, a government decision clothed in such terms can seriously inhibit the possibility of the dismissed employee thereafter successfully seeking non-government positions. That danger becomes especially acute under circumstances such as the present case in which loss of certification will impose upon petitioner "a 'badge of infamy,' . . . fixing upon him the stigma of an official defamation of character." (Norton v. Macy, supra, 417 F.2d 1161, 1164, fns. 8 & 9.)

Our conclusion affords no guarantee that petitoner's life diplomas cannot be revoked. If the Board of Education believes that petitioner is unfit to teach, it can reopen its inquiry into the circumstances surrounding and the implications of the 1963 incident with Mr. Schneringer. The board also has at its disposal ample means to discipline petitioner for future misconduct. [1 Cal.3d 240]

Finally, we do not, of course, hold that homosexuals must be permitted to teach in the public schools of California. As we have explained, the relevant statutes, as well as the applicable principles of constitutional law, require only that the board properly find, pursuant to the precepts set forth in this opinion, that an individual is not fit to teach. Whenever disciplinary action rests upon such grounds and has been confirmed by the judgment of a superior court following an independent review of the evidence, this court will uphold the result.

The judgment of the superior court denying the writ of mandate is reversed, and the cause is remanded to the superior court for proceedings consistent with this opinion.

Traynor, C. J., Peters, J., and Mosk, J., concurred.

SULLIVAN, J., dissented.

I dissent.

We deal here with the right and duty of respondent State Board of Education (Board) to discipline public schoolteachers for immoral or unprofessional conduct. The precise question before us is this: Did the Board properly revoke petitioner's life diplomas upon determining that petitioner, while employed as a teacher, had committed homosexual acts and engaged in a homosexual relationship with a fellow teacher and that such acts constituted immoral and unprofessional conduct within the meaning of sections 13202 and 13209 of the Education Code?

The record is clear and without dispute. . . .

The trial court concluded that petitioner committed homosexual acts involving moral turpitude and that such acts constituted immoral and unprofessional conduct within the meaning of sections 13202 and 13209 of the Education Code; and that the action of the Board in revoking the life diplomas

"Our conclusion affords no guarantee that petitoner's life diplomas cannot be revoked."

was correct "in that petitioner demonstrated he was *unfit for service as a teacher in the California public school system within the meaning*" (italics added) of the above sections. The court entered judgment discharging the alternative writ and denying the petition for the peremptory writ.

On appeal the Court of Appeal, Second Appellate District, Division Two, affirmed the denial of mandate in an opinion prepared by Presiding Justice Roth and concurred in by Justice Herndon and Justice Fleming, in which they declared that "we cannot say there is no rational connection between petitioner's homosexual conduct and his fitness for service in the public school system." I am firmly convinced that the superior court and the Court of Appeal correctly disposed of the matter. I must disagree with the analysis proffered by the majority opinion of this court. I would affirm the judgment.

Section 13202 of the Education Code which is at the center of this controversy provides in pertinent part: "The State Board of Education shall revoke or suspend for immoral or unprofessional conduct, . . . or for any cause which would have warranted the denial of an application for a certification document or the renewal thereof, or for evident unfitness for service, life diplomas, documents, or credentials issued pursuant to this code." Section 13129 of the same code provides that the Board" . . . may deny any application for the issuance of a credential or a life diploma . . . made by an applicant who . . . (e) Has committed any act involving moral turpitude. . . ." Although the first section is couched in mandatory terms and the second in permissive terms (§ 36), I do not think this is an issue since the Board did in fact impose discipline under section 13202.

"The crucial question before us is whether the homosexual acts and relationship . . . constituted immoral or unprofessional conduct . . ."

The crucial question before us is whether the homosexual acts and relationship in which petitioner engaged constituted immoral or unprofessional conduct within the meaning of section 13202. [1 Cal.3d 243]

We have said that "The term 'immoral' has been defined generally as that which is hostile to the welfare of the general public and contrary to good morals. Immorality has not been confined to sexual matters, but includes conduct inconsistent with rectitude, or indicative of corruption, indecency, depravity, dissoluteness; or as wilful, flagrant, or shameless conduct showing moral indifference to the opinions of respectable members of the community, and as an inconsiderate attitude toward good order and the public welfare."

(Orloff v. Los Angeles Turf Club (1951) 36 Cal.2d 734, 740 [227 P.2d 449].)

In Sarac v. State Board of Education (1967) 249 Cal.App.2d 58 [57 Cal.Rptr. 69], the court upheld the Board's revocation of a general secondary teaching credential pursuant to section 13202 upon the rationale that homosexual acts constituted immoral and unprofessional conduct within the compass of that section. In that case the acts were committed on a public beach and the teacher was arrested for violation of Penal Code section 647, subdivision (a), and convicted, on his plea of guilty, of violation of a municipal ordinance. However, the accusation filed before the Board charged that he was unfit for service in the public school system under section 13202 because of his conduct as well as because of the criminal proceedings occasioned by his conduct.

There, as in the instant case, the trial court on review of the administrative proceedings concluded that the teacher had committed a homosexual act involving moral turpitude which conduct constituted both immoral and unprofessional conduct within the meaning of section 13202. There, as in the instant case, the trial court concluded that the teacher had demonstrated that he was unfit for service in the public school system. There, as in the instant case, on appeal from the trial court's denial of a writ of mandate, the teacher challenged the Board's action on the ground among others that it had failed to establish any rational connection between his homosexual conduct and ". . . immorality and unprofessional conduct as a teacher on his part and his fitness for service in the public schools; . . ." (249 Cal.App.2d at p.62.)

The court's rejection of the appeal in that case is a convincing answer to the question now confronting us: ". . . Homosexual behavior has long been contrary and abhorrent to the social mores and moral standards of the people of California as it has been since antiquity to those of many other peoples. It is clearly, therefore, immoral conduct within the meaning of Education Code, section 13202. It may also constitute unprofessional conduct within the meaning of that same statute as such conduct is not limited to classroom misconduct or misconduct with children. It certainly constitutes evident unfitness for service in the public school system within the meaning of that statute. (Cf. Ed. Code, [1 Cal.3d 244] §§ 13206–13208.)

Here is a key aspect of the disagreement between the two sides in this case: Is homosexuality, in and of itself, evidence of immoral and unprofessional conduct? The dissenting justices in the *Morrison* case seem to believe that it is. The justices concurring with the majority opinion disagree.

*"I cannot say . . . that there
is no rational connection
between petitioner's homosexual acts and his fitness for
service in the public school
system."*

In view of appellant's statutory duty as a teacher to 'endeavor
to impress upon the minds of the pupils the principles of
morality' (Ed. Code, § 7851) and his necessarily close association with children in the discharge of his professional
duties as a teacher, there is to our minds an obvious rational connection between his homosexual conduct on the
beach and the consequent action of respondent in revoking
his secondary teaching credential on the statutory grounds
of immoral and unprofessional conduct and evident unfitness for service in the public school system of this state."
(249 Cal.App.2d at pp. 63–64.)

In view of the foregoing, as I have already said, I am in
agreement with the trial court and the Court of Appeal, and
like them, I cannot say on this record that there is no rational
connection between petitioner's homosexual acts and his fitness for service in the public school system.

A considerable part of the majority opinion is devoted to a
consideration of the terms "immoral conduct," "unprofessional conduct," and "moral turpitude" in a wide variety
of contexts other than that of the teaching profession and
in reference to numerous occupations having no relevance
to the instant problem, which need not be enumerated and
require no attention other than to say they cover a range from
barbers to veterinarians. . . .

In sum, the majority opinion boils down to this: ". . . the
Board failed to show that petitioner's conduct in any manner affected his performance as a teacher" and "petitioner
is entitled to a careful and reasoned inquiry into his fitness
to teach by the Board of Education before he is deprived of
his right to pursue his profession." Taking this position, the
majority remand this case to the superior court presumably,
although they do not say so, to be remanded by that court in
turn to the Board.

I feel it my duty to observe, with all due respect to the majority, that this action is taken without proper recognition of
our function of review in cases of administrative boards as
recently spelled out by this court unanimously in the Merrill
case.

Were petitioner's acts immoral or not? Or was he perhaps
correct after all in maintaining they were not? The majority
do not answer this question; nevertheless they reverse the
judgment and remand the cause to the trial court for further

proceedings. I would think that under the circumstances the question should be answered for the guidance of the court below on retrial; that court, as well as the Board, should be told whether or not they were in error in concluding that petitioner's homosexual acts were immoral and involved moral turpitude. As I said at the beginning, this is the pivotal question and I think it was correctly answered by the Board, the trial judge and the three appellate justices. . . .

I would affirm the judgment of the trial court.

McComb, J., concurred. Burke, J., concurred with a separate dissenting opinion.

Source: *Morrison v. The State Board of Education,* 1 Cal. 3d 214.

"Full Moon over the Stonewall"

Howard Smith's Article in the *Village Voice*

July 2, 1969

INTRODUCTION

The police raid on June 28, 1969, of the Stonewall Inn, a Christopher Street hangout for GLBT individuals in the Greenwich Village section of Manhattan, gave rise to several days of rioting in the tavern and in the streets outside. The so-called Stonewall Riots became a rallying cry for those pushing for greater acceptance of homosexuals and fairer treatment of them and probably the single most important incident leading to cries for gay liberation. In this article, published by the *Village Voice,* reporter Howard Smith writes about how he became trapped inside the Stonewall with police officers as they confronted angry patrons and protestors of the raid. This article and a companion story by Lucien Truscott were published on July 2, giving rise to a new round of rioting that night.

During the "gay power" riots at the Stonewall last Friday night I found myself on what seemed to me the wrong side of the blue line. Very scary. Very enlightening.

I had struck up a spontaneous relationship with Deputy Inspector Pine, who had marshalled the raid, and was following him closely, listening to all the little dialogues and plans and police inflections. Things were already pretty tense: the gay customers freshly ejected from their hangout, prancing high and jubilant in the street, had been joined by quantities of Friday night tourists hawking around for Village-type excitement. The cops had considerable trouble arresting the few people they wanted to take in for further questioning. A strange mood was in the crowd—I noticed the full moon. Loud defiances mixed with skittish hilarity made for a more dangerous stage of protest; they were feeling their impunity. This kind of crowd freaks easily.

Terms such as "dyke," which today would be considered pejorative and insensitive, were used more freely during the early days of the gay power movement in America. Because gender issues were just starting to be discussed publicly, there had not yet formed a lexicon of terms and phrases for how to refer to gays. In fact, the term "gay" was not being used that much at the time; "homosexual" was the more standard term. And about the "pigs" reference, this was an intentionally derisive term used by protestors who saw police as blindly enforcing unfair and unjust laws created by leaders of the establishment.

The turning point came when the police had difficulty keeping a dyke in a patrol car. Three times she slid out and tried to walk away. The last time a cop bodily heaved her in. The crowd shrieked, "Police brutality!" "Pigs!" A few coins sailed through the air. I covered my face. Pine ordered the three cars and paddy wagon to leave with the prisoners before the crowd became more of a mob. "Hurry back," he added, realizing he and his force

of eight detectives, two of them women, would be easily overwhelmed if the temper broke. "Just drop them at the Sixth Precinct and hurry back."

The sirened caravan pushed through the gauntlet, pummeled and buffeted until it managed to escape. "Pigs!" "Faggot cops!" Pennies and dimes flew. I stood against the door. The detectives held at most a 10-foot clearing. Escalate to nickels and quarters. A bottle. Another bottle. Pine says, "Let's get inside. Lock ourselves inside, it's safer."

"You want to come in?" he asks me. "You're probably safer," with a paternal tone. Two flashes: if they go in and I stay out, will the mob know that the blue plastic thing hanging from my shirt is a press card, or by now will they assume I'm a cop too? On the other hand, it might be interesting to be locked in with a few cops, just rapping and reviewing how they work.

In goes me. We bolt the heavy door. The front of the Stonewall is mostly brick except for the windows, which are boarded within by plywood. Inside we hear the shattering of windows, followed by what we imagine to be bricks pounding on the door, voices yelling. The floor shudders at each blow. "Aren't you guys scared?" I say.

"No." But they look at least uneasy.

The door crashes open, beer cans and bottles hurl in. Pine and his troop rush to shut it. At that point the only uniformed cop among them gets hit with something under his eye. He hollers, and his hand comes away scarlet. It looks a lot more serious than it really is. They are all suddenly furious. Three run out in front to see if they can scare the mob from the door. A hail of coins. A beer can glances off Deputy Inspector Smyth's head.

Pine, a man of about 40 and smallish build, gathers himself, leaps out into the melee, and grabs someone around the waist, pulling him downward and back into the doorway. They fall. Pine regains hold and drags the elected

Smith is using the first-person narrative format to convey the drama of this night. This is a format not used as much in the 1960s as it is today by reporters. And he is using present-tense verbs and heavy amounts of dialogue, re-created from memory to add more depth to the events being described and the mood of those, including himself, involved.

protester inside by the hair. The door slams again. Angry cops converge on the guy, releasing their anger on this sample from the mob. Pine is saying, "I saw him throwing somethin," and the guy unfortunately is giving some sass, snidely admits to throwing "only a few coins." The cop who was cut is incensed, yells something like, "So you're the one who hit me!" And while the other cops help, he slaps the prisoner five or six times very hard and finishes with a punch to the mouth.

It was a different era in the way that police were allowed to react to protestors. The *Miranda* ruling of the Supreme Court was barely three years old, requiring suspects to be read their rights before being arrested and restraining police in the way they dealt with criminal suspects. Even in a heat of battle situation as this scene could be described, many would argue that the police action described by Smith would be over the top and would constitute police brutality. In any event, this description shows how ferocious the scene inside the Stonewall was on the night of this June 28 police raid.

They handcuff the guy as he almost passes out. "All right," Pine announces, "we book him for assault."

The door is smashed open again. More objects are thrown in. The detectives locate a fire hose, the idea being to ward off the madding crowd until reinforcements arrive. They can't see where to aim it, wedging the hose in a crack in the door. It sends out a weak stream. We all start to slip on water and Pine says to stop.

By now the mind's eye has forgotten the character of the mob; the sound filtering in doesn't suggest dancing faggots any more. It sounds like a powerful rage bent on vendetta. That was why Pine's singling out the guy I knew later to be Dan Van Ronk was important. The little force of detectives was beginning to feel fear, and Pine's action clinched their morale again.

A door over to the side almost gives. One cop shouts, "Get away from there or I'll shoot!" It stops shaking. The front door is completely open. One of the big plywood windows gives, and it seems inevitable that the mob will pour in. A kind of tribal adrenaline rush bolsters all of us; they all take out and check pistols. I see both policewomen busy doing the same, and the danger becomes even more real. I find a big wrench behind the bar, jam it into my belt like a scimitar. Hindsight: my fear on the verge of being trampled by a mob fills the same dimension as my fear on the verge of being clubbed by the TPF.

Pine places a few men on each side of the corridor leading away from the entrance. They aim unwavering at the door. One detective arms himself in addition with a sawed-off baseball bat he has found. I hear, "We'll shoot the first motherfucker that comes through the door."

Pine glances over toward me. "Are you all right, Howard?" I can't believe what I'm saying: "I'd feel a lot better with a gun."

I can only see the arm at the window. It squirts a liquid into the room, and a flaring match follows. Pine is not more than 10 feet away. He aims his gun at the figures.

He doesn't fire. The sound of sirens coincides with the whoosh of flames where the lighter fluid was thrown. Later, Pine tells me he didn't shoot because he had heard the sirens in time and felt no need to kill someone if help was arriving. That was close.

While the squads of uniforms disperse the mob out front, inside we are checking to see if each of us [is] all right. For a few minutes we get the post-tension giggles, but as they subside I start scribbling notes to catch up, and the people around me change back to cops. They begin examining the place.

It had lasted 45 minutes. Just before and after the siege I picked up some more detached information. According to the police, they are not picking on homosexuals. On these raids they almost never arrest customers, only people working there. As of June 1, the State Liquor Authority said that all unlicensed places were eligible to apply for licenses. The police are scrutinizing all unlicensed places, and most of the bars that are in that category happen to cater to homosexuals. The Stonewall is an unlicensed private club. The raid was made with a warrant, after undercover agents inside observed illegal sale of alcohol. To make certain the raid plans did not leak, it was made without notifying the Sixth Precinct until after the detectives (all from the First Division) were inside the premises. Once the bust had actually started, one of Pine's men called the Sixth for assistance on a pay phone.

It was explained to me that generally men dressed as men, even if wearing extensive makeup, are always released; men dressed as women are sometimes arrested; and "men" fully dressed as women, but who upon inspection by a policewoman prove to have undergone the sex-change operations, are always let go. At the Stonewall,

It is interesting that police conducting the raids seem to distinguish degrees of alternative gender expressions and consider some more worthy of arrest than others. In 1969, there seemed to be confusion among law enforcement agents as to who should be arrested and who should not be within the GLBT community.

out of the five queens checked, three were men and two were changes, even though all said they were girls. Pine released them all anyway.

Here Smith attempts to balance his observations out by including the position of the owners and managers of the Stonewall Inn. It is not hard to see how—in today's climate—the assertion that their due process rights had been violated is a statement that would be supported by many people.

As for the rough-talking owners and/or managers of the Stonewall, their riff ran something like this: we are just honest businessmen who are being harassed by the police because we cater to homosexuals, and because our names are Italian so they think we are part of something bigger. We haven't done anything wrong and have never been convicted in no court. We have rights, and the courts should decide and not let the police do things like what happened here. When we got back in the place, all the mirrors, jukeboxes, phones, toilets, and cigarette machines were smashed. Even the sinks were stuffed and running over. And we say the police did it. The courts will say that we are innocent.

Who isn't, I thought, as I dropped my scimitar and departed.

Source: Howard Smith, "Full Moon over the Stonewall," *Village Voice,* July 3, 1969, http://blogs.villagevoice.com/runninscared/2014/06/full_moon_over_the _stonewall_howard_smiths_account_of_the_stonewall_riots.php. Used by permission of Cass Smith.

Notes

1. Milt Ford, "A Brief History of Homosexuality in America," Grand Valley State University, http://www.gvsu.edu/allies/a-brief -history-of-homosexuality-in-america-30.htm.

2. Leila Rupp, "The Persistence of Transnational Organizing: The Case of the Homophile Movement," *American Historical Review* 116(4) (October 2011): 1014–1039.

3. "Key Dates in U.S. Policy on Gay Men and Women in the Military Service," U.S. Naval Institute, as accessed on April 17, 2014, at http://www.usni.org/news-and-features/dont-ask-dont-tell/ timeline.

4. Ibid.

5. Sam LeGrone, "Updated: History of U.S. Policy and Laws on Gays in the Military," by USNI News, June 26, 2013, http://news .usni.org/2013/06/26/a-history-of-gays-in-the-military.

6. Ford, "A Brief History of Homosexuality in America."

7. Ibid.

Chapter 7

A Voice from the Past, Demanding to Be Heard: The Native American

Introduction

The American Indian has been a native of the North American continent for more than five centuries. As Europeans began arriving in America in the 17th century and beyond, these Native Americans saw their culture and existence first threatened, then compromised, and next displaced by a new breed of immigrants and settlers. Progress to the pioneers often meant steps backward for the American Indian. Underlying much of that was the clash of cultural values between Indians and white settlers.

Intercultural communications scholars point to one of several dimensions or scales that differentiate one culture from the next. One of these dimensions is how a culture perceives its relationship to nature and the land. While one culture might feel that its role is to adapt to the environment and live in harmony with it, another might feel that its role and right is to master it. On this scale, the American Indian favored adaptation, while the white settler usually favored mastery. To Native Americans, the idea of carving up open territory into sections to be owned by individuals didn't make sense. It also threatened their existence and way of life. The conflict that resulted in the American West was inevitable. Shoved into smaller and smaller spaces, displaced to new homes far away from their native lands, and victimized by broken treaties with the federal government, Indians became assimilated into the larger population of latter-day Americans. The reservations remain, but life on them is often hard, and the voices of those choosing to stay there have not been heard in resounding volume in Washington, D.C.

As Lindsay G. Robertson wrote in his essay "Native Americans and the Law," however, American Indians today still living in their tribes and on their assigned lands do have control over what goes on in those reservations:

> Native American tribal governments are an integral part of the political fabric of the United States. As the Supreme Court of the United States determined in its 1831 decision in Cherokee Nation v. Georgia, 30 U.S. (5 Peters) 1, tribal governments are not "states" in a constitutional sense, nor are they "foreign states," at least for purposes of Article III original jurisdiction. Instead, they are "domestic dependent nations," with many sovereign powers retained from the pre-contact period. As tribal governments have grown in political and economic power, the Supreme Court, the United States Congress, the federal executive, and the tribes have engaged in an increasingly important discussion to determine the scope of their powers. States, municipalities and individual citizens have all contributed to this conversation. The result is a legal regime of fascinating complexity.[1]

More than 500 tribal governments are recognized by the U.S. government. Some have large membership bases and control vast domains. The Navajos, for example, have a population of more than 225,000 and govern lands totaling in excess of 15 million acres spread over three southwestern states. The largest tribe in terms of membership is the Cherokee Nation, which has more than 300,000 citizens. Most tribes, however, have fewer than 1,000 members. Approximately 40 percent of all federally recognized tribes are village groups in Alaska. The smallest tribal reservation is smaller than 100 acres. The state with the largest Indian population is California, with Oklahoma a close second. Alaska is the state with the highest percentage of Native Americans residing within its borders.

In the 1960s, the voice of the American Indian was added to the other voices of underrepresented groups in America seeking change and, most of all, equal treatment under the law. This protest movement did not jell until the late 1960s and carried into the decade of the 1970s.

The formal history of the highest-profile Native American activist group—the American Indian Movement (AIM)—began in 1968, although Native Americans would point out that the movement has existed for five centuries without a name. The modern-day movement is steeped in that longer history and pays homage to those Indians who survived and prospered for so long. As AIM historians Laura Waterman Wittstock and Elaine J. Salinas explain, the AIM movement was founded "to turn the attention of Indian people toward a renewal of spirituality which would impart the strength of resolve needed to reverse the ruinous policies of the United States, Canada, and other colonialist governments of Central and South America. At the heart of AIM is a deep spirituality and a belief in the connectedness of all Indian people."[2] Minneapolis is the headquarters for AIM, although it has many branches in other cities, rural areas, and Indian nations. Over the years, the movement has successfully filed lawsuits against the federal government for the protection of the rights of native nations that have long been guaranteed by treaties, sovereignty, the U.S. Constitution, and other laws. AIM believes in the philosophy of self-determination and strives to keep alive traditional Indian spirituality, history, language, and culture.

"On the Art of Stealing Human Rights"

Gerry Gambill's Speech at a Conference on Human Rights
August 1968

INTRODUCTION

In the speech below, Indian activist Gerry Gambill outlines (in a somewhat sarcastic yet heartfelt manner) how the federal government is oppressing Indians and using tactics of misdirection, obfuscation, and condescension to keep them from realizing their rights guaranteed under various treaties as well as the U.S. Constitution.

Gambill begins his "instructions" as if he were talking to politicians and government officials intent on denying American Indians their rights under the law and existing treaties, advising them that it will go even smoother if the government can enlist the support of the victimized Indians themselves.

The art of denying Indians their human rights has been refined to a science. The following list of commonly used techniques will be helpful in "burglar-proofing" your reserves, and your rights if you can do it with his own cooperation:

As far-fetched as this technique may seem, this kind of depiction has been seen many times in American history, often in movies where the Indians of the American West are supplied liquor to keep them happy or just steal it from the trading post and go on a tribal binge. One such movie done in 1965 was the comedy (some call it a "mockumentary") *The Hallelujah Trail,* from a novel of the same title by author William Gulick. In the story, a group of Indians steal booze, get drunk, and have a raucous run-in with an army caravan. While humorous, this kind of depiction served as a basis for lingering views of the American Indian as something less than a reasoning person.

1. Make him a non-person. Human rights are for people. Convince Indians their ancestors were savages, that they were pagan, that Indians are drunkards. Make them wards of the government. Make a legal distinction, as in the Indian Act, between Indians and persons. Write history books that tell half the story.

2. Convince the Indian that he should be patient, that these things take time. Tell him that we are making progress, and that progress takes time.

This was one of the hardest messages for protest groups to swallow: that the process takes time. It was often interpreted by activists as a delaying or sandbagging tactic on the part of politicians and the government whom, activists felt, had no real intention of acting but were simply trying to wait out the protesters.

3. Make him believe that things are being done for his own good. Tell him that you're sure that after he has experienced your laws and actions that he will realize how good they have been. Tell the Indian he has to take a little of the bad in order to enjoy the benefits you are conferring on him.

4. Get some Indian people to do the dirty work. There are always those who will act for you to the disadvantage of their own people. Just give them a little honor and praise.

This is generally the function of band councils, chiefs and advisory councils. They have little legal power, but can handle the tough decisions such as welfare, allocation of housing, etc.

5. Consult the Indian, but do not act on the basis of what you hear. Tell the Indian he has a voice and go through the motions of listening. Then interpret what you have heard to suit your own needs.

As with many of these other points that Gambill makes, they can be interpreted two totally different ways. Government officials would say that it is only right to involve tribal leaders in the process of improving conditions and that not doing so would be wrong. To protesting Native Americans, however, these are seen as condescending tactics meant to obfuscate real government inaction. The effect, to many Native Americans hearing Gambill's speech, would be to wonder what to believe at all: Is the government trying to help our cause or hurt it?

6. Insist that the Indian "GOES THROUGH THE PROPER CHANNELS." Make the channels and the procedures so difficult that he won't bother to do anything. When he discovers what the proper channels are and becomes proficient at the procedures, change them.

7. Make the Indian believe that you are working hard for him, putting in much overtime and at a great sacrifice, and imply that he should be appreciative. This is the ultimate in skills in stealing human rights: when you obtain the thanks of your victim.

8. Allow a few individuals to "MAKE THE GRADE" and then point to them as examples. Say that the "HARD WORKERS" and the "GOOD" Indians have made it, and that therefore it is a person's own fault if he doesn't succeed.

If the logic of this point was followed by Native Americans, it would seem to have the effect of distrusting those achievers in the tribe who managed to make a success of themselves by going through channels or by taking advantage of opportunities afforded them by federal law.

9. Appeal to the Indian's sense of fairness, and tell him that even thought things are pretty bad, it is not right for him to make strong protests. Keep the argument going on his form of protest and avoid talking about the real issue. Refuse to deal with him while he is protesting. Take all the fire out of his efforts.

10. Encourage the Indian to take his case to court. This is very expensive, takes lots of time and energy and is very safe because the laws are stacked against him. The court's ruling will defeat the Indian's cause, but makes him think he has obtained justice.

11. Make the Indian believe that things could be worse, and that instead of complaining about the loss of human

This argument is one we have seen in debates involving other issues, such as the argument some used against the Equal Rights Amendment. It basically says that the government had better leave things as they are because you never know what negative effects a change might bring, even for the group wanting that change. Interestingly, it was still being used in 2014. For example, after a federal judge overturned a ban on same-sex marriages in Kentucky, the governor of that state appealed the decision and cited the possible negative effect that could occur on the future birth rate of the state if gays were allowed to marry. Although he didn't specify how the birthrate would actually be affected, he said that such a change in allowing gays to marry would have an effect and that the state had an economic interest in keeping the birthrate at a certain level. In other words, better leave things as they are, because you never know what change will bring.

rights, to be grateful for the human rights we do have. In fact, convince him that to attempt to regain a right he has lost is likely to jeopardize the rights that he still has.

12. Set yourself as the protector of the Indian's human rights, and then you can choose to act on only those violations you wish to act upon. By getting successful action on a few, minor violations of human rights, you can point to these as examples of your devotion to his cause. The burglar who is also the doorman is the perfect combination.

Indians, whether in the United States or neighboring Canada, saw this as another attempt by the government at obfuscation and delaying action. By shifting the blame from the government to characteristics of the Indians, the government was putting the responsibility on their shoulders and releasing themselves from needing to act with legislation.

13. **Pretend that the reason for the loss of human rights is for some other reason than that the person is an Indian. Tell him some of your best friends are Indians, and that his loss of rights is because of his housekeeping, his drinking, his clothing. If he improves in these areas, it will be necessary for you to adopt another technique of stealing his rights.**

14. Make the situation more complicated than is necessary. Tell the Indian you will have to take a survey to find out just how many other Indians are being discriminated against. Hire a group of professors to make a year-long research project.

15. Insist on unanimity. Let the Indian know that when ALL the Indians in Canada can make up their minds about just what they want as a group, THEN you will act. Play one group's special situation against another group's wishes.

16. Select very limited alternatives, neither of which has much merit, and then tell the Indian that he indeed has a choice. Ask, for instance, if he could or would rather have council elections in June or December, instead of asking if he wants them at all.

17. Convince the Indian that the leaders who are the most beneficial and powerful are dangerous and not to be trusted. Or simply lock them up on some charges like driving with no lights. Or refuse to listen to the real leaders and spend much time with the weak ones. Keep the people split from their leaders by sowing rumor. Attempt to get the best leaders into high-paying jobs where they have to keep quiet to keep their paycheck coming in.

18. Speak of the common good. Tell the Indian that you can't consider yourselves when there is the whole nation to think of. Tell him that he can't think only of himself. For instance, in regard to hunting rights. Tell him we have to think of all the hunters, or the sporting good industry.

19. Remove rights so gradually that people don't realize what has happened until it is too late. Again, in regard to hunting rights, first restrict the geographical area where hunting is permitted, then cut the season to certain times of the year, then cut the limits down gradually, then insist on licensing, and then Indians will be on the same grounds as white sportsmen.

20. Rely on reason and logic (your reason and logic) instead of rightness and morality. Give thousands of reasons for things, but do not get trapped into arguments about what is right.

21. Hold a conference on HUMAN RIGHTS, have everyone blow off steam and tension, and go home feeling that things are well in hand.

Source: Gerry Gambill, "On the Art of Stealing Human Rights," speech given at a Conference on Human Rights in New Brunswick, August 1968, as printed in *NARP Newsletter,* June–July 1969, http://archive.lib.msu.edu/DMC/AmRad/americanindianmovement/ABW.pdf.

"The Meaning of AIM"

Birgil Kills Straight's Letter to the Editor
1973

INTRODUCTION

Birgil Kills Straight is an Oglala Sioux tribal leader and among 15 core members who led the planning of the proposed Crazy Horse Tribal National Park on the Pine Ridge Indian Reservation in South Dakota. As of this writing, the proposed park was still going through public hearings and had not yet been constructed. If approved, it would be the first Native American tribal national park in America. Straight's mother was one of the original landowners on the tribal land. Straight was a leader in the American Indian Movement, and here he describes why the movement exists.

Things won't ever be quite the same again, and that's what the American Indian Movement is all about.

They are respected by many and hated by some, but they are never ignored.

They are the shock troops of Indian sovereignty.

They intend to raise questions in the minds of all; questions which have gone to sleep in the minds of Indians and non-Indians alike.

What most Americans saw, and thus perceived regarding protest movements such as AIM, were the demonstrations by these groups that sometimes turned violent. In some cases, such as the civil rights demonstrations in the South, the violence was precipitated by police and not by the groups themselves. Nevertheless, the physical confrontations made for good television, and these were the images that stuck in the minds of TV viewers. What most Americans did not witness were the events and provocations that led to many of these protest demonstrations in the first place. This is what Kills Straight is alluding to here: the reason these movements came into existence in the first place.

From the outside, AIM people are tough people. They have had to be. AIM was born out of the dark violence of police brutality and the voiceless despair of injustice in the courts of Minneapolis. AIM was born because a few who knew that it was enough, enough to endure for themselves and others like them who were people without power or rights. All people have known the Indians of jails, the long wait, the "no appeal" of the courts for Indians because many of these were there.

The AIM idea spread rapidly into the Great Lake cities because other Indians knew the power of local Indian police watchmen, of local legal aid, of a place to live where you could hold your head up and joke.

And from the inside, AIM people are cleansing them-selves. Many have returned to the old religions of their tribes, away from the confused notions of a society which has made slaves of their own unguided lives. AIM is first a spiritual movement, a religion's rebirth, and then a rebirth of Indian dignity. It succeeds because it has beliefs to act on. AIM is attempting to connect the realities of the past with the promises of tomorrow.

In times of trouble and injustices—perceived or real—different subcultures within America often reunite around the culture and traditions of the past. These are the things that made them a unique group in the first place, and there is a natural reason that these traditions become the bonding point for these groups. Such was the case with AIM. Native Americans have always been a proud people, even in the face of attempts to subdue that pride by others for what they might see as progress or the need for assimilation.

They are people in a hurry because they know the dignity of a person can be finally broken or greatly hurt by despair and a belt in a cell in a city jail. They know the deepest hopes of the old people could die with these, they know that the "Indian way" is not tolerated in America because it is not acknowledged as a decent way to be.

Sovereignty, laws, and culture cannot endure if a person is not at peace

AIM is a new warrior class of this century, bound by the bond of a drum, who vote with their bodies instead of with their mouths.

Their business is hope.

Source: Letter published in the *Rapid City Journal* as found in the American Indian Institute Collection, Box 1, Folder 39, Western History Collections, University of Oklahoma Libraries, Norman, Oklahoma.

The NARP Eight-Point Program

Article from the Native Alliance for Red Power Newsletter

June–July 1969

INTRODUCTION

The American Indian Movement (AIM) published the *NARP Newsletter,* and archived copies can be found in a collection at Michigan State University. The newsletter promoted the concept of "Red Power," similar obviously to the "Black Power" phrase in use during the 1960s. The term "Red Power" is often attributed to the author Vine Deloria and refers to the intertribal unity of Native Americans that surfaced in the late 1960s. That unity extended across the U.S.-Canadian border and joined Indians in Canada and America into the spirit of a united front. In states along the Canadian border, there was—and continues to be—intermingling of American and Canadian tribespeople who have shared the same goals and frustrations regarding their governments. The eight-point program that follows is directed at the Canadian government and conditions that Indians faced in Canada. It is presented here because members of AIM drew inspiration from it and voiced many of the same concerns about the American government that their Canadian brothers and sisters were sharing about their government. Although the newsletter does not define "NARP," it appears to refer to the Native Alliance of Red Power, whose newsletter is listed by Michigan State as an AIM document. "NARP" is not spelled out in this article from one of these newsletters, although clearly it refers to the major points and goals of the red power movement, of which AIM was at the center.

The Canadian Indian Act, passed in 1951 but built upon many other previous treaties and acts between the Canadian government and Indians, was the principal federal act dealing with Indian status and the management of tribal lands, local governments, and communal finances. The Indian Branch of the Canadian government was charged with administering the act's provisions. The act has been amended several times to allow Indians to have grater control over their affairs.

1. **We will not be free until we are able to determine our destiny. Therefore, we want power to determine the destiny of our reservations and communities. Gaining power in our reservations and communities, and power over our lives will entail the abolishment of the "Indian Act" and the destruction of the colonial office (Indian Affairs Branch).**

2. **This racist government has robbed, cheated and brutalized us, and is responsible for the deaths of untold numbers of our people. We feel under no obligation to support this government in the form of taxation. Therefore, we want an end to the collection of money from us in the form of taxes.**

3. **The history of Canada was written by the oppressors, the invaders of this land. Their lies are perpetrated in the educational system of today. By failing to expose the true history of this decadent Canadian society, the schools facilitate our continued oppression. Therefore, we want an education that teaches us our true history and exposes the racist values of this society.**

These two points echo the logic behind other revolutionary movements, most notably the American Revolution, that it is not the revolutionaries who are breaking the contract with the existing government. Rather, it is government that has broken the contract with its people. The logic, in spirit, harkens back to ideas of such philosophers as John Locke, who discussed what he called the "social contract" in which both the government and its people have obligations to uphold their part of the arrangement; if one fails, the contract fails. In contemporary times, this philosophy is still uttered by groups such as those promoting secession of their states following President Barack Obama's election and reelection.

4. In this country, Indian and Metis [one of the aboriginal people of Canada tracing their descent to mixed first nations and Europeans] represent 3 percent of the population, yet we constitute 80 percent of the inmates in prisons and jails. Therefore, we want an immediate end to the unjust arrests and harassment of our people by the racist police.

5. **When brought before the courts of this country, the redman cannot hope to get a fair hearing from white judges, jurors and court officials. Therefore, we want natives to be tried by a jury of people chosen from native communities or people of their racial heritage. Also we want freedom for those of our brothers and sisters now being unjustly held in the prisons of this country.**

This point, along with point 4, is a sentiment that has been echoed by minority groups in America. The percentages may be different, but the logic is the same when this question is asked: Why does a group consisting of only a minority of the population have such a majority of inmates in prison, having lost a much larger percentage of its felony trials?

6. The treaties pertaining to fishing, hunting, trapping, property rights and special privileges have been broken by this government. In some cases, our people did not engage in treaties with the government and have not been compensated for their land. Therefore, for those of our people who have not made treaties, we want fair compensation. Also, we want the government to honour the statutes, as laid down in these treaties, as being supreme and not to be infringed upon in any way by any legislation whatsoever.

7. The large industrial companies and corporations that have raped the natural resources of this country are responsible, along with their government, for the extermination of the resources upon which we depend for food, clothing, and shelter. Therefore, we want an immediate end to this exploitation, and compensation from these thieves. We want the government to give foreign aid to the areas comprising the Indian Nation, so that we can start desperately needed programs concerning housing, agriculture, and industrial cooperatives. We want to develop our remaining resources in the interests of the redman, not in the interest of the white corporate elite.

8. The white power structure has used every possible method to destroy our spirit, and the will to resist. They have divided us into status and non-status, American and Canadian, metis and Indian. We are fully aware of their "divide and rule," tactic, and its effect on our people.

Red power is the spirit to resist.
Red power is pride in what we are.
Red power is love for our people.
Red power is our coming together to fight for liberation.
Red power is now!

Source: *NARP Newsletter,* June–July 1969, MSU Libraries, Michigan State University, http://archive.lib.msu.edu/DMC/AmRad/americanindianmovement/ABW.pdf.

Establishing the National Council on Indian Opportunity

Lyndon B. Johnson's Executive Order 11399

March 6, 1968

INTRODUCTION

President John F. Kennedy and President Lyndon B. Johnson had both wanted to do something to draw attention to the plight of the American Indian. In the face of growing pressure from Native Americans and their supporters, Johnson decided to enact an executive order to create the National Council on Indian Opportunity in 1968. This was meant to be an organizing council to focus attention on ways of improving opportunities for Native Americans.

WHEREAS the United States has initiated a number of programs in various Departments that should be made available for the development and benefit of the Indian population; and

WHEREAS these programs should be adapted and coordinated in such manner that Indians will participate in and be benefited by them:

NOW, THEREFORE, by virtue of the authority vested in me as President of the United States, it is ordered as follows:

SECTION 1. Establishment of Council. There is hereby established The National Council on Indian Opportunity (hereinafter referred to as the "Council").

The Council shall have membership as follows: The Vice President of the United States who shall be the chairman of the Council, the Secretary of the Interior, the Secretary of Agriculture, the Secretary of Commerce, the Secretary of Labor, the Secretary of Health, Education, and Welfare, the Secretary of Housing and Urban Development, the Director of the Office of Economic Opportunity, and six Indian leaders appointed by the President of the United States for terms of two years.

The seriousness of this effort is underscored by the fact that Johnson appointed the vice president and four cabinet heads as active members of this council. The hope was that this would show the Native American population that the council was meant to produce results in seeking out greater economic opportunities for American Indians.

SEC. 2. Functions of the Council. The Council shall:

(a) Encourage full use of Federal programs to benefit the Indian population, adapting them where necessary to be available to Indians on reservations in a meaningful way.

(b) Encourage interagency coordination and cooperation in carrying out Federal programs as they relate to Indians.

(c) Appraise the impact and progress of Federal programs for Indians.

(d) Suggest ways to improve such programs.

SEC. 3. Compensation and per diem. Members of the Council who are officers of the Federal government shall receive no additional compensation by reason of this order. Other members of the Council shall be entitled to receive compensation and travel expenses, including per diem in lieu of subsistence, as authorized by law for persons in the government service employed intermittently (5 U.S.C., 3109, 5703).

Here the president orders that all relevant government agencies and departments offer their support, as needed, to the efforts of the council and that the administrative services be provided by the Department of the Interior, the agency generally charged with handling Native American overseer functions.

SEC. 4. Assistance to the council. (a) Each Federal department and agency, represented on the Council shall furnish such necessary assistance to the Council as may be authorized by section 214 of the Act of May 3, 1945, 59 Stat. 134 (31 U.S.C. 691), or other law. The Department of the Interior shall furnish necessary administrative services for the Council.

(b) The staff of the Council shall include an Executive Director, who shall be appointed by the chairman of the Council, and such other employees as may be necessary, who shall be assigned by the departments and agencies represented on the Council.

SEC. 5. Meetings. The Council shall meet on call of the chairman.

LYNDON B. JOHNSON

Source: "Lyndon B. Johnson: Executive Order 11399—Establishing the National Council on Indian Opportunity, March 6, 1968," The American Presidency Project, http://www.presidency.ucsb.edu/ws/?pid=76359.

"Eighteen Thousand Pages"

A Guide to the Microfilm Edition of the FBI Files on the American Indian Movement

1986

INTRODUCTION

The following document, although published after the protest era had concluded, is included in this discussion of the protest movement in support of Native Americans because it summarizes the rise and fall of the American Indian Movement (AIM) by analyzing the thousands of pages of files on AIM amassed by the Federal Bureau of Investigation (FBI) during the 1960s and 1970s. This introduction to this microfilm collection of FBI files on AIM serves as a means of seeing how this high-profile movement began, turned violent, and ultimately failed, following the tragic deaths of two FBI agents who were investigating it. This introduction accompanied the guide to the microfilm project, compiled by Martin Schipper and published by University Publications of America in 1986.

Formed in 1968 as a local Indian-support organization, the American Indian Movement (AIM) quickly expanded well beyond its roots in Minnesota and broadened its political agenda to include a searching analysis of the nature of social justice in America. Under the leadership of Dennis Banks and Clyde Bellecourt, AIM developed into a national vehicle for protest during the Nixon administration. Calling for the reorganization of the U.S. Bureau of Indian Affairs (BIA) and for strict observance of past treaties between American Indians and the U.S. government, AIM took an activist and increasingly militant stance in support of its claims.

In 1972, to dramatize their demands, AIM members occupied the BIA building in Washington, D.C. The following year, in a protest that gained worldwide attention, about two hundred AIM militants seized the village of Wounded Knee, an Oglala Sioux hamlet on the Pine Ridge Reservation in South Dakota, and waged what came to be known as the "Second Battle of Wounded Knee." On the same reservation, in 1975, a shoot-out took the lives of two FBI agents; this episode led to the largest manhunt in FBI history and, eventually, to the indictment of four AIM members on murder charges.

These were the incidents—especially the latter two—that catapulted AIM into the militant category and ensured that it received national media coverage. Much of this coverage, however, was framed as a group breaking the law and, in the case of the deaths of the FBI agents, a case of extremist tactics being used by members of the militants. This news coverage polarized people about AIM and caused many of its followers to abandon the movement as being an outlaw group. The FBI didn't come out clean in the minds of many, however, and questions of excessive force and law enforcement reaction were raised, as they would be years later in the storming of the Branch Davidian complex in Waco, Texas.

These FBI files provide detailed information on the evolution of AIM as an organization of social protest and on the occupation of Wounded Knee.

J. Edgar Hoover is universally credited with making the FBI the most modern and sophisticated criminal investigative agency in the world. He integrated scientific methods into the solving of crimes and turned crime-fighting into a science. But Hoover was also heavily criticized for his heavy-handedness at the FBI and his myopic vision that paralleled paranoia. Such was the case with his view of protest movements of the 1960s. Hoover often believed that communists were behind some of these movements and that they all threatened the peace and, in a larger vein, American values in general.

The AIM and Wounded Knee files also illuminate the policies and activities of the FBI during the years just before and after the death of J. Edgar Hoover, a period marked by often severe criticism from outside the Bureau and increasingly by frequent dissent from within. The history of the Bureau in the Nixon "Watergate" era was often a troubled one, and changes in Bureau leadership frustrated efforts to develop clear and consistent policies in response to the fervid politics of the early 1970s.

These files offer a significant source of documentation on the intelligence and law enforcement programs of the Bureau in an era of increasingly militant social activism.

The breadth and depth of this kind of FBI surveillance over a period of years became an issue in and of itself in the 1960s and 1970s among many American citizens. Much of the country was worried that the government had spies everywhere and that files were being kept on many people, whether they were involved in any conspiracy or not. This kind of reaction prompted Congress to look into the question of whether surveillance by the federal government into the lives of everyday citizens who were upset about government policies was too much.

The FBI elected to maintain separate files on the American Indian Movement and the 1973 occupation of Wounded Knee. As might be expected the AIM file is much larger than the Wounded Knee file—eighteen thousand pages for the former to eight thousand pages for the latter. . . . The AIM file covers the ten-year period from 1969 through 1979, a period that witnessed AIM's rise to national prominence and its subsequent demise as a politically and culturally viable force. During the course of its surveillance, the FBI developed an extensive network of information concerning AIM's leadership, its policies, its strategies, and its role in the civil rights movement and the politics of the New Left. Within several months of the organization's initial success in the Minneapolis–Saint Paul area, AIM-inspired demonstrations and takeovers proliferated throughout the country. For an entire decade the files in this collection supply details on every such incident of any consequences involving AIM.

AIM achieved national recognition as an effective organization after its successful intervention in the town of Gordon, Nebraska, to protest the death of Raymond Yellow Thunder at the hands of four white men in February 1972. Yellow Thunder lived on the nearby Pine Ridge Reservation, and many of the Sioux welcomed AIM to their reservation, which retained some of the worst living conditions of any Indian reservation. In general, AIM's influence and support blossomed as a result of the Gordon affair. Volume three of the AIM file depicts the Gordon incident in great detail.

Encouraged by the success at Gordon, AIM decided to embark upon a "Trail of Broken Treaties" to protest the government's failure to honor its many Indian treaties. The plan entailed assembling two groups on the West Coast, one from Seattle and one from San Francisco. The groups were to travel east, picking up followers and support along the way, and were to arrive in Washington, D.C. in early November just before the 1972 presidential election.

In the minds of many white Americans, these treaties that the government had made with the Indians in the 19th and early 20th centuries were ancient history, and they couldn't understand why these Native Americans couldn't bring themselves into the modern era and turn loose of the past. But to many American Indians, such was not the case. These treaties, and the memories of how so many were broken, formed part of their culture and worldview. To those still living on reservations, this was even more the case. This was not ancient history, and the broken treaties were still having an effect on them and their lifestyles.

Although AIM leaders maintain that they had not planned a violent confrontation, the group occupied the headquarters building of the Bureau of Indian Affairs on November 1, barricaded themselves in, and stayed under November 9, when President Nixon's aides granted them amnesty. Volume one, two, four, and five deal with the Trail of Broken Treaties. Volume two also includes negotiator Hank Adams's account of the bargaining at the BIA building.

Immediately following the BIA confrontation, on November 21, 1972, the FBI issued a directive to intensify its efforts against AIM; to develop informants and sources of information concerning extremists in the group, and to have the Extremist Intelligence Section of the Domestic Intelligence Division assume supervision of the investigation. This directive, combined with an almost frenetic increase in AIM activity, makes the files much richer for the next several years.

FBI records indicate that, although AIM was benefitting from the enormous publicity it had generated, it also had managed to alienate much of the established Indian leadership and dry up a good deal of its financial support from government and church sources.

This is the risk that any activist movement takes when it decides to turn to extremist methods to gain public attention and get its point across. AIM was not designed originally to be a militant group, nor did all of its members follow this path. Those who did become militant, however, polarized the AIM effort in the minds of many Americans and—as mentioned earlier—cost them followers and supporters.

Another significant event in this period involved the riot at Custer, South Dakota, on February 6, 1973, that was precipitated by the stabbing death of AIM member Wesley Bad Heart Bull at nearby Guvvalo Gap. When Custer county authorities charged Bad Heart Bull's white assailant with second degree manslaughter (rather than with a first degree murder charge), AIM leaders decided to demonstrate at Custer to protest what they considered another example of white injustice. The Custer riot, which led to prison terms for both Dennis Banks and Russell Means, is carefully detailed in volume twelve.

Aware that it must move quickly to capitalize on its high visibility, AIM sought to gain control of the Pine Ridge Reservation in early 1973 by attempting to impeach tribal chairman Richard Wilson. When the Pine Ridge Tribal Council refused to impeach Wilson, AIM and its Pine Ridge allies occupied Wounded Knee. Events concerning the occupation are, of course, treated most fully in the Wounded Knee file. . . .

The AIM file documents the numerous demonstrations in support of the occupation throughout the country and identifies many individuals and groups who sympathized with the takeover. While at the height of its national prominence, AIM received financial support from a variety of sources, including church groups, government programs, and private donations. As the AIM file indicates, the FBI took a great interest in these sources. Volume thirty-two details the sources for almost one million dollars of AIM support. During their investigation the FBI recovered a briefcase owned by AIM leader Vernon Bellecourt, brother of Clyde, that contained excellent examples of Aim fund-raising proposals. Volume thirteen offers a complete analysis of the contents of Bellecourt's briefcase.

This network of supporters from other protest movements showed the kind of unity that existed among groups and individuals who were supporting different causes but had empathy with their brothers and sisters who were protesting different issues. We saw this when members of the civil rights movement came to the aid of women seeking equal rights, and vice versa.

In addition to financial support, AIM established a network of support groups, mostly from the New Left organizations such as the Black Panthers, Vietnam Veterans against the War, Venceremos, Students for a Democratic Society, La Rasa Unida Party, Workers Student Alliance, and the October League. Altogether, the FBI identified some fifty-one organizations that either attempted to enter or did gain entry into Wounded Knee during the takeover.

AIM also worked closely with various government agencies established to assist minority groups. These included various agencies of the Office of Economic Opportunity, the Office of Health, Education, and Welfare, and the Justice Department's Community Relations Service. The FBI files thus form a useful introduction to the coherent network of activist groups that supported AIM and similar organizations.

Wounded Knee also represents an important chapter in the history of the conflict between militant social activism and federal law enforcement. The FBI was on the scene from the beginning of the seventy-one day occupation and was forced to maintain a contingent of approximately one hundred agents in a paramilitary endeavor unique to the history of the organization. Never have the inherent shortcomings of the FBI been more exposed and never have agents been more critical of their role in an operation. For the first several weeks the FBI, acting on instructions from the Department of Justice, participated in direct negotiations with the AIM occupiers in an attempt to end the takeover. Those acquainted with the FBI realize that engaging in negotiations of this sort, as well as manning roadblocks and laying siege to areas, are not typical of the Bureau's role in law enforcement. The Bureau's paperwork documents the Wounded Knee episode and the FBI's role in response to the takeover in enormous detail. The FBI communications, interviews, reports, and analyses contained in the Wounded Knee file provide a day-to-day portrait of the occupation. For example, all of the negotiations and maneuvers that took place are minutely dissected. In addition, interviews and reports make it clear that AIM— as well as the FBI—was troubled by dissension, mistrust, and a lack of cohesiveness throughout the ordeal. . . .

The FBI files detail AIM's rapid disintegration after Wounded Knee. Efforts to gain support at reservations around the country were, for the most part, frustrated. Attempted to hold national AIM conventions—at White Oak, Oklahoma, in 1973; at the Standing Rock Reservation near Mobridge, South Dakota, in 1974; and at Farmington, New Mexicao, in 1975—netted disappointing results. All were poorly attended and were characterized by factionalism and rancor. Each of their meetings is covered in detail in the AIM file. The file also reveals that as early as the summer of 1974, virtually no AIM chapters were in operation. The only chapter that still exhibited much vitality was Minneapolis–St. Paul.

The demise of AIM as a national organization was furthered by dissension at the upper echelons of its leadership, most dramatically seen at the White Oak meeting when Carter Camp shot Clyde Bellecourt on August 27, 1973, apparently over money matters. Bellecourt survived

"Never have the inherent shortcomings of the FBI been more exposed and never have agents been more critical of their role in an operation."

As has been seen with other protest organizations of the 1960s and 1970s, the zeal for the cause did not mean that internal politics came into play with these groups. Any organization develops a hierarchy and methods for carrying out goals. Dissension in the ranks often arises over these methods, and ambitions rise and vie among individuals to take leadership roles in these movements. All of this was true in the AIM movement as with others before it.

and was named to Camp's position in December, 1973. By Februaruy 1974, Dennis Banks publicly announced that Camp might be an FBI informer. Camp retaliated by sending a letter to AIM members claiming Banks and Means acted in a cowardly manner during the Wounded Knee occupation. By May 1974, AIM leades meeting at Cumberland, Wisconsin, recalled all memberships in a clearly defined thrust at dissident members of the movement. Banks announced that AIM intended to change its militant image.

"Militants from around the country flocked to Pine Ridge."

Allegations that AIM was infiltrated by FBI informers were substantiated in March 1975 when Chicago television broke the story that Douglass Durham, AIM's top security officer and Banks's personal pilot, was employed by the FBI. AIM leaders had confronted Durham with their evidence, and he admitted to the charge in a television news conference. The entire interview can be found at the end of volume forty-four.

Meanwhile, the Pine Ridge Reservation had become a caldron of violence after Means failed to defeat Wilson in a disputed election early in 1974. Militants from around the country flocked to Pine Ridge. On June 26, in spite of official warnings to use extreme caution, two FBI agents, Jack Coler and Ron Williams, were ambushed and murdered on the Jumping Bull ranch near Oglala, just as Dennis Banks' trial for the Custer riot was beginning.

Unfavorable publicity concerning the murder of Coler and Williams, combined with Banks's political asylum in California and Means's incarceration in South Dakota, effectively ended any hope that AIM would remain a viable national organization. By September 1976 the Senate Internal Security Subcommittee, using Durham as its key witness, branded AIM "a frankly revolutionary organization which is committed to violence." Interviewed in jail, Means stated, "Nationally, AIM is in terrible shape." By July 1979, the FBI closed the full investigation of AIM with the following directive: "If informants reporting on AIM cannot be redirected, they should be discontinued." Some information concerning AIM can be found in the file after that date, but the FBI's judgment was essentially accurate.

Source: Rolland Dewing, "Introduction," in *A Guide to the Microfilm Edition of the FBI Files on the American Indian Movement and Wounded Knee*, edited by Rolland Dewing and compiled by Martin Schipper (Frederick, MD:

University Publications of America, 1986), http://cisupa.proquest.com/ksc
_assets/catalog/2141_FBIAmIndMovWoKnee.pdf.

Notes

1. Lindsay G. Robertson, "Native Americans and the Law: Native Americans under Current United States Law," June 2001, University of Oklahoma School of Law, http://thorpe.ou.edu/guide/robertson.html.

2. Laura Waterman Wittstock and Elaine J. Salinas, "A Brief History of the American Indian Movement," American Indian Movement Grand Governing Council, at http://www.aimovement.org/ggc/history.html.

Chapter 8

The Fight in the Fields: Latino Protests of the Era

Introduction

The 1960s also gave rise to protests of the Mexican American community in America, and the epicenter of this movement was in California and Arizona. Its leader—the Latino community's version of Martin Luther King Jr.—was Cesar Estrada Chavez. The movement he founded was the United Farm Workers (UFW), and the cause was better treatment for migrant farmworkers and equal opportunity for those who felt enslaved by the agribusiness system then existing in the United States.

The history of migrant Mexican farmworkers goes back to the 1930s and the drought that crippled southwestern farmers. When farms shut down or laid off workers, the neediest of these moved to California, where conditions were better and there was a greater demand for farm labor. In 1951, Public Law 78 was enacted. Under it, American farmers were allowed to hire Mexican laborers, or braceros, to work in the fields if there was a shortage of American farmhands. California farmers took advantage of the situation and wound up hiring mostly Mexican braceros, because entire bracero families would work for much less (as little as 20 cents for three hours of work) and would tolerate working conditions that American laborers would not. These families would work and live in run-down shanties or tents. Entire camps of these migrant laborers would form, and it wasn't long before these braceros began talking about their conditions and looking for a leader who could articulate their demands. That leader was Chavez.

The story of Chavez began in 1927 in a small village in Arizona, where his family would be cheated out of their small farm, and ended with his death in 1993, with the UFW firmly established in America. As evidence of Chavez's immense contribution to equality and justice, President Bill Clinton awarded the Medal of Freedom to his widow, Helen Chavez, in 1994 at a White House ceremony.

"Viva La Causa"

Statement of Senator Robert F. Kennedy at a Rally of the United Farm Workers
March 10, 1968

INTRODUCTION

The work of the United Farm Workers (UFW), founded in 1962 under the leadership of Cesar Chavez, had made an impression on some leaders in Congress, among them Senator Robert F. Kennedy, who would challenge President Lyndon B. Johnson for the Democratic nomination for the presidency in 1968 before Johnson withdrew from the race. Kennedy was then assassinated in June of that year. What had begun as a grape workers' strike in Delano, organized by Chavez, became known as La Causa (The Cause). In the statement that follows, Kennedy voices support for the UFW and Chavez at a rally in Delano, California. Six days after this speech, Kennedy made his official election announcement that he would seek the nomination.

This is a historic occasion. We have come here out of respect for one of the heroic figures of our time—Cesar Chavez. But I also come here to congratulate all of you, you who are locked with Cesar in the struggle for justice for the farmworker, and the struggle for justice for the Spanish-speaking American. I was here two years ago, almost to the day. Two years ago your union had not yet won a major victory. Now, elections have been held on ranch after ranch and the workers have spoken. They have spoken, and they have said, "We want a union."

You are the first—not the first farm workers to organize—but the first to fight and triumph over all the odds, without proper protection from federal law.

You have won historic victories.

Others, inspired by your example, have come to offer help—and they have helped. But the victories are yours and yours alone. You have won them with your courage

This rally at which Kennedy spoke followed by a year the start of the famous Delano grape strike and grape boycotts that had been organized by Filipino farmworkers and Chavez to put pressure on the California grape growers to treat the migrant farmworkers better. Along with a well-publicized 360-mile march by farmworkers to Sacramento, the strike was leverage used to form the first Hispanic farmworkers' union, which the infant UFW had become. In his statement here, Kennedy decries the fact that there was no effective federal protection for these migrant workers in pursuing their cause. When he says that they were not the first farmworkers to organize, he was referring to the Filipino farmworkers who had formed the Agricultural Workers Organizing Committee in 1965. The Filipinos and Mexican Americans worked together to bring about improved conditions for migrant farm laborers.

and perseverance. You stood for the right—you would not be moved.

And you will not be moved again.

This is not just vacant political rhetoric on Kennedy's part; it is an important acknowledgment of what the migrant farmworkers— under Chavez—had done for themselves. In the black power movement, which was going on concurrently with the migrant farmworkers' struggle, leaders such as Stokeley Carmichael were calling on African Americans to distrust any laws created or help given by anyone outside the black community. That which can be given, Carmichael said, can also be taken away. But here, Kennedy is saying that what these laborers have earned for themselves cannot be taken by someone else.

The world must know, from this time forward, that the migrant farm worker, the Mexican-American, is coming into his own rights. You are winning a special kind of citizenship: no one is doing it for you—you are winning it yourselves—and therefore no one can ever take it away.

And when your children and grandchildren take their place in America—going to high school, and college, and taking good jobs at good pay—when you look at them, you will say, "I did this. I was there, at the point of difficulty and danger." And though you may be old and bent from many years of labor, no man will stand taller than you when you say, "I marched with Cesar."

But the struggle is far from over. And now, as you are at midpoint in your most difficult organizing effort, there are suddenly those who question the principle that underlies everything you have done so far—the principle of non-violence. There are those who think violence is some shortcut to victory.

Here Kennedy raises the discussion of the inevitable struggle that occurred in protest groups of the 1960s: whether to try to reach the goals through nonviolence or violence. This was the debate that was polarizing part of the African American community, with Dr. Martin Luther King Jr. advocating nonviolence and Stokeley Carmichael and others advocating violence. Kennedy and Chavez both knew that if the migrant farm laborers resorted to violence, they could lose everything they had achieved by giving the companies who owned the farms a reason to bring law enforcement against them for disrupting the peace and causing threats to well-being.

Let me say that violence is no answer. And those who organized the steel plants and the auto plants and the coal mines a generation ago learned from bitter experience that that was so. For where there is violence and death and confusion and injury, the only ones who benefit are those who oppose your right to organize. Where there is violence, our nation loses. Violence destroys far more than it can ever create. It tears at the fabric of our society. And let no one say that violence is the courageous route. It takes far greater commitment, far more courage to say, "We will do what must be done through an organization of the people, through patient, careful building of a democratic organization."

That road is far more difficult than lighting a match or firing a weapon. That road requires far greater militancy. But along that road lies success. Along that road lies the building of institutions and cooperative businesses, of clinics and schools and homes.

So we come here, you and I, in a great pilgrimage to demonstrate our commitment to non-violence, to democracy itself. Just a few miles from here is the tower of the Voice of America—broadcasting across vast oceans and whole continents, the greatness of America. And we say together, we will build, we will organize, we will make America fulfill its promise and we will make our voices heard. We will make America a better place for all Americans.

But if you come here today from such great distances and at such great sacrifice to demonstrate your commitment to non-violence, we in government must match your commitment. That is our responsibility.

We must have a federal law which gives farm workers the right to engage in collective bargaining—and have it this year.

We must have more adequate regulation of green-card workers, to prevent their use as strikebreakers—and we must have that this year.

We must have equal protection of the laws. Those are the words of the Fourteenth Amendment to the Constitution of the United States. The California Labor Code, the Federal Immigration Laws, the Federal Labor Department Regulations—these are laws which are supposed to protect you. They must be enforced. From now on.

Kennedy here pledges the support of the federal government to La Causa's efforts, something not within his control as a junior senator from New York but certainly within his control were he to become president. And Kennedy was only a week away from announcing that he would seek the Democratic nomination for president.

So I come here today to honor a great man, Cesar Chavez. I come here today to honor you for the long and patient commitment you have made to this great struggle for justice. And I come here to say that we will fight together to achieve for you the aspirations of every American—decent wages, decent housing, decent schooling, a chance for yourselves and your children. You stand for justice, and I am proud to stand with you.

Viva La Causa.

Source: "Robert F. Kennedy Statement on Cesar Chavez, March 10, 1968," Robert F. Kennedy Papers, Senate Papers, Speeches and Press Releases, 03/01/1968–03/10/1968, National Archives and Records Administration, http://research.archives.gov/description/194027.

"Men Are Not Angels"

Cesar Chavez's Letter from Delano
April 4, 1969

INTRODUCTION

The following letter was an important one written in 1969 by Chavez to E. L. Barr Jr., president of the California Grape and Tree Fruit League, during the United Farm Workers (UFW) grape boycott. It is often called "The Letter from Delano," which referred to Chavez's home of Delano, California.

To: E. L. Barr, Jr., President
California Grape and Tree Fruit League
717 Market St., San Francisco, California

Dear Mr. Barr:

I am sad to hear about your accusations in the press that our union movement and table grape boycott have been successful because we have used violence and terror tactics. If what you say is true, I have been a failure and should withdraw from the struggle; but you are left with the awesome moral responsibility, before God and man, to come forward with whatever information you have so that corrective action can begin at once.

If for any reason you fail to come forth to substantiate your charges, then you must be held responsible for committing violence against us, albeit violence of the tongue. I am convinced that you as a human being did not mean what you said but rather acted hastily under pressure from the public relations firm that has been hired to try to counteract the tremendous moral force of our movement. How many times we ourselves have felt the need to lash out in anger and bitterness.

Today on Good Friday 1969 we remember the life and the sacrifice of Martin Luther King, Jr., who gave himself

Chavez is responding to statements made by Barr in media interviews that claimed that the UFW, a union based on nonviolent responses to perceived injustices, was using violence and intimidation in its organized consumer boycott to achieve better pay and benefits for its workers. These accusations were largely unsubstantiated. The UFW's initial consumer boycott in 1965 was called against the Schenley Liquor Company, which owned most of the grape vineyards in California's San Joaquin Valley. The boycott was successful and resulted in labor contracts from the grape producers, so the UFW spread its boycott efforts over the next four years to all producers of all table grapes. Chavez stated that "The consumer boycott is the only open door in the corridor of nothingness, down which farm workers have had to walk for many years. It is a gate of hope through which they expect to find the sunlight of a better life for themselves and their families."[1]

Once again, the protests of one minority group in the 1960s is seen to invoke the name and support of other protest groups. In this case, Chavez remembers Dr. Martin Luther King Jr. and his efforts, comparing the struggles for equality by African Americans to those of the migrant Mexican farmworkers.

totally to the nonviolent struggle for peace and justice. In his "Letter from Birmingham Jail" Dr. King describes better than I could our hopes for the strike and boycott: "Injustice must be exposed, with all the tensions its exposure creates, to the light of human conscience and the air of national opinion before it can be cured."

"[W]e have seized upon every tactic and strategy consistent with the morality of our cause . . ."

For our part I admit that we have seized upon every tactic and strategy consistent with the morality of our cause to expose that injustice and thus to heighten the sensitivity of the American conscience so that farm workers will have without bloodshed their own union and the dignity of bargaining with their agribusiness employers.

By lying about the nature of our movement, Mr. Barr, you are working against nonviolent social change. Unwittingly perhaps, you may unleash that other force which our union by discipline and deed, censure and education has sought to avoid, that panacea shortcut, that senseless violence which honors no color, class or neighborhood.

You must understand—I must make you understand—that our membership and the hopes and aspirations of the hundreds of thousands of the poor and dispossessed that have been raised on our account are, above all, human beings, no better and no worse than any other cross-section of human society; we are not saints because we are poor, but by the same measure neither are we immoral. We are men and women who have suffered and endured much, and not only because of our abject poverty but because we have been kept poor.

Here, Chavez elevates the complaints of the UFW from better pay and working conditions to a level that resonated with many Americans who knew little of the specific demands of the migrant farmworkers' movement. Chavez instead speaks of the dignity of humans who are waging battle against oppressors. This was a common theme of all protest groups in the 1960s and in part ensured them a wider group of sympathizers and supporters beyond members of those knowledgeable of their groups.

The colors of our skins, the languages of our cultural and native origins, the lack of formal education, the exclusion from the democratic process, the numbers of our men slain in recent wars—all these burdens generation after generation have sought to demoralize us, to break our human spirit. But God knows that we are not beasts of burden, agricultural implements, or rented slaves; we are men. And mark this well, Mr. Barr, we are men locked in a death struggle against man's inhumanity to man in the industry that you represent.

And this struggle itself gives meaning to our life and ennobles our dying.

As your industry has experienced, our strikers here in Delano and those who represent us throughout the world are well trained for this struggle. They have been under the gun, they have been kicked and beaten and herded by dogs, they have been cursed and ridiculed, they have been stripped and chained and jailed, they have been sprayed with the poisons used in the vineyards; but they have been taught not to lie down and die nor to flee in shame, but to resist with every ounce of human endurance and spirit. To resist not with retaliation in kind but to overcome with love and compassion, with ingenuity and creativity, with hard work and longer hours, with stamina and patient tenacity, with truth and public appeal, with friends and allies, with nobility and discipline, with politics and law, and with prayer and fasting.

They were not trained in a month or even a year; after all, this new harvest season will mark our fourth full year of strike and even now we continue to plan and prepare for the years to come. Time accomplishes for the poor what money does for the rich. This is not to pretend that we have everywhere been successful enough or that we have not made mistakes. And while we do not belittle or underestimate our adversaries—for they are the rich and the powerful and they possess the land—we are not afraid nor do we cringe from the confrontation. We welcome it! We have planned for it! We know that our cause is just, that history is a story of social revolution, and that the poor shall inherit the land.

Once again, I appeal to you as the representative of your industry and as a man. I ask you to recognize and bargain with our union before the economic pressure of the boycott and strike takes an irrevocable toll; but if not, I ask you to at least sit down with us to discuss the safeguards necessary to keep our historical struggle free of violence. I make this appeal because as one of the leaders of our nonviolent movement, I know and accept my responsibility for preventing, if possible, the destruction of human life and property.

For these reasons, and knowing of Gandhi's admonition that fasting is the last resort in place of the sword, during a most critical time in our movement last February 1968 I undertook a 25-day fast. I repeat to you the principle enunciated to the membership at the start of the fast: if to build our union required the deliberate taking of life, either the life of a grower or his child, or the life of a farm worker or his child, then I choose not to see the union built.

"Time accomplishes for the poor what money does for the rich."

After invoking the memory of Dr. King earlier in his letter, Chavez makes prominent note of Mahatma Gandhi, another advocate of nonviolent protest, and vows to follow his philosophy, so much so that Chavez undertook two life-threatening hunger strikes. This passage of the letter ends, however, with a veiled threat that "men are not angels" and if pushed to extreme limits of despair may resort to violence.

Mr. Barr, let me be painfully honest with you. You must understand these things. We advocate militant nonviolence as our means for social revolution and to achieve justice for our people, but we are not blind or deaf to the desperate and moody winds of human frustration, impatience and rage that blow among us. Gandhi himself admitted that if his only choices were cowardice or violence, he would choose violence. Men are not angels, and time and tide wait for no man. Precisely because of these powerful human emotions, we have tried to involve masses of people in their own struggle. Participation and self-determination remain the best experience of freedom, and free men instinctively prefer democratic change and even protect the rights guaranteed to seek it. Only the enslaved in despair have need of violent overthrow.

This letter does not express all that is in my heart, Mr. Barr. But if it says nothing else, it says that we do not hate you or rejoice to see your industry destroyed; we hate the agribusiness system that seeks to keep us enslaved, and we shall overcome and change it not by retaliation or bloodshed but by a determined nonviolent struggle carried on by those masses of farm workers who intend to be free and human.

An interesting afterthought comes from a May 1, 2014, Associated Press story by Katherine Corcoran, who notes that Chavez is largely unknown in Mexico today and that many of those who have heard of him have only done so because of the film *Cesar Chavez,* starring Michael Pena, that premiered in 2014. "That Chavez is barely known in Mexico shocks most Americans," Corcoran writes. "That he was a U.S. civil rights hero with streets, schools, parks and a day in his honor surprises many Mexicans. Most of the moviegoers interviewed before an afternoon showing of the film in Mexico City said they only knew about Chavez because of the Mexican actor Diego Luna, who directed 'Chavez' as his first English-language film. . . . Chavez wasn't a Mexican citizen. He was born in Yuma, Arizona."[2]

Sincerely yours,
Cesar E. Chavez
United Farm Workers Organizing Committee, A.F.L.-C.I.O.
Delano, CA

Source: TM/© 2012 the Cesar Chavez Foundation, www.chavezfoundation.org. Used by permission.

"The Boycott Is Our Major Weapon"

Dolores Huerta's Statement to Congress
July 15, 1969

INTRODUCTION

Dolores Huerta, a native of New Mexico who moved to California at a young age, was a school-teacher who taught children of migrant farmworkers and became deeply concerned over the plight of their families. In 1960 she organized the Agricultural Workers Association and lobbied legislators for allowing migrant workers without U.S. citizenship to receive benefits such as public assistance and pensions. Huerta also lobbied for Spanish-language voting ballots and driving tests. In 1962 she cofounded a workers' union with Cesar Chavez that became the United Farm Workers (UFW). Huerta was a leader in the organization's strikes and boycotts in the 1960s and 1970s that paved the way to success for the UFW.

My name is Dolores Huerta. I am the Vice-President of the United Farm Workers Organizing Committee (UFWOC), AFL-CIO. It is a pleasure to come before your committee to discuss a very serious matter for our union and for all farm workers—obstacles to farm worker organizing.

As you know, UFWOC has undertaken an international boycott of all California-Arizona table grapes in order to gain union recognition for striking farm workers. We did not take up the burden of the boycott willingly. It is expensive. It is a hardship on the farm worker families who have left the small valley towns to travel across the country to boycott grapes.

But, because of the table grape growers' refusal to bargain with their workers, the boycott is our major weapon and our last line of defense against the growers who use foreign labor to break our strikes. It is only through the pressure of the boycott that UFWOC has won contracts with major California wine grape growers.

Throughout the history of America, it has been organized labor efforts such as the UFW's strikes and boycotts that have often overcome the reluctance of company management to negotiate for better pay and working conditions for its employees. Although the migrant farmworkers were not full-time employees, in most cases the efforts of Chavez, Huerta, and their UFW were able to bring about the same results using the same tactics as many other unions had before them. Their overarching principle of nonviolent protest generally stayed intact.

At this point, the major obstacles to our efforts to organize farm workers are obstacles to our boycott. Our boycott has been met with well-organized and well-financed opposition by the growers and their sympathizers.

The John Birch Society is an ultraconservative movement begun in 1958 and still active (although in more limited form) today. It championed the causes of anticommunism and limited government and often has seen labor unions as communist-backed or at least socialist-backed movements in America. The Agricultural Workers Freedom to Work Association was founded as an antiunion movement and used a name similar to Huerta's Agricultural Workers Association. Some perceived this as an attempt to confuse Mexican workers as to which movement belonged to which cause.

Most recently, several major California grape growers joined with other agribusiness interests and members of the John Birch Society to form an employer-dominated "union", the Agricultural Workers Freedom to Work Association (AWFWA), for the sole purpose of destroying UFWOC.

AWFWA's activities have been described in a sworn statement to the U.S. Government, which Senator [Walter] Mondale has placed in the Congressional Record. In spite of this type of anti-union activity, our boycott of California-Arizona table grapes is successful. It is being successful for the simple reason that millions of Americans are supporting the grape workers strike by not buying table grapes. After six weeks of the 1969–1970 table grape harvest, California table grape shipments to 36 major United States cities are down 20 percent from last year, according to United States Department of Agriculture reports. The price per lug for Thompson Seedless grapes is at least $1.00 less than it was at this time of last year's harvest.

It is because of the successful boycott that, on Friday, June 13, 1969, ten major California growers offered to meet with UFWOC under the auspices of the Federal Mediation Service. UFWOC representatives and ranch committee members met with the growers for two weeks. Progress is being made in these negotiations, which are presently recessed over the issue of pesticides.

Now that the boycott has brought us so close to a negotiated settlement of this three-year old dispute, we learn that the United States Department of Defense (DOD) has doubled its purchases of table grapes. We appear to be witnessing an all out effort by the military to bail out the growers and break our boycott.

Let me review the facts behind this imposing federal obstacle to farm worker organizing. The DOD is doubling its purchases of table grapes this year. DOD bought 6.9 million pounds of table grapes in FY 1968, and 8 million pounds in the first half of FY 1969, with an estimated climb to over 16 million this year (according to an article in THE FRESNO BEE, 4/25/69 by Frank Mankiewicz and Tom Braden). DOD table grape shipments to South Vietnam this year have increased by 400 percent. In FY 1968, 550,000 pounds were shipped to S. Vietnam. In the first half of FY 1969 alone, these shipments totaled 2,047,695 pounds. This data on completed FY year purchases of table grapes come directly from a DOD Fact Sheet entitled "Use of Table Grapes", dated March 28, 1969. Commercial shipments of fresh table grapes to South Vietnam in 1968 have risen nine times since 1966, according to U.S. Department of Commerce statistics.

In 1966, S. Vietnam imported 331,662 pounds of U.S. grapes and was the world's 23rd largest importer of U.S. fresh table grapes. In 1967, when the UFAVOC boycott of Giumarra table grapes began, S. Vietnam's imports of U.S. table grapes jumped to 1,194,988 pounds, making it the world's 9th largest importer. Last year, 1968, S. Vietnam became the world's 5th largest importer of this luxury commodity, by buying 2,855,016 pounds of U.S. table grapes.

"This could not have occurred," states the AFL-CIO News of June 14, 1969, "without both DOD and Agriculture Dept. encouragement."

It is worth remembering—in this discussion of South Vietnamese purchasing of table grapes—that American military troop buildup was continuing to increase mightily in Vietnam during these very years, and this could have contributed to the greater need in South Vietnam for table grapes. It is also worth noting that the administration of Richard Nixon took over the White House in 1968 and was not known for its indulgence of labor unions.

These are the facts as to how the Grapes of Wrath are being converted into the Grapes of War by the world's richest government in order to stop farm workers from waging a successful boycott and organizing campaign against grape growers.

The title of the 1939 book *The Grapes of Wrath* is being used here by Huerta, who compares that metaphor to her own idea of "the Grapes of War," meaning that the government purchase of these grapes is creating an unfair advantage for the grape growers in their fight with the farmworkers.

The DOD argues in its Fact Sheet that "The total Defense Supply Agency purchases of table grapes represent less than one percent of U.S. table grape production."

Data from the California Crop and Livestock Reporting Service indicate, however, that table grapes may be utilized in three different ways: fresh for table use; crushed for wine; or dried as raisins. . . . It is clear that DOD purchases of table grapes for fresh use represents nearly 2.5% of all U.S. fresh table grape production! Table grape prices, like those of other fruits and vegetables, are extremely susceptible to minor fluctuations in supply. DOD purchases of table grapes are probably shoring up the price of all grapes and, at a critical point in the UFWOC boycott, are permitting many growers to stand firm in their refusal to negotiate with their workers.

It is obvious that the DOD is taking sides with the growers in this dispute. The DOD Fact Sheet states that "The basic policy of the DOD with regard to awarding defense contracts to contractors involved in labor disputes is to refrain from taking a position on the merits of any labor dispute. This policy is based on the premise that it is essential to DOD procurement needs to maintain a sound working relationship with both labor and management."

Nevertheless, many unions in the United States are decrying this fantastic increase in DOD table grape purchases. The AFL-CIO notes that "union observers point out, however, that DOD does become involved in a labor dispute when it so greatly increases its purchase of boycotted grapes." It seems that the DOD is violating its own policy and endangering its working relationship with labor, and we hope that the committee will explore this fully.

"The history of our struggle against agribusiness is punctuated by the continued violations of health and safety codes by growers . . ."

The history of our struggle against agribusiness is punctuated by the continued violations of health and safety codes by growers, including many table grape growers. Much of this documentation has already been submitted to the Senate Subcommittee on Migratory Labor. Such violations are so well documented that Superior Judge Irving Perluss recently ruled that a jobless worker was within his rights when he refused to accept farm labor work offered him through the California Department of Employment on grounds that most of such jobs are in violation of state health and sanitation codes. . . .

If the federal government and the DOD is not concerned about the welfare of farm workers, they must be concerned with protecting our servicemen from contamination and disease carried by grapes picked in fields without toilets or washstands.

The UFW was not concerned with just low pay, bad working conditions, and lack of public assistance for migrant farmworkers; it was also concerned about the harmful effects of pesticides such as DDT on workers and about the rampant use of Mexican child labor in the grape fields.

Recent laboratory tests have found DDT residues on California grapes. Economic poisons have killed and injured farm workers. Will they also prove dangerous to U.S. military personnel? Focusing on other forms of crime in the fields, we would finally ask if the DOD buys table grapes from the numerous growers who daily violate state and federal minimum wage and child labor laws, who employ illegal foreign labor, and who do not deduct social security payments from farm worker wages?

The DOD increasing purchase of table grapes is nothing short of a national outrage. It is an outrage to the millions of American taxpayers who are supporting the farm workers struggle for justice by boycotting table grapes.

How can any American believe that the U.S. Government is sincere in its efforts to eradicate poverty when the military uses its immense purchasing power to subvert the farm workers' non-violent struggle for a descent, living wage and a better future?

No action of Congress is perceived the same by everyone in America, nor does congressional action affect everyone and every group in the same way. What might normally be seen as a benign act of increasing the government purchase of table grapes became a sign to the UFW that the government was opposing—even sabotaging—its efforts at boycotting these grapes to gain leverage for improving conditions of migrant farm laborers.

Many farm workers are members of minority groups. They are Filipino- and Mexican-American and African-American. These are the same farm workers who are on the front lines of battle in Vietnam. It is a cruel and ironic slap in the face to these men who have left the fields to fulfill their military obligation to find increasing amounts of non-union grapes in their mess kits.

In conclusion let me say that our only weapon is the boycott. Just when our boycott is successful the U.S. military doubles its purchases of table grapes, creating a major obstacle to farm worker organization and union recognition. The DOD is obviously acting as a buyer of last resort for scab grapes and is, in effect, providing another form of federal subsidy for anti-union growers who would destroy the efforts of the poor to build a union.

UFWOC calls on all concerned Americans and on the members of the Senate Subcommittee on Migratory Labor to protest this anti-union policy of the military and the Nixon administration.

Source: *Migrant and Seasonal Farmworker Powerlessness: Hearings before the Subcommittee on Migratory Labor of the Committee on Labor and Public Welfare, United States Senate, 91st Congress, 1st Session, on Efforts to Organize; Part 3-A, July 15, 1969* (Washington, DC: U.S. Government Printing Office, 1970), 551–562, http://www.archive.org/details/migrantseasonalf03unit.

Notes

1. Claire Peterson and Susana Diaz, "Exploring the United Farm Workers History," Center for LifeLong Learning & Design (L3D), http://l3d.cs.colorado.edu/systems/agentsheets/New-Vista/grape-boycott/History.html.

2. Katherine Corcoran, "Who was Cesar Chavez? Most Mexicans Don't Know," Associated Press, May 1, 2014, http://bigstory.ap.org/article/who-was-cesar-chavez-most-mexicans-dont-know.

Timeline of Key Events in the Protest Era of the 1960s

January 20, 1960   *Fannie Mae Clackum v. United States* is heard in the United States Court of Claims. The case involves an airman in the U.S. Air Force who had been discharged from the service in 1952 "under conditions other than honorable" for being homosexual. Clackum insisted that the discharge was invalid and filed for back pay for the eight years since her discharge. The court agreed with her that her discharge was invalid.

April 15, 1960   The Student Nonviolent Coordinating Committee (SNCC) is created in Raleigh, North Carolina, to provide young blacks an organized way of promoting civil rights in America.

December 1960   Six years after the country of Vietnam is divided into North and South Vietnam under a treaty signed by the United States and Russia, armed insurgents led by North Vietnamese communists (known as the Viet Cong) begin appearing in the U.S.-supported South Vietnam. This lays the foundation for what has been called the first of the "proxy" wars between the United States and the Soviet Union during the Cold War era.

May 4, 1961   A year after the first black sit-ins at restaurants in the South, a group of civil rights protestors (both black and white) climb aboard buses in Washington, D.C., to head south and protest the system of segregation. These protests will lead to sometimes violent clashes with whites and police and are meant to put pressure on President John F. Kennedy to follow through on his commitment to civil rights legislation.

December 1961   The United States starts increasing its presence in South Vietnam by way of troops sent to advise South Vietnamese forces on how to fight the Viet Cong and North Vietnamese communists.

January 1962	The East Coast Homophile Organizations (ECHO) is founded in Philadelphia as an organizing coalition of smaller localized homophile organizations.
February 14, 1962	President Kennedy announces that if fired upon, U.S. military advisers in South Vietnam will shoot back to defend themselves. The American troop buildup continues in that country.
June 1962	The first Convention of the Students for a Democratic Society (SDS) is held to protest the war in Vietnam and other perceived injustices. The *Port Huron Statement: Agenda for a Generation* is compiled and published by the Students for a Democratic Society.
1963	Women's rights advocate Betty Friedan launches the modern feminist movement with the publication of her book *The Feminist Mystique*.
June 11, 1963	The federal government is pitted against states' rights advocates in the South when two black teens present themselves at the all-white University of Alabama for registration as students. Governor George Wallace, flanked by Alabama state troopers, tries to block that registration but stands down after President Kennedy issues Presidential Proclamation 3542 ordering the governor to let the students register. A confrontation with the Alabama National Guard and the Alabama state troopers is narrowly averted.
June 11, 1963	The night of the Alabama confrontation, President Kennedy delivers his "Address on Civil Rights" speech to the nation. He calls for passage of national civil rights legislation.
August 28, 1963	Dr. Martin Luther King Jr. delivers his famous "I Have a Dream Speech" in Washington, D.C., during the Civil Rights March on Washington. Some 250,000 people crowd the Mall to hear King and others, such as John Lewis, leader of the SNCC, speak for civil rights in front of the Lincoln Memorial.
August 31, 1963	The first convention of ECHO is held in Philadelphia in the Drake Hotel. The theme is "Homosexuality: Time for Reappraisal."
November 22, 1963	President Kennedy is assassinated in Dallas, Texas. Shortly after moving into the Oval Office, President Lyndon B. Johnson announces that he will continue the push to eradicate the Viet Cong from South Vietnam.
July 2, 1964	The U.S. Congress passes the Civil Rights Act, prohibiting discrimination on the basis of race, color, religion, sex, or national origin.

August 2, 1964	After a debated incident in the Gulf of Tonkin alleging an attack on the U.S. warship *Maddox*, Congress gives President Johnson the power to conduct a war against North Vietnam without a formal declaration of war. This is known as the Gulf of Tonkin Resolution.
September 1964	The Society for Individual Rights (SIR) is founded in San Francisco. It is a kind of West Coast version of ECHO but differs from other homophile organizations in becoming more assertive and vocal. SIR sees itself as more liberationist and democratic. Soon it opens the first openly gay bar in San Francisco.
November 3, 1964	President Johnson defeats Republican challenger Barry Goldwater, a declared hawk on the war in Vietnam. Johnson declares that he is for de-escalating the conflict. When he wins, however, he takes the opposite tack and greatly increases U.S. military troop strength in South Vietnam.
December 2, 1964	Mario Savio, a student at the University of California at Berkeley, becomes the de facto leader of the Free Speech Movement when he arouses fellow Berkeley students to sit down and block passage into the Sproul Hall administration building on the UC campus.
March 2, 1965	The United States begins a massive air war against North Vietnam to interrupt support for Viet Cong insurgency in South Vietnam. The bombing campaign is called Operation ROLLING THUNDER.
March 15, 1965	President Lyndon Johnson delivers his "We Shall Overcome" speech to a national television audience and calls for effective civil rights legislation, especially in the area of voting rights. The speech comes just seven months after the passage of the Civil Rights Act and paves the way for the Voting Rights Act, which would be passed and signed into law five months later.
March 24, 1965	Three weeks after Operation ROLLING THUNDER begins, Students for a Democratic Society (SDS) and college faculty against the war hold the first Anti–Vietnam War Teach-In, which draws 3,000 supporters, and the protest of the Vietnam War begins in earnest in America.
September 5, 1965	The word "hippie" is introduced to America by way of a series of stories in the *San Francisco Examiner* written by Michael Fallen. The stories discuss the evolution of the beatnik culture of North Beach to the lower-rent district of Haight-Ashbury, which became the epicenter of hippies.
September 15, 1965	Cesar Chavez agrees to have his fledgling National Farm Workers Union join a fellow Filipino union in a strike against the Delano-area grape growers, protesting low pay

and unsafe working conditions. The strike proves a success, capped by a march to Sacramento, and the strike eventually spreads across the country to other grape growers who employ migrant farm laborers. The strikes turn into boycotts as well and last until 1970.

November 14, 1965	The first major ground engagement between U.S. military troops and North Vietnamese regular army troops begins in the Ia Drang Valley in South Vietnam. The battle lasts until November 18, and the United States claims a 10 to 1 "kill ratio." The battle provides the blueprint for future battles wherein the North Vietnamese and Viet Cong neutralize U.S. air support by engaging in close-in physical attack of U.S. troops.
June 1966	The Underground Press Syndicate (UPS), which was later called the Alternative Press Syndicate, is formed as a network of counterculture newspapers and magazines. Included were the *Berkeley Barb,* the *San Francisco Oracle, The Paper,* and many others.
June 16, 1966	Black activist Stokely Carmichael takes over the leadership of the Student Nonviolent Coordinating Committee (SNCC) on a platform that rejects nonviolence as an effective form of civil rights protest. He inaugurates the slogan "Black Power."
June 30, 1966	The National Organization for Women is launched with the goal of true equality for women in America.
October 15, 1966	Bobby Seale and Huey Newton found the Black Panther Party in Oakland, California, endorsing violence as a feasible tactic to reach goals of civil rights for blacks.
January 5, 1967	Police in Los Angeles stage a mass raid on the Black Cat Bar, a gay hangout that had been open for only two months. Sixteen patrons are arrested, and the raid sparks outrage among the gay community.
Summer 1967	The so-called Summer of Love unfolds in San Francisco, and the hippie movement is now in full bloom. Thousands of young people crowd into Haight-Ashbury over the summer vacation.
August 15, 1967	Some 400,000 protestors march on the United Nations in New York City to protest the war and state other grievances. Speeches are delivered by Dr. Martin Luther King Jr., Dr. Benjamin Spock, and others.
January 30, 1968	Despite declarations by President Johnson that America is winning the war in Vietnam, the Viet Cong stage the massive two-day Tet Offensive in various locations in South Vietnam, costing the lives of 2,500 American soldiers and sparking a stronger wave of war protests in America.

March 6, 1968	President Johnson signs Executive Order 11399, creating the National Council on Indian Opportunity. Johnson said, "The time has come to focus on the plight of the American Indian." This same year, the Minneapolis American Indian Movement (AIM) Patrol is created to address issues of extreme police brutality against Native Americans. This is the beginning of the national AIM movement.
August 1968	Native American activist Gerry Gambill delivers a speech titled "On the Art of Stealing Human Rights" at a conference on human rights in New Brunswick, Maine, on the Tobique Reserve. The speech focuses on the many ways that Native Americans are being denied their rights by the federal government.
November 5, 1968	Shirley Chisholm becomes the first African American woman to be elected to Congress. She will become a leader in the fight for women's rights and the Equal Rights Amendment.
November 5, 1968	Richard M. Nixon narrowly defeats Democrat Hubert H. Humphrey and is elected president. Nixon continues to press the war in Vietnam and pursue a policy of "peace with honor." He creates an "enemies list," and many war protestors are on it.
May 21, 1969	Representative Shirley Chisholm delivers her "Equal Rights Speech" to the House of Representatives, calling for passage of the Equal Rights Amendment to the Constitution and giving that long-running effort a boost as the 1960s draws to a close.
July 27, 1969	The funeral of singer and actress Judy Garland attracts many gay mourners to New York City, and many of them gather at the Stonewall Tavern. One of the mourners resists arrest when police arrive, and a confrontation breaks out that is well publicized. The incident is usually credited as the start of the gay liberation movement in America.
August 15, 1969	For three days music, free-spirited love, and peace rhetoric flow out of Woodstock, the gigantic festival that takes place near Bethel, New York, on a dairy farm. Some 200,000 young people are expected to come hear some of the best bands and pop singers of the day, but police estimate that one million are trying to crowd in.
October 15, 1969	A one-day nationwide action, the Peace Moratorium, is the largest demonstration in U.S. history. Protestors include many first-time activists. Events include religious services, street rallies, public meetings, school seminars, and marches. Participants wear black armbands to signify opposition to the Vietnam War and honor the dead. The event in Washington, D.C., draws 250,000 people.

November 3, 1969   President Nixon goes on the air to deliver his "Silent Major-
                     ity Speech." Nixon called for a "Vietnamization" of the war
                     whereby South Vietnamese troops would take over more of
                     the fighting from American troops and called upon the "silent
                     majority" of Americans to rise up in the face of vocal war
                     protestors and stand with him and his "peace with honor"
                     strategy for bringing the war to an end. The Vietnam War
                     would last another four years, however.

November 20, 1969   The California Supreme Court hears the case of *Morrison
                     v. State Board of Education* to decide whether a teacher's
                     dismissal from a public school and removal of certification
                     was valid simply because the teacher showed a proclivity
                     toward homosexuality. The court finds the school board's
                     action invalid, agreeing with the petitioner.

November 29, 1969   Native American protestors move in to occupy the San Fran-
                     cisco Bay island of Alcatraz, attempting to reclaim it as their
                     own. Although they don't succeed in gaining legal title to
                     the island, the incident is well publicized in the media and
                     inspires a larger American Indian Movement (AIM).

Further Reading

Banks, Dennis. *Ojibwa Warrior: Dennis Banks and the Rise of the American Indian Movement*. Norman: University of Oklahoma Press, 2011.

Boyd, Joe. *White Bicycles: Making Music in the 1960s*. London: Serpent Tail, 2010.

Callan, Jim. *America in the 1960s*. New York: Facts on File, 2005.

Carson, Clayborn. *The Autobiography of Martin Luther King, Jr.* New York: Hachette, 2001.

Carter, Dan T., Robert Cohen, and David J. Snyder. *Rebellion in Black and White: Southern Student Activism in the 1960s*. Baltimore: Johns Hopkins University Press, 2013.

Carter, David. *Stonewall: The Riots That Sparked the Gay Revolution*. Boston: St. Martin's Press, 2010.

Cohen, Robert. *Freedom's Orator: Mario Savio and the Legacy of the 1960s*. Oxford: Oxford University Press, 2009.

Cohen, Robert, and Reginald E. Zelnik. *The Free Speech Movement: Reflections on Berkeley in the 1960s*. Berkeley: University of California Press, 2002.

Collins, Gail. *When Everything Changed: The Amazing Journey of Women From 1960s to the Present*. Boston: Little, Brown, 2009.

Cortwright, David, and Howard Zinn. *Soldiers in Revolt: GI Resistance during the Vietnam War*. Chicago: Haymarket, 2005.

Dancis, Bruce. *Resister: A Story of Protest and Prison during the Vietnam War*. New York: Cornell University Press, 2014.

Farber, David. *The Age of Great Dreams: America in the 1960s*. New York: Hill and Wang, 1994.

Farber, David, and Beth Bailey. *The Columbia Guide to America in the 1960s*. New York: Columbia University Press, 2010.

Ferriss, Susan, Richardo Sandoval, Diana Hembree, and Gary Soto. *The Fight in the Fields: Cesar Chavez and the Farm Workers Movement*. New York: Houghton Mifflin Harcourt, 1998.

Flamm, Michael W. *Law and Order: Street Crime, Civil Unrest, and the Crisis of Liberalism in the 1960s*. New York: Columbia University Press, 2005.

Flamm, Michael W., and David Steigerwald. *Debating the 1960s: Liberal, Conservative, and Radical Perspectives*. Lanham, MD: Rowman and Littlefield, 2007.

Gitlin, Todd. *The Sixties: Years of Hope, Days of Rage.* New York: Bantam, 2013.

Goodlad, Lauren M. E., Lilya Kaganovsdky, and Robert A. Rushing, eds. *Mad Men, Mad World: Sex, Politics, and Style in the 1960s.* Durham, NC: Duke University Press, 2013.

Gustafson, S. Melanie, Kristie Miller, and Elisabeth Israels Perry. *"We Have Come to Stay": American Women and Political Parties, 1880–1960.* Albuquerque: University of New Mexico Press, 1999.

Halberstam, David. *The Best and the Brightest.* Foreword by John McCain. New York: Modern Books, 2002.

Howard-Pitney, David. *Martin Luther King, Jr., Malxolm X, and the Civil Rights Struggle of the 1950s and 1960s.* Boston: Bedord/St. Martin's, 2004.

Isserman, Maurice, and Michael Kazin. *America Divided: The Civil War of the 1960s.* Oxford: Oxford University Press, 2011.

Klatch, Rebecca E. *A Generation Divided: The New Left, the New Right, and the 1960s.* Berkeley: University of California Press, 1999.

Kohl, Herbert, and Marian Wright Edelman. *She Would Not Be Moved: How We Tell the Story of Rosa Parks and the Montgomery Bus Boycott.* New York: New Press, 2005.

Kuhn, Betsy. *Gay Power! The Stonewall Riots and the Gay Movement.* Springfield, MO: 21st Century, 2011.

Mansbridge, Jane J. *Why We Lost the ERA.* Chicago: University of Chicago Press, 1988.

Marqusee, Mark. *Wicked Messenger: Bob Dylan and the 1960s.* New York: Seven Stories, 2011.

Matusow, Allen J. *The Unraveling of America: A History of Liberalism in the 1960s.* Athens: University of Georgia Press, 2009.

McCleary, John Bassett. *Hippie Dictionary: A Cultural Encyclopedia of the 1960s And 1970s.* Berkeley: Ten Speed, 2013.

McKersie, Robert B., and James R. Ralph. *A Decisive Decade: An Insider's View of the Chicago Civil Rights Movement of the 1960s.* Carbondale: Southern Illinois University Press, 2013.

O'Neill, William. *Coming Apart: An Informal History of America in the 1960s.* Lanham, MD: Ivan R. Dee, 2004.

O'Neill, William. *Dawning of the Counterculture: The 1960s.* Santa Monica, CA: Now and Then Reader, 2011.

Pawel, Miriam. *The Crusades of Cesar Chavez: A Biography.* New York: Bloomsbury, 2014.

Reilly, Edward J. *The 1960s: American Popular Culture through History.* Santa Barbara, CA: Greenwood, 2003.

Small, Melvin. *Antiwarriors: The Vietnam War and the Battle for America's Hearts and Minds.* Lanham, MD: Rowman and Littlefield, 2002.

Smith, Chaat, and Robert Allen Warrior. *Like a Hurricane: The Indian Movement from Alcatraz to Wounded Knee.* New York: New Press, 1997.

Ward, Brian, ed. *The 1960s: A Documentary Reader.* Oxford, UK: Wiley-Blackwell, 2009.

Washington, James M., ed. *A Testament of Hope: Essential Writings and Speeches of Martin Luther King, Jr.* New York: HarperOne, 2003.

Williams, Lee. *Servants of the People: The 1960s Legacy of African American Leadership.* New York: Palgrave Macmillan, 2008.

Yapp, Dick. *The 1960s.* New York: Konnemann, 1998.

Index

About the Author

Jim Willis is a writer and university professor of journalism and mass communication and holds a PhD in journalism from the University of Missouri. He is a veteran reporter and editor for the *Dallas Morning News* and *The Oklahoman* and has authored more than a dozen books on American and German history, the news media, and college football. Willis has been a frequent lecturer in Europe for the U.S. State Department and German universities, has held endowed professorships at the University of Oklahoma and the University of Memphis, and has chaired academic departments at Boston College, Ball State University, and Azusa Pacific University, where he is now a professor of journalism. He is often a special correspondent for newspapers and has covered such stories as the 1995 Oklahoma City bombing, and the 10th, 20th, and 25th anniversaries of the fall of the Berlin Wall. He lives in southern California with his wife Anne and has two sons and three stepdaughters.